Counting Coup
AND
Cutting Horses

Counting Coup
AND
Cutting Horses

INTERTRIBAL WARFARE
ON THE NORTHERN PLAINS
1738-1889

Anthony McGinnis

CORDILLERA PRESS, INC.

Publishers in the Rockies

Library of Congress Cataloging-in-Publication Data

McGinnis, Anthony.
  Counting coup and cutting horses: intertribal warfare on the northern plains, 1738-1889 / Anthony McGinnis. — 1st ed.
    p.   cm.
  Includes bibliographical references and index.
  ISBN 0-917895-29-0 : $14.95
    1. Indians of North America — Great Plains — Wars. 2. Indians of North America — Great Plains — History — 18th century. 3. Indians of North America — Great Plains — History — 19th century. I. Title.
E78.G73M42   1990
978'.02—dc20
                                                                    90-45306
                                                                        CIP

First Edition
1 2 3 4 5 6 7 8 9

Printed in the United States of America

Front Cover Photograph: "When Sioux and Blackfeet Meet," by Charles M. Russell, watercolor on paper. *Courtesy The Thomas Gilcrease Institute of American History and Art, Tulsa, Oklahoma.*

Back Cover Photograph, Upper Left: Medicine Crow. *Courtesy Smithsonian Institution National Anthropological Archives, Bureau of American Ethnology Collection.*

Back Cover Photograph, Lower Right: Curley. *Courtesy Smithsonian Institution National Anthropological Archives, Bureau of American Ethnology Collection.*

Cover and Book Design: Shadow Canyon Graphics, Evergreen, Colorado.

Cordillera Press, Inc.
Post Office Box 3699
Evergreen, Colorado 80439
(303) 670-3010

CONTENTS

ACKNOWLEDGEMENTS

I owe a great debt of gratitude to a number of people for their help in writing this book. My graduate school advisor, the late Robert G. Athearn of the University of Colorado, was instrumental in his suggestions and encouragement toward publication. Many thanks go to my other advisor, Ralph Mann, also of the University of Colorado, for his precise assistance. I am particularly indebted to my fellow historian Jay Fell for his assistance in bringing this work to print. Great help in researching this book came from the staffs of Norlin Library of the University of Colorado; the National Archives in Washington, D.C.; and the Federal Archives and Records Centers of Kansas City, Missouri, and Denver, Colorado. I am particularly grateful to Robert Svennigson, archivist of the Denver Records Center. For helping me tour the northern Plains Indian country, I am especially appreciative of the efforts of John Face, Henry Old Coyote, Mickey Old Coyote, and Sonny Joe Reed, men who tried to help me better understand the depth of Indian tribal culture. Special gratitude goes to my parents, Bert and Roberta McGinnis, who raised me with an appreciation for the importance of learning. My largest and most affectionate thanks go to my family — my children, Anne, Del, Gray, and Tucker, who put up with a lot, and especially my wife, Jean, without whose ideas, editing, understanding, and patience this book could not have been researched and written.

Note to Readers: In this book, quotations have been left in the form of the original document, regardless of spelling, in order to provide authenticity and not to clutter the text with an excessive use of the word sic. In showing the locations of historical events, for the convenience of the reader I have often used modern, twentieth-century names for states, provinces, cities, towns, and other places, even though these names may not have existed at the time of the event.

For Jean

In the many years of exploration, settlement, and exploitation of the American West first by the Spanish, then the French, the Russians, the English, and, finally, the Americans, no region excited quite the interest as did the flat, treeless grasslands of the Great Plains. It was a different land. It contradicted the landscapes already known: the eastern forests; the rolling, grassy, tree-studded prairies; the arid, rocky Southwest; and the watery northwest wilderness. Francisco Vasquez de Coronado penetrated the southern portion of the plains at an early date, and Spanish military expeditions followed in the 1600s and 1700s. French traders also traversed the region in the 1700s. But the northern high plains remained relatively unknown and untouched by Europeans until the trading and exploratory expeditions of the late 1700s and early 1800s. Then, during the hundred years after these beginnings, British, Americans, and others gradually learned the secrets of this land and its people. The newcomers found the Indians engaged in constant warfare, continually raiding each other across the open country. Steady tribal migration compounded the hostilities. Recently obtained horses and firearms made the fighting more intense. The plains environment fit this raiding lifestyle, and Indian warriors perfectly adapted to the wild and dangerous existence.

If one word could describe this land fought over by the tribes it would be vast. Bounded on the west by the massive Rocky Mountain barrier, the northern plains stretched from the Platte River in the south to the Saskatchewan River in the north, a river which spread its tributaries out across present-day western Canada. The widesweeping Missouri River dominated the scene. The Indians called it the Big River, and it rolled from the mountains eastward through yellow and green hills like a great, unstoppable, muddy carpet. In the central part of North Dakota it turned southward toward its junction with the Mississippi River. Along this stretch the Missouri formed the eastern boundary of the northern plains.

Other rivers flowing from the mountains joined the bluff-lined banks of the Big River at various intervals. The Yellowstone, or Elk River to the Indians, was the largest of these tributaries, slicing diagonally across Montana. It and other easterly and northeasterly running rivers, such as the Little Missouri and the Cheyenne, formed a generally parallel pattern across the northern plains. These rivers in a parched land provided wood, water, and pathways east and west for native and newcomer alike.

When the fur traders and explorers looked out over the vast land traced by these rivers, they found an elevated region of short buffalo grass. Though the country was generally flat, as the Europeans and Americans moved west, they found that the plains varied widely in particulars. The rich grasslands of central South Dakota contrasted with the barren badlands farther west. The flat areas of eastern Montana differed from the rolling Nebraska sand hills. In the western portion of the plains, long series of buttes and hills thrust out as extensions of the mountains to provide reliable reservoirs of wood, water, and protection.

As white people made more and more inroads into this varied landscape during the eighteenth and nineteenth centuries, they gradually learned about the complex intertribal rivalries that prevailed among many of the tribes migrating into and throughout the area. The tribes had different cultures and languages, and while most of them were nomadic buffalo hunters, some tribes on the border of the plains lived a partially sedentary, farming existence. A few tribes were even in the process of changing from sedentary to nomadic ways of life.

The sovereign tribes were ready to fight any other bands in a widespread rivalry that was carried on by individuals in order to obtain wealth and glory. Compared with more modern warfare, however, this was a limited conflict. Tribes whose survival depended on the men, who hunted buffalo, could not afford numerous military losses. In addition, Indian raiding was ambivalent; it was often stopped in order to establish a truce or for the nomadic bands to trade with sedentary tribes for agricultural produce.

From the beginning, the Europeans and Americans became irrevocably involved in these conflicts, often influencing them with firearms, trade goods, and alliances. In particular, guns and horses brought by the Europeans gave a large technological boost to Indian fighting. As the United States Army became more visible on the northern plains in the role of protecting white settlers, it used tribal rivalries to gain allies against hostile Indians. But most importantly, the American government created a policy to end the wars between the tribes. This policy was hard to establish and took most of the nineteenth century to carry out. Eventually, the army was able to end tribal war, but the destruction of the buffalo herds was just as important because it ended the independence of the nomadic bands.

CHAPTER ONE

From Time Immemorial . . . Deadly Enemies

INTERTRIBAL WARFARE, 1738-1800

In early December of 1738, a cautious band of Assiniboin Indians brought a small group of Frenchmen to a pole stockade surrounding a Mandan village near present-day Bismarck, North Dakota. Against their better judgment, the Assiniboins had ventured through territory east of the Missouri River — territory increasingly dominated by enemy Sioux — to escort a French explorer and trader, Pierre Gautier de Varennes de la Verendrye, to the Mandan settlement.

The village that Verendrye walked into was tightly packed with circular, earth-covered lodges. It teemed with barking dogs that served as much for the stew pot as for pets. People of all ages talked noisily as they perched on top of their mound-shaped dwellings, peering curiously at the strange white men. It was an auspicious arrival.

Verendrye was something of a self-made man. He had come from an important but relatively poor family in Quebec. After a career in the army, he had risen to a high station in New France's important fur trade and the exploration that was integral to it. By the time he visited the Mandans, he had had years of trading experience in the lake country of southern Canada.

Verendrye quickly noticed that the Mandans were different from the lake country Indians to the northeast with whom he was familiar. The Mandans, like their nearby friends and allies the Hidatsas, were of the prairie culture. Even though they inhabited the edge of the plains, they lived a partially sedentary, agricultural life along the Missouri, or Big River. Their settlements served as important trading centers for eastern tribes as well as for the nomads of the plains farther west. The Mandans and Hidatsas, like most Indians, had a varied existence that allowed them, when necessary, to fall back on a second and even a third means of survival. Women farmed and gathered

1

edible plants. Men defended the villages and ranged afar on horseback to trade, hunt buffalo, and raid other tribes.

Normally, the Mandans and the Assiniboins were at war. What had ended the hostility between them was one of the warfare's periodic truces, this one designed to facilitate Verendrye's visit. Known for their open-handed hospitality, the Mandans no doubt provided the hungry French and Assiniboin travellers with fresh corn and squash as well as boiled dog, a delicacy in those parts. But eventually, the Assiniboins, who had voracious appetites, overstayed their welcome. So the Mandans spread the rumor that a large Sioux war party lurked nearby, resulting in a hasty departure by the Assiniboins.

Verendrye, however, stayed behind. He represented the governor of New France and His Majesty Louis XV in the frantic French attempts to counter the growing competition in the fur trade from Great Britain's Hudson's Bay Company to the north. Thus, Verendrye was to establish commerce with the tribes, as well as search for a trade route to the elusive Western Sea, or Pacific Ocean.

Making the necessary arrangements to resolve intertribal rivalries was part of Verendrye's job. He had a reputation as a mild man who possessed a surprisingly firm hand in Indian relations, and he used those talents in negotiating agreements with the Mandans as part of his effort to expand French trade west of the Great Lakes.

When Verendrye returned east, he left two of his men to winter at the Mandan village and learn the language. During the winter these two Frenchmen heard numerous war stories from plains tribes coming to trade. The warlike Sioux, although a major force in the prairie lands east of the Missouri River, were not yet part of the tribal conflicts on the high plains. Instead, said the nomadic Indians coming to trade, the Shoshonis were the tribe to be feared the most, especially during the long, dangerous trading expeditions to the Mandan villages. Called the Snakes by their enemies — Gens du Serpent by the French — the Shoshonis in the 1700s were the strongest tribe on the northern plains.[1]

In 1742, four years after Verendrye's visit, two of his sons led an expedition to the Mandan villages. There they found that the continuous tribal conflicts still focused on Shoshoni power. The warfare was rooted in strong feelings of tribalism. Each tribe called itself "The People," or a term with similar meaning, and each was hostile toward most outsiders.

The Verendryes discovered these chauvinistic feelings when, guided by the Mandans and later by some Crows, they explored the plains southwest of the Mandan villages. The journal of the elder

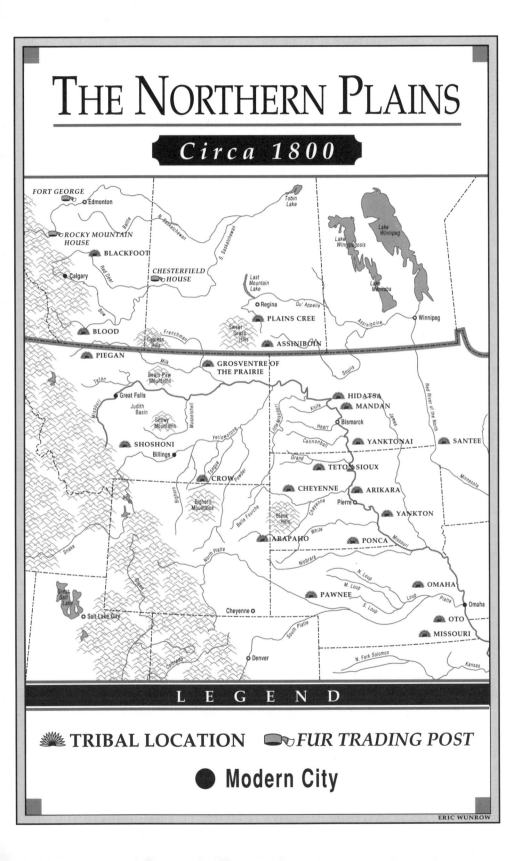

THE NORTHERN PLAINS

Circa 1800

LEGEND

🌾 **TRIBAL LOCATION**   🪶 *FUR TRADING POST*

⬤ **Modern City**

ERIC WUNROW

brother, the Chevalier de la Verendrye, illuminated an internecine conflict involving courageous warriors and tribes. The warfare was often bloody. On occasion, large war parties tore apart small villages, slaughtering the men and killing or capturing the women and children. At one point the Frenchmen met a band of Indians called the Gens du Chevaux, or People of the Horses, who were deep in mourning because the Shoshonis had destroyed one of their villages. The Shoshonis, the chevalier wrote, had no friends and were constantly attacking their enemies, endeavoring to "keep up the war from spring to autumn."[2]

No one tribe, not even the Shoshonis, could completely prevail, however. On one occasion the chevalier joined a band called the Gens du l'Arc, or People of the Bow, which, the Frenchman learned, was the one tribe brave enough to stand against the Shoshonis. When the Gens du lÁrc forced the Shoshonis to retreat from a skirmish, however, they fled themselves, fearing that the Shoshonis might return with reinforcements.[3]

The French were not familiar with this type of combat. European rules of warfare did not countenance killing civilians, much less the slaughter or mistreatment of women and children. And in battles like the one involving the Gens du l'Arc, the warriors seemed more concerned about individual bravery and spiritual power than the outcome of the fight. A tribal victory had little importance except in defending a village or discovering that an opponent was very weak.

This way of war meant little to the French. In Europe, officers went to war dressed in the latest fashion of topcoat and silk stockings, accompanied by servants and silver plates, not with paint and feathers on barebacked horses. Pierre de la Verendrye was an excellent example, particularly in his actions at the Battle of Malplaquet, fought between France and England in 1709. There, the French revived their military reputation by stopping the famous Duke of Marlborough's advance on Paris. The young Lieutenant Verendrye, fresh from Canada, fought gallantly amid the smoke and carnage of the battlefield. He received four saber wounds, a gunshot through the body, and was left for dead on the battlefield. Fortunate enough to recover from his wounds, Verendrye returned home to Canada, having willingly shed his blood for God, King Louis XIV, and France, something the Indians of the northern plains would not have understood — sacrifice for an ideal or a leader rather than for oneself.[4]

The expedition of Verendrye's two sons was the last major French effort to establish a fur trade on the northern Great Plains. The wars with the English for control of the upper Ohio Valley intensified in the 1740s and 1750s, and the French needed to consolidate their widespread outposts. But before they retired from the plains, the French became the first Europeans to discover the violent tribal warfare of the region. The French also recognized that they had to control the warring in order to create effective commerce, because the traders had already found similar conflicts east of the plains. Verendrye had had both a son and a nephew killed by Indians jealous of French trade with tribal enemies. Verendrye himself told his superiors in 1742 that he could not pursue his exploration for the Western Sea while intense intertribal raiding continued.

When he retired in 1744, Verendrye defended what his superiors apparently saw as failure. His defense was that he had tried to control the intertribal warfare in the lake country, but that this was impossible without a long-term government policy "to pacify all these tribes who from time immemorial have been deadly enemies." He was correct about government policy, but it would take another 150 years before such an effort was successful.[5]

When the French retired from the northern plains, they left the fur trade to the English. It was not long before the Hudson's Bay Company began sending traders up the Saskatchewan River to trade with those Assiniboins and their Cree allies who were migrating west to the plains. These tribes were already two of England's oldest trading partners, but the British also wanted to begin an exchange with the large Blackfoot nation that had preceded the Crees and Assiniboins west. As early as 1743, James Isham, a factor, or fur trading agent, for the Hudson's Bay Company, had suggested opening trade with the Blackfeet. To do this, however, the British had to make peace between the Blackfeet and their enemies because, as Isham noted, the conflicts were "a hinderance to their Coming to the English Setlements to trade. . . ."[6]

As a result, the Hudson's Bay Company tried to attract trade from the western plains all the way to York Factory, the firm's important post on Hudson's Bay. To establish this commerce, in 1754, Anthony Hendry travelled from York Factory westward to the plains and up the South Saskatchewan River as far as Red Deer River at the present boundary between Saskatchewan and Alberta. He negotiated with the Assiniboins and was probably the first white man to visit the Blackfeet. Hendry noted that the Blackfeet were mounted, that the Assiniboins were beginning to use horses, and that the Blackfeet were friendly with at least some of the Assiniboins.

Despite these peaceful relations, however, Hendry wrote that warfare was quite lively, especially between the Blackfeet and the Crees.

Both sides used captives as slaves, and Hendry, who apparently had an appreciative eye for women, mentioned the many "fine Girls who were captives." He also noted the brutal death of one slave girl at the hands of the owner's jealous wife, a death that could have resulted from the angry slash of a knife or the crushing blows of a war club.[7]

Eighteen years later, in 1772, Matthew Cocking of the Hudson's Bay Company followed Hendry's trail west to the Blackfoot land. Like Hendry, he observed the Blackfeet using captives as slaves. While the Indians often brutally mistreated the older captives, they frequently adopted the younger ones into the tribe. Cocking agreed with Hendry that the Blackfeet were at peace with a small portion of the Assiniboin tribe. On the whole, Cocking was greatly impressed with the Blackfeet and made the judgment that they excelled other tribes in all things, notably riding and hunting.

In 1775, Andrew Graham of the Hudson's Bay Company was taken with the prowess of the Assiniboins in the same way that Cocking had been impressed by the Blackfeet. The Assiniboins were unsurpassed as warriors, wrote Graham, particularly in their frequent horse raids against the Blackfeet. Traders' opinions such as these varied widely, depending to a large degree on specific observations and the quality of the traders' experiences with a particular tribe.

Despite their reputations as fighters, the Assiniboins and Blackfeet were still threatened by the Shoshonis. With their Flathead and Kutenai allies, the Shoshonis had obtained horses at an early date, which changed the nature of warfare. Mounted on large horses and dressed in quilted leather armor, the Shoshonis launched thundering attacks on small villages and made themselves the terror of the plains.[8]

The Shoshoni threat made it too dangerous for the Blackfeet and the Assiniboins to make the long journey east to York Factory for British goods. The Hudson's Bay Company needed posts farther west, and so did its rival, the North West Company. During the 1780s and 1790s both firms built trading posts along the various tributaries of the mighty Saskatchewan River in present-day Manitoba, Saskatchewan, and Alberta. This had an unexpected consequence: As the traders flooded the northern plains to compete for furs, they inevitably became involved in the wars between the tribesmen who traded furs for weapons and other goods.

As the fur trade increased, so did the intensity of intertribal conflict. In the early 1700s, Spanish horses had reached the plains, generally by way of the tribes west of the Rocky Mountains. Firearms arrived in the same era, but at a slower pace, by way of British trade from the East. Although horses and firearms spread slowly from tribe to tribe,

A Mandan village, painted by George Catlin in the 1830s. The villages that the Verendryes visited in the 1730s and 1740s must have looked similar to this. *Courtesy National Museum of American Art, Smithsonian Institition.*

they had an important impact on warfare as one tribe or another gained an advantage of mobility or firepower.[9]

The person who best understood the northern plains conflict was David Thompson, a trader first for the Hudson's Bay Company and later for the North West Company. He was a short, stocky man with long, dark hair cropped square around a ruddy face with friendly features. He was something of an anomaly on a frontier characterized by rough, uneducated, and often violent men. Thompson had a keen, penetrating mind and was generous in sharing his ideas with others. He had high moral standards — he refused to use liquor in the Indian trade — and he was pious without being self-righteous. In addition to taking an interest in Indian cultures, Thompson was a close and accurate observer. His *Narrative*, written in 1840, remains an important source in the ethnohistory of the northern plains.[10]

Thompson learned much of Blackfoot culture, history, and warfare during the winter of 1787 when he stayed with the Piegan Indians near present-day Calgary, Alberta. The Piegans were the largest of the three tribes of the Blackfoot nation (the others being the Blood and the Blackfoot proper). Unlike many white men, Thompson seemed to enjoy the sights, sounds, and smells of an Indian village, and he was not afraid of the Piegans' warlike ways and strange unfamiliar customs (to Europeans). He spent long winter evenings at the lodge of an old man named Saukamappe. Thompson, like many Indians, was a natural storyteller, and the two spent many hours swapping tales over the smoky fire of buffalo chips that clouded the interior of a plains tipi.

The 75- or 80-year-old Saukamappe was actually a Cree who had joined the Piegan tribe many years earlier. His wife had left him in the easy type of divorce used by plains people. Saukamappe reacted by leaving the Crees and going off to live permanently with the Piegans, whom he had been helping in war anyway.

Saukamappe spoke of the time during his youth, probably the 1720s and 1730s, when the Blackfeet, with the Piegans in the lead, had moved west along the South Saskatchewan River. They found a new home, but the powerful Shoshonis and their allies, the Kutenais and Flatheads, quickly challenged the Blackfoot presence. Saukamappe's description of the Shoshonis' ferocity matched Verendrye's stories of the Shoshonis' violence farther south. The Shoshonis travelled in large war parties to attack small enemy camps, killing the men and capturing the women and children — normal objectives in plains warfare.

Major battles occurred only when sizable war parties encountered each other. Each time, said Saukamappe, both sides practiced the same tactics. The warriors lined up facing each other in almost theatrically rehearsed poses. Protected by large shields, they sometimes jumped out into the open and shouted and gestured wildly to insult the enemy. In between, they crouched and shot arrows from behind shields that, according to Saukamappe, could not be penetrated even by iron-tipped arrows. Many hours or whole days might be spent in this indecisive fighting without either side suffering many casualties.

These battles must have been rather monotonous, the only excitement coming when one group of warriors leaped to their feet and charged madly across the field, waving their clubs and lances at the enemy. Saukamappe told of one such incident when the Piegans, encouraged by their leaders, charged a Shoshoni line. The Shoshonis broke and ran. Given this chance, the Piegans pursued with a vengeance, lancing and clubbing the panic-stricken Shoshonis at will as the defeated warriors scattered over the prairie.[11]

Despite this defeat, the Shoshonis were a serious threat to the newly arrived Blackfeet. The Blackfoot solution was to seek aid from their occasional enemies, the Crees and Assiniboins, and work together against the common threat. With the developing fur trade already having an effect on tribal war, the Crees and Assiniboins had the advantage of metal and guns obtained from long years of dealing with the British and French. For their part, the Blackfeet provided the forward elements in the fight to hold onto the lucrative hunting grounds at the edge of the mountains.

Saukamappe made his first trip to Piegan country, probably in the 1720s, as a member of a Cree war party led by his father. The Cree men were equipped with bows, steel knives, and metal-tipped arrows and spears. Only a few carried firearms. Later, during the 1730s, Saukamappe led his own war parties, armed with British guns, to help the Blackfeet, and during one of these expeditions his warriors used their firearms to rout a Shoshoni war party.

Of course, the Shoshonis were also trying to enhance their own power. About the same time that the Blackfeet were obtaining help and a few guns from the Crees and Assiniboins, the Shoshonis were acquiring horses, probably from their Comanche relatives, who were slowly migrating from their northern mountain habitat toward the southern plains.

After the 1730s, guns and horses helped cause a gradual change in intertribal conflict. Mounted Shoshoni warriors, swinging the long-handled stone war clubs for which they were famous, could break their enemies' long battle lines. Some opponents, struck with fear at the sight of the great animals, panicked and ran. On the other hand, Shoshoni shields were not much protection against Blackfoot muskets. Saukamappe maintained that after one victory in which the Piegans and Crees chased the Shoshonis from the battlefield, the Shoshonis began to change to more cautious tactics. "The terror of that battle," he said, "has prevented any more general battles, and our wars have since been carried on by ambuscade and surprize of small camps. . . ."[12]

Tactics, perhaps, did not change as rapidly as the old Cree implied, but the tribes did develop new methods. The relatively small hunting bands could not afford the casualties that resulted from large battles using guns and horses. The Blackfeet, Crees, and Assiniboins, because of their close connection with traders, first gained the technological advantage over other northern plains tribes. Supplies of guns increased as white traders came in greater numbers. By the 1750s, the Blackfeet were mounted, and, to a limited extent, so were the Assiniboins. The Shoshonis, on the other hand, had no such commercial sources. They traded for horses from other tribes and from the Spanish, but the Spanish authorities in faraway Santa Fe refused to sell the Indians guns. Ultimately, the imbalance in the white man's "gifts" to the Indians helped bring about the Shoshonis' demise.

In the 1780s and 1790s, when the Blackfeet gradually drove the

Shoshonis, Flatheads, and Kutenais from the plains, they had plenty of help from other tribes. Not only did the Crees and Assiniboins assist as temporary allies, but also the Blackfeet increased their number of friends and developed a confederacy. The tiny Sarsi tribe, living to the north, united with the Blackfeet. So, too, did the warlike Atsina tribe, known to the French as Grosventres, or "Big Bellies."

South of the Missouri River, other tribes also pressured the Shoshonis. The Crows attacked them from the upper Yellowstone country using horses and guns obtained from the Mandans and Hidatsas. The Arapahos, who were relatives of the Grosventres and who had recently migrated to the Black Hills, also took up the fight against the Shoshonis.

By 1800, these tribes controlled the lands the Shoshonis had once dominated. The Arapahos were ensconced around the Black Hills and the upper North Platte River, where the Cheyennes later joined them. The Crows inhabited the upper Yellowstone country, and the Blackfoot confederation controlled the land from the Missouri to the North Saskatchewan River.[13]

This shift in the balance of power reflected a profound transition taking place throughout the Great Plains in the 1780s and 1790s — a transition producing major changes in plains culture and its inherent warfare. First, tribal migrations into and within the plains raised the level of competition for hunting grounds. Not only did tribes move to find more productive areas, but also the growing white American and English settlement farther east set off a chain of Indian migrations that reached all the way to the Great Plains. The result was that, on the northern plains, the Blackfeet, Crows, and others took up the old Shoshoni lands, and to the south the Comanches drove out most of the Apache tribes remaining on the southern plains.

Second, the growing presence of American, Canadian, and European goods had a profound effect on the plains tribes. Horses, introduced by the Spanish during the sixteenth and seventeenth centuries, spread gradually from the south and west across the plains, revolutionizing the plains culture in terms of transportation, hunting, and war. The fur trade, which greatly expanded in the 1780s and 1790s, brought more guns and other commodities the Indians came to use and depend upon. The most noticeable was liquor, which flowed freely from the trading posts and exacerbated the quarrelsome qualities of warrior societies. Another factor was disease. Of all the elements the traders brought to the plains, new diseases had the most devastating impact on the indigenous American culture. In the decades to come, smallpox, cholera, and other diseases would kill more Indians than anything else.

The smallpox epidemic of 1780-1781 was particularly devastating. It began in the Spanish settlements in Texas, spread quickly to the southern tribes, then made its way far north to the Saskatchewan River and the Red River of the north. Smallpox hit the sedentary river tribes the hardest; the Mandans and Hidatsas probably lost half their populations. The disease devastated the tribes that frequented trading posts — the Blackfeet, Assiniboins, Crees, and Grosventres of the Prairie. Portions of the Comanche and Kiowa tribes near the northern plains, along with the Shoshonis, Crows, and Arapahos, were also hit hard. Traditional remedies such as sweat baths or the spiritual healing powers of medicine men or medicine women were of no use. With no natural immunity, Indians died by the thousands.[14]

Evidence suggests that this disastrous epidemic caused the tribes to decrease their warring for a time. Even the belligerent Comanches briefly sought peace with the Spanish. In the northern plains, Saukamappe maintained that war changed after the Blackfeet caught smallpox from a raid on an infected Shoshoni village. He explained the strange disease as the anger of the bad spirit toward his children for their overindulgence in war. "We were fond of War, even our Women flattered us to war and nothing was thought of but Scalps for singing and dancing," he told Thompson. "Now think of what has happened to us all, by destroying each other and doing the work of the Bad Spirit; the Great Spirit became angry with our making the ground red with blood; he called the Bad Spirit to punish and destroy us, but in doing so not to let one spot of the ground to be red with blood, and the Bad Spirit did it as we all know."[15]

Saukamappe defended the opinion, held by at least part of his adopted tribe, that it would be preferable to have less full-scale war that destroyed entire villages and instead concentrate on small expeditions for "cutting out," or stealing, horses. In fact, Saukamappe said, horse stealing took greater bravery than destroying a small enemy camp because "it required great courage and conduct, to be for several days in the face of a large camp undiscovered; and each of you to bring away a horse from the enemy instead of leaving your own scalps."[16]

Saukamappe described the new approach to warfare that gradually spread through the northern plains during the late 1700s. Although disease was a factor, horses and guns were the major reasons for changing tactics. The large numbers of major battles that had been described by the old Cree and the chevalier de la Verendrye were no longer feasible. Mounted and well-armed adversaries greatly increased the possibility of casualties. As a result, warriors tended to focus more on capturing horses, now the major form of wealth, superseding booty and captured women. This type of warfare was destined to reach a high degree of sophistication by the 1830s.

The diminished use of war expeditions also reflected the nature of nomadic hunting societies kept small by the spread of epidemics and the search for food. Because able-bodied adult males numbered perhaps one-fourth of a band's population, no band could afford to lose many men in battle. Men were needed to defend the camp and supply buffalo meat. But there was still a paradox: While a band's requirements limited warfare, fighting existed for what the individual could safely attain for himself. In war, the tribe was important only insofar as it supported the individual warrior and his combat and in the fact that the tribe's noncombatants — the women, children, and old men — needed to be defended.[17]

Since most early traders worked the northern portions of the Great Plains, more observations of tribal warfare occurred in that area. In the 1780s, the Hudson's Bay Company became more active. Then in the 1790s, the enterprising and aggressive North West Company, carrying on an often violent competition with its rival, founded trading posts along the Saskatchewan River and its tributaries. This great river, the pathway west for Blackfeet, Crees, and Assiniboins, drained the land north of the Missouri River basin. Thus, the trading forts could draw customers from many scattered tribes.

A number of traders wrote journals in which they described incessant tribal conflict. To them, raiding appeared to be strengthening after some decline in the decade following the smallpox epidemic. By now the Blackfeet, Assiniboins, Crows, and others were pushing the last remnants of the Shoshoni, Flathead, and Kutenai tribes from the plains. The country swarmed with war parties.

Control of the rich buffalo hunting grounds was an important motive for intertribal war, but hardly the only one. John McDonnell, a partner in the North West Company, emphasized the widespread horse stealing, no matter from whom. Referring to the Assiniboins, he noted, "Stealing horses is quite a necessary trade among them, and they steal them from their own traders as well as from the Indians of the Missouri and of Fort des Prairies. . . ." The horse, now the key item of wealth in plains society, was a primary objective, but there were other types of plunder. Duncan M'Gillivray, brother of one of the important partners of the North West Company, maintained that warriors pillaged for anything and whenever possible, as long as it was done with little cost to themselves. The famous explorer Alexander MacKenzie, crossing the continent from 1789 to 1793, noted other motives, especially revenge and the goal of proving one's courage.[18]

English traders constantly found themselves in the middle of raids and counter-raids. Indians had come to depend upon whites for blankets, metal pots, and knives, as well as guns and ammunition, which meant that the trading posts often became the locations for important intertribal activity, violent and otherwise. It was not unusual for a war party, en route to or from a raid, to stop at a fort. Warriors would abruptly appear before the stockade gate, brightly painted for battle and wearing their warshirts, which were richly decorated with porcupine quills and embroidery. The purpose of the visit was often trade or, perhaps, just socializing. War parties, however, were not above stealing horses or goods from the trader, especially if the Indians had not been successful on the warpath.

Duncan M'Gillivray, a tall handsome man known as something of a swashbuckler, carefully described some of the dramatic events that took place at his post, Fort George on the North Saskatchewan River, a hundred miles east of present-day Edmonton, Alberta. In 1794, he reported that the British trade was of such importance to the Blackfeet and their enemies, the Assiniboins and Crees, that the Indians, with the help of company employees, arranged temporary truces at the fort in order to trade. Other tribes were not so fortunate. In February 1795, M'Gillivray described the brave but vain attempts of the Kutenais to avoid Blackfoot war parties in order to reach Fort George to buy guns. The numerous Blackfeet and their new Grosventre friends were fairly successful in keeping enemy tribes away from the fur posts and so maintain their own superiority in arms.

Because of this Blackfoot policy, the situation around some forts got so heated that war parties clashed nearby, sometimes in full view of the inhabitants. In both 1794 and 1795, M'Gillivray noted skirmishes on the flat prairies near Fort George. Though brief, the confrontations included young warriors galloping through swirls of dust into the enemy ranks, hoping to get close enough to strike an opponent, or count coup, and thus gain an important war honor.[19]

The Grosventres of the Prairie, though recent arrivals to the region, were quite active in this resurging tribal war that often flourished around the trading posts. Although the Grosventres became members of the Blackfoot confederation, they often seemed to outdo even that nation of warriors in the wide range of their raiding and in their reputation for courage. The Grosventres not only raided the mountain tribes, but also travelled far to the southeast to fight the Mandans and Hidatsas. The increased range of warfare, made practical by horses, created a difficult trading situation between the Missouri River tribes and the British in Canada. John McDonald, who worked as a clerk, first at Fort George and later at Chesterfield House on the South Saskatchewan River, wrote in his autobiography that the Mandans and Hidatsas resented the near monopoly that the Crees, Assiniboins, and Blackfeet held at the British trading forts. The Mandans and Hidatsas claimed they had difficulty reaching the posts because of enemy war parties and, on one occasion, they complained that the traders favored their enemies too much and threatened to attack the white men.[20]

The traders were in a quandary. There was the lure of profit on the one hand and the danger from the increasingly embittered warriors on the other. Because the tribes demanded European products such as guns, knives, blankets, and pots and saw the advantages of controlling the commerce with their enemies, there was no clear-cut solution to the problem. The alternative for the Englishmen would have been to give up many customers; the result was that the traders' attempts to control the conflicts, while occasionally successful, did not supersede the goals of developing a lucrative business.

Farther south on the Missouri River, however, one fur man had some success in controlling tribal war in order to develop a more efficient trading system. This was Jean Baptiste Trudeau. Although he remains a shadowy figure, Trudeau was one of a number of St. Louis traders who worked for Spanish companies (France having ceded Louisiana to Spain in 1762). The Spanish wanted to establish a solid Indian trade from St. Louis, but to do this they had to combat the competition of the British North West Company, which was beginning to move south to the Missouri to accommodate the river tribes' desire for goods.

To fulfill this objective, a Spanish company hired Trudeau to establish a trading post among the Arikaras, who lived along the Missouri River near present-day Pierre, South Dakota, and in 1795, he visited the Arikara villages. Trudeau believed that the tribe was relatively small — only 2,000 to 3,000 people — as a result of the recent smallpox epidemic, but that it was larger than the Mandans and Hidatsas combined. Like their neighbors to the north, the Arikaras were a prairie culture — they farmed and hunted. And their villages, protected by five-foot barricades made of forked stakes covered with brush and mud, surrounding the earth lodges, served as a trading center for the surrounding area tribes.

Both the Mandan-Hidatsa and the Arikara trade centers were in the middle of the westward migration paths of the Cheyenne and the Teton Sioux. The Crows, Arapahos, and those portions of the Kiowas and Comanches still in the process of moving south lived to the west and south of the Arikaras. The Crees, Assiniboins, Blackfeet, and Grosventres of the Prairie were to the north and northwest. Trudeau found that all these tribes traded with the village tribes living along the Missouri River.

But tribal relations were ambiguous. Even on the day immediately following an exchange of goods, warriors from the plains tribes might return to raid the horse herds or the desirable gardens of corn and squash belonging to the Arikaras. Compared to the multitude of nomadic warriors surrounding them, the village Indians were small in number and vulnerable because of their immobility. But like the Mandans and Hidatsas, the Arikaras, though small in number, were by no means passive. They had a warlike reputation. The men often took to the warpath against any of the surrounding tribes, leaving home for months at a time and travelling as far as the Rocky Mountains.[21]

The coming of European traders meant arms for the sedentary tribes. This gave them more power, and their villages provided the traders with natural trading locations. The intertribal conflict, however, was more complicated and ambiguous than in the British commercial area. Warfare created problems for Trudeau, but he overcame the difficulty to some degree. While present in the Arikara villages, he stopped some war parties from attacking the Crows and Sioux by threatening to withhold his goods. He also arranged a temporary peace between the Arikaras and the Mandans and Hidatsas. What helped Trudeau was the assistance of some of the older men. They were readier for peace than the hot-blooded young warriors looking for ways to prove themselves.[22]

Trudeau's mission to the Arikara villages was important because it showed the advantages of setting up trade along the Missouri River — advantages the British posts on the tributaries of the Saskatchewan did not possess. The traders could keep their wares — guns, metal products, blankets, tobacco, and liquor — safe in the earth lodge of a respected chief. Equally important, Indian customers were already used to frequenting the established trading centers. This facilitated the truces necessary for trade. From the villages the traders easily reached many tribes. Even more significant, through this system and, later, with more centralized trading posts, the Indians grew increasingly dependent on the goods the traders provided. This dependence, part of the evolution of war during the 1780s and 1790s, was interrelated with migrations, disease, and changing military tactics.

By 1800 the military scene on the vast landscape of the northern plains had changed. With the help of European guns, the Blackfoot nation had driven the dominant Shoshoni tribe into the mountains and become a powerful force in the Northwest. According to Alexander MacKenzie's figures, the Blackfeet must have numbered from 6,000 to 8,000 people, with the Grosventres adding at least 2,000 more. David Thompson said the Blackfoot lands stretched from the northernmost plains down to the Missouri River and then eastward from the Rocky Mountains, a distance of 300 miles. Meanwhile, a new and very numerous nation, the Sioux, was moving from the prairie lands east of the Missouri across the river and into the plains. In time these people would dominate most of the northern plains as the Shoshonis had in the 1700s.[23]

As the balance of power shifted, so, too, did the conflict itself. It gradually evolved toward an activity in which strong and reckless young men could prove themselves in what amounted to almost individual combat in the company of like-minded tribesmen and enemies. Despite fewer large battles and massacres, intertribal raiding became the most important element of the small, nomadic societies. Using a horse to hunt buffalo, the staple of the wandering lifestyle, did not take a large portion of a man's time. It was his military feats that gave him status. Women, though exposed to death from enemies and also suffering indirectly from the death of male relatives, still supported war. Their vocal inspiration was present in many songs of encouragement sung before or even during battle. Their self-mutilation in mourning made prompt revenge necessary. And women greatly preferred to marry men who had impressive war honors.

The Europeans' increasing numbers complicated, changed, and intensified tribal warfare. White settlement in the east indirectly affected tribal migrations. Indians eagerly sought manufactured goods and eventually came to depend on traders. Inevitably, the white men got caught up in this strange fighting. The Europeans' presence, along with their trade goods, contributed to the violence. Then, in turn, the traders often sought to end the hostilities. The arrival on the Missouri of men like Trudeau was a precursor of the intensified exploration and trade that would come with the nineteenth century. More British traders appeared, as well as representatives from the new United States. As intertribal conflict became more widespread and complex, white influence also became more all-encompassing and pervasive.

CHAPTER TWO

Killed Them Like Birds

EXPLORERS, TRADERS, AND INTENSIFIED WARFARE, 1804-1810

The American purchase of Louisiana from France in 1803 signaled the beginning of a steady movement of settlers into the northern Great Plains. Neither the British trade nor the minimal Spanish commerce on the upper Missouri River matched the Americans' interest in their new land. Formal exploration quickly began in earnest, prompted by President Thomas Jefferson's political realism and scientific curiosity. He not only recognized the need to claim the land physically and gain the Indians' allegiance, but also wanted to know everything about the geography, plants, animals, and the human inhabitants of the vast region drained by the Mississippi River.

To accomplish these objectives, as well as find a profitable trade route to the Pacific Ocean, Jefferson sent Meriwether Lewis and William Clark to explore the continent. Their expedition opened a new and important chapter in the history of the Far West, but, unknown to Jefferson, this came just as intertribal warfare on the plains intensified. Jefferson's choice to lead the first exploration of Louisiana was his own secretary — tall, handsome Meriwether Lewis. Lewis had the right qualifications. He had broad military experience, including heroic action while serving under "Mad Anthony" Wayne at the Battle of Fallen Timbers in 1794. Jefferson thought Lewis would be a natural leader for the expedition because of his education, his keen observation skills, and his knowledge of the wilderness. Lewis's speculative and, at times, mercurial qualities provided the imaginative and scientific approach necessary to carry out Jefferson's objectives.

To share the command, Lewis approached his longtime friend and army associate, Captain William Clark. Like Lewis, Clark had both frontier and military experience, but Clark also possessed practical experience in handling boats, solving engineering problems, and dealing with the Indians. Clark agreed to go.

The explorers set out from St. Louis in May 1804, heading up the Missouri River. By late summer they had entered the territory of the prairie tribes — the small, allied Oto and Missouri tribes, the Omahas, and the Poncas — who lived near the mouth of the Platte River in what is now eastern Nebraska. The powerful and numerous Pawnee tribes resided farther west on the Platte River. Lewis and Clark learned that some of these tribes fought among themselves as well as against the Iowa, the Osage, and other tribes who lived east of the Missouri, outside the arena of plains warfare.

As they travelled upriver, Lewis and Clark also learned of the changing balance of power. The westernmost portions of the migrating Sioux tribes now constituted the greatest force along the Big River where it flowed north to south in the central portions of present North and South Dakota. The large Yanktonai tribe residing east of the Missouri and the seven Teton tribes west of the river had begun to raid the Mandans, Hidatsas, and all the other tribes in the vicinity. In effect, the Sioux tribes had begun their domination, which would continue for decades.[1]

Jefferson had instructed Lewis and Clark to make treaties between the rival tribes and to ensure that the Indians stayed at peace with the United States. The new nation's short experience in Indian affairs had already demonstrated the benefit of such treaties. During August and September of 1804, Lewis and Clark met with the various tribes, first at present-day Council Bluffs, Iowa, and then farther upriver at today's Yankton, South Dakota. They brought together such rivals as the Omahas and the Otos and Missouris, and the Pawnees and the Omahas. Lewis and Clark also negotiated with several Sioux tribes.

At the various councils, Lewis and Clark made treaties and distributed the usual trade trinkets and peace medals bearing Jefferson's image; yet there is little evidence that the conferences had any permanent influence in ending tribal warfare. Lewis and Clark had no more success than Verendrye and Trudeau before them. The Indians were unwilling to go for long without raiding. In retrospect, it seems that the explorers simply encouraged the brief truces already common in intertribal relations.

Certainly, there was no let-up from the growing Sioux threat. The western Sioux, or Tetons, were migrating to the western plains. Already in 1804, they had swooped down on the Poncas in southeast South Dakota, killed sixty people, and forced the tribesmen to seek refuge with their distant relatives the Omahas. But the two tribes together could rally only a few hundred warriors, a meager number, for the common defense. That was not enough to counter the Sioux threat.[2]

From eastern Nebraska, Lewis and Clark proceeded up the Big River to the Arikara villages in central South Dakota. There, in a settlement of domed earth lodges, they met the French-Canadian trader Pierre Antoine Tabeau, who had been recommended to them as a good contact. Tabeau had worked along the Missouri River since the 1790s, operating out of both St. Louis and the British fur posts in Canada.

Having spent many years with the Arikaras, Tabeau was well acquainted with their ways. By this time the Sioux tribe dominated — almost "enslaved" — the Arikaras, said Tabeau. The Sioux supplied them with meat and hides and in return got all the corn they desired. But there was no equality. The Sioux made the Arikaras dependent by keeping the buffalo herds far from the Arikara villages. Not only that, the Sioux raided the hapless Arikaras whenever they wanted, at random, said Tabeau, then crushed any attempts at revenge.

Tabeau's close commercial relationship with the Arikaras made him exaggerate the Sioux domination. True, the Arikaras' small numbers and sedentary life hindered their position, but other observers noted their extremely warlike habits. And certainly, the nomadic tribes depended upon the sedentary tribes for food and firearms. Whatever the Arikara position, Lewis and Clark found some members of the tribe ready to make peace with their old enemies, the Mandans and Hidatsas. Such peace would give the Arikaras a partial buffer against the intermittent attacks of the Sioux and other tribes.[3]

During Lewis and Clark's stay with the Arikaras, one of the chiefs asked them to help make peace with the Mandans and Hidatsas. When the expedition continued on upriver, this man went along to the enemy villages. Although he represented only one of the Arikara bands, he succeeded in making a peace treaty. Though a small step, it was a beginning to what became by midcentury a firm alliance of the three river tribes. The Sioux, of course, tried to disrupt the truce because they feared a possible alliance against them. According to Tabeau, ". . . they would lose, in the Ricaras, a certain kind of serf, who cultivates for them and who, as they say, takes, for them, the place of women."

The Mandans themselves played no small part in the Arikaras' decision. Fed up with the Arikara raids, they had recently abandoned their usual peaceable nature in favor of an intense and bloody vengeance that had cost the Arikaras dearly. One Mandan leader told

Clark that his tribe had stayed peaceful until the Arikaras had killed some chiefs. Then the Mandans had "killed them like birds" and by the time of the peace "were tired" of killing them.

Tabeau supported this view. He denigrated the Arikaras' fighting ability. "The Ricaras, especially," he wrote, "are considered the best runners of all the nations and it is probably before the enemy that they have gained this reputation." This was somewhat unfair. The derogatory views of the Arikaras seemed to result in part from the huge, unstoppable Teton Sioux migration that flowed westward through the lands of the small river tribes and threatened them all. Later observers saw the Arikaras in a more warlike mode, although their luck in battle did not necessarily improve.[4]

When Lewis and Clark arrived in the Mandan and Hidatsa country in October 1804, they reached another area of intense tribal competition. The Mandan and Hidatsa villages were strung out for several miles below the mouth of the Knife River in today's central North Dakota. Lewis and Clark found the Indians quite friendly and hospitable, and the red men were particularly curious about Clark's black servant, York, who was different from any white man they had ever seen. Called "Great Medicine" by the Indians because of his great size and dark skin, York contributed much to the expedition with his frontier skills and his talents as an interpreter.

Taking advantage of the Mandans' friendliness, the Americans built a fort nearby to wait out the winter and prepare for their departure to the mountains in the spring. That done, they busied themselves in learning more about the land to the west and trying to convince the Indians of the importance of the Great White Father. Jefferson had instructed Lewis and Clark to examine intertribal warfare. These instructions illustrated the thorough thinking of these men of the Enlightenment. The semi-literate Clark copied them into his notebook: ". . . at what season of the year do they usially go to war? Do their women ever accompany them on their hostile experditions?"[5]

As the fierce winter winds of the northern plains howled around Fort Mandan, Lewis and Clark set to work to learn about the confusing system of plains conflict. What they discovered was a complex group of rivalries. The settlements of tribes such as the Mandans not only provided important trade goods such as vegetables and guns, but also contained tempting horse herds and cornfields for the stealthy thief. Lewis and Clark also found that the sedentary nature of the prairie Indians made it possible for the nomadic tribes to exert a certain amount of control over them, as seen in the Sioux-Arikara relationship. A similar situation existed to the north, with the Assiniboins and

Crees having a certain control over the Mandans and Hidatsas.

The Teton Sioux and the Cheyennes also attacked the Mandans and Hidatsas. The Cheyennes, steadily moving west from their home near the Great Lakes because of Sioux and Ojibwa pressure, had recently been farmers near the Missouri River. A hardy and adaptive people, they had now crossed the river and were becoming a nomadic tribe. They were friends of the Arikaras, but fought the Mandans and Hidatsas.

At first glance, the large tribes appeared to dominate intertribal conflict along the Missouri River. The Sioux had overwhelming numbers; the Crees and Assiniboins boasted reputations as inexhaustible horse thieves. But this did not adequately describe the character of tribal warfare. Alexander Henry, a partner in the North West Company, explained this character in some of his voluminous journals. Though Henry lacked that sympathy for the Indians shown by his contemporary David Thompson, he provided accurate, detailed descriptions. and close attention to detail.

As part of his numerous business trips, Henry periodically journeyed south from Canada to trade at the Mandan and Hidatsa villages. Like Lewis and Clark, he found the Mandans reluctant to conduct offensive raids, but noted that they "had the reputation of defending themselves to the last moment when attacked by an enemy; let the number be ever so great against them, they scorn to fly, and fight to the last man." The Hidatsas, often called Minatarees, were more aggressive and were "perpetually at war." For years this small tribe had taken long expeditions as far as the Blackfoot land or against the Shoshonis, now living in the mountains. Almost suicidal military operations such as these by small tribes against powerful opponents could only exist within the framework of a limited warfare.⁶

The objectives and methods of intertribal war partly explained its limited nature, but its ambivalent character was also a factor. Lewis and Clark learned that the tribes periodically curtailed their bloody rivalries in order to trade. Henry and other Canadian traders encountered just such a truce when they made a trading trip to the Mandans and Hidatsas in the summer of 1806, shortly before the Lewis and Clark expedition returned down the Missouri.

From the Hidatsa villages Henry and his men accompanied a group of Mandans and Hidatsas on a trading trip under the leadership of a famous Hidatsa chief the French called "Le Borgue." They travelled south to an enemy Cheyenne village located on the Cheyenne River in present-day central South Dakota. The Cheyennes welcomed the chance to barter but did not like the sudden arrival of a small Assini-

Mandans attacking Arikaras, drawn by George Catlin. Although Catlin did not observe this battle, he reported that the Mandans were victorious. *Courtesy National Museum of American Art, Smithsonian Institution.*

boin band following the trading party. The Cheyennes were on the verge of killing the Assiniboins, who were not supposed to be part of the trade negotiations, but the Hidatsas and Mandans managed to soothe the angry feelings and protect the Assiniboins until they reached the camp. (Most tribes observed a code of hospitality, according to which anyone on a friendly mission could not be harmed once he reached the physical confines of an enemy village.)

A specific ceremony officially cleared the air of disagreeable feelings. To signify his sincerely peaceful motives, Le Borgue symbolically adopted a Cheyenne leader. Then the Mandans and Cheyennes exchanged gifts and the bartering began. Such trading truces were not at all unusual because they permitted the nomadic, horse-borne Indians to supply the river tribes with hides and horses and obtain vegetables and firearms in return.

This ambiguity between war and peace confused Europeans and Americans, but it was an integral part of Indian life. Indians gave gifts to friends and received gifts in return; they stole from enemies. Trade could take place with friends or enemies or within a relationship somewhere in between. This type of exchange included certain obligations, which, in this case, included Le Borgue's adoption ceremony.[7]

The widespread system of war, interspersed with occasional periods of peace, created a shifting situation. Peace never lasted long because warfare held the utmost social importance. According to Tabeau, the Indians saw "the advantages of peace and seem[ed] to desire it," but because it was a basic custom, war was "necessary to them." Tabeau pointed out that a young man had no social position without taking part in war since he had "no right to answer the insults of a warrior." He was admitted "neither to an important feast nor to certain assemblies." Beyond this, "even love is not favorable to him and a brave is the rival who wins most often in love affairs."[8]

Honors in war also decided tribal leadership. Lewis witnessed a good example of this during the winter he spent at Fort Mandan. Several older Hidatsas, having already collected war honors and retired from the warpath, agreed in theory with Lewis' suggestion of a permanent state of intertribal peace. But one young man spoke for the rest of the warriors when he raised a pertinent question: What would the tribe do for leaders, ". . . taking as granted that there could be no other mode devised for making Cheifs [sic] but that which custom had established through the medium of warlike ac[h]ievements"? The unspoken problem was that if raiding stopped, the young men would have no way to gain the status that the older men already possessed.[9]

The social components of warfare made the job of treaty making doubly difficult for the Americans. Despite these obstacles, a major part of Jefferson's instructions was to make friendship agreements between the tribes. The president considered intertribal peace essential to the development and control of the new territory. He later voiced this view in his message to an Indian delegation that came east after the Lewis and Clark expedition: "I have already told you that you are my children, and I wish you to live in peace and friendship with one another as brethren of the same family ought to do." Lewis and Clark had some small success in carrying out that policy, especially in their treaty between a portion of the Arikaras and the Mandans and Hidatsas. On occasion, Clark was even able to convince men to give up plans for war parties.[10]

Jefferson's ideas inaugurated the first specific policy to curtail tribal warfare on the northern plains. His policy went well beyond the fragmented attempts of the French and British traders and would remain government policy throughout the nineteenth century.

From the first, however, certain inherent problems were difficult to overcome. As the French and British had discovered in the 1700s, the fur trade created jealousies between tribes and traders. The Hidatsas and Mandans, for instance, resented the attempts of Alexander Henry and others to trade with the Cheyennes. The white man's trade also undermined both the Indians' commerce and their efforts to defend their villages against enemies armed with British guns. In addition, the treaty makers often took sides to defend the interests of their favorite tribes. The brave but impetuous William Clark, for example, at one point prepared to join a Mandan and Hidatsa war party to help avenge a killing. Clark and others also failed to realize that to the Indians these treaties were little different from their own temporary, nonbinding truces. The Indians usually did not intend to change their ways; rather, they simply wanted the white man's aid.

The Sioux, Cheyennes, and other enemies of the Arikaras, Mandans, and Hidatsas recognized this favoritism and sometimes turned against the white men who began to help the river tribes with trade goods and arms. In February 1805, Tabeau sent word from the Arikara villages to Lewis and Clark that the Teton Sioux, with the help of their Yanktonai relatives east of the river, planned "to come to war in a Short time against the nations in this quarter, and will kill everry white man they See."[11]

In April 1805, after a long but cozy winter at Fort Mandan spent making treaties, spreading good will, and collecting ethnological information, Lewis and Clark again led their men up the Big River. It ran muddy brown now from the early snow melt and moved massively between its high banks now green with the new spring grass. By now, a crusty old French fur trader, Toussaint Charbonneau, had joined the expedition to act as an interpreter. Charbonneau was something of a contrary and arbitrary personage, not greatly liked by the leaders of the group. Lewis and Clark included him more for the possible services of one of his wives, Sacagawea, or Bird Woman.

The slim, young Sacagawea was a Shoshoni who could interpret for the explorers when they reached the mountain fastness of her tribe. She was, in a sense, heading home to her people. Some years earlier, her village had camped near present-day Butte, Montana, close to where the Jefferson, Madison, and Gallatin rivers combine to form the Missouri. It was a good place to hunt and pick wild berries. But the Shoshonis were not on guard. Abruptly, a large party of whooping Hidatsa warriors charged into the camp. The outmanned and outarmed Shoshoni men mounted their horses and fled, and the Hidatsas captured a number of women and children, among them Sacagawea. She lived as a captive with the Hidatsas for several years. For a woman, this meant marriage, adoption, or slavery. Slavery usually meant almost constant work, sleeping outside with little more than rags to wear, and frequent beatings from the tribe's women. Eventually, the Hidatsas gave or sold Sacagawea to Charbonneau as a wife.

When the Lewis and Clark expedition reached Sacagawea's homeland in July, it entered another theater of warfare. The Blackfeet and others raided the mountain strongholds of the Flatheads, Kutenais, and Shoshonis, whom they had pushed off the plains in the late 1700s. The Shoshonis, often labelled the Eastern Shoshonis to distinguish them from many other Shoshonean-speaking tribes living in the Great Basin and Columbia Plateau, suffered continually from Blackfoot raids.[12]

The frightened behavior of Sacagawea's people at the time of her capture perhaps in part indicated the unequal war between the mountain Indians and their aggressive, well-armed neighbors on the plains. On the eastern border of the plains, the river tribes were at a disadvantage because they were sedentary and their populations small. But guns had given them some help in battles against large tribes. Here in the mountains on the western border of the plains, however, the Indians were at a greater disadvantage because they not only were few in number but also lacked firearms. These obstacles had ended the Shoshonis' days of power.

The Shoshonis' weak position made them so shy that it was difficult for Lewis to contact them. At first, the Shoshonis mistook his men for Blackfoot raiders. Hunting on the eastern slope of the Rockies and on the plains was quite dangerous, but the Shoshonis, Flatheads, and others also had to watch out for Blackfeet while at home in the heart of the mountains. Despite the Shoshonis' elusiveness, Sacagawea helped bring together the explorers and a band that happened to be led by her brother. This meeting and happy homecoming occurred far into the mountains across the Continental Divide, just west of Lemhi Pass in present-day central Idaho.[13]

Even though the Shoshonis were very cautious, they by no means avoided war. Like the plains tribes, they considered personal bravery a man's primary virtue, and leaders had to prove their bravery to a high degree. Young Shoshonis were no different from young men of the plains tribes; what the Shoshonis lacked was not courage but guns. In the past, Spain had been their only source for European goods, but the Spanish steadfastly refused to sell the Indians guns. Lewis wrote that the mountain tribes complained that the Spanish "put them off by telling them that if they suffer them to have guns they will kill each other, leaving them [the Spanish] defenceless and an easy prey to their bloodthirsty neighbors to the East of them. . . ." The Spanish, like other white men, recognized the usefulness of Indian protection against more hostile tribes. From the day of the earliest traders until the late 1800s, first Europeans and then Americans allied with friendly Indians in order to further their economic objectives, political policies, or military goals.

Unlike the Spanish, Lewis and Clark responded to the needs of the weak mountain tribes, as they had with the village tribes on the Missouri River. Lewis told the Shoshonis that he had forced the Arikaras, Mandans, and Hidatsas to agree not to attack them. He promised to try to arrange the same understanding with the Gros-ventres of the Prairie, but in this he was not successful. Lewis and Clark also assured the Shoshonis that American trade would eventually supply them with guns and other items that would help eliminate their military disadvantage.

After leaving the Shoshonis, now fast friends, the explorers completed their journey to the Northwest coast, then began their return to St. Louis in the spring of 1806. On the way back, they heard requests for peace from such diverse tribes as the Blackfeet, and the Nez Percés. Fishermen, hunters, gatherers, and expert horse trainers, the Nez Percés were part of the plateau culture inhabiting the Columbia River drainage, but they also crossed the Rocky Mountains to hunt buffalo on the plains. Thus, they were often involved in the plains conflicts. But as elsewhere, Lewis and Clark found that these western tribes included many people who desired peace — generally old men and others who could see in peace a way to gain the Americans as allies and trading partners. None of the tribes wholeheartedly favored peace, however. Warfare was too much a way of life.[14]

In their efforts to regulate intertribal relationships, Lewis and Clark offended some tribes and befriended others. They also offered the smaller, weaker tribes convenient support and a sympathetic ear. But however altruistic their approach, Lewis and Clark perceived the resolution of the struggle from their own culture's view that happiness was inextricably tied to economic advance and peaceful coexistence. Among the tribes of the northern plains, however, economic advancement and personal status depended on the warfare that men pursued so assiduously.

Lewis and Clark, however, were objective enough to recognize the negative influence that their fellow white men had upon tribal culture and warfare. In 1809, shortly before he took his own life, a greatly depressed Lewis wrote that he saw little cause for optimism for the tribes of the upper Missouri. In his "Observations and Reflections on Upper Louisiana," he noted that Spanish, American, and particularly British traders were the main cause of Indian trouble. Lewis accused them of "stimulating or exciting by bribes or otherwise, any nations or bands of Indians, to wage war against other nations or bands, or against the citizens of the United States or against citizens or subjects of any power at peace with the same." This indictment was too all-in-

Skirmishing Crow Indians, painted by Alfred Jacob Miller. The Crows obtained horses earlier than most other tribes on the Northern Plains. *Courtesy Public Archives of Canada.*

clusive, but, certainly, the traders had profits, not the Indians' welfare, foremost in their minds. And the Indians' demand for firearms and other items useful in war involved the fur trade in tribal rivalry regardless of the traders' efforts.[15]

During and after the Lewis and Clark expedition, British traders continued to be close observers of tribal warfare. In the early 1800s, they moved south from Canada to include in their trade network the tribes of the Missouri River and beyond. They travelled as far as the Crow territory on the upper Yellowstone — what the Indians called the Elk River — in present-day Montana. Here the Crows, something of a power in those parts, occupied a land known for its abundant timber, water, and game.

Francois Antoine Larocque, a man known for his courage and the great energy he devoted to his work, led the first North West Company contingent to visit the Crows. Hardly the typical French-Canadian trader, he was studious, well-read, and fluent in two languages. Before retiring to a quiet, academic life, Larocque made close observations of the Mandans and Hidatsas and was one of the few traders who visited the Crow territory in the early 1800s. In 1804 he led a small trading expedition south from Canada to the Mandan and Hidatsa villages. The next summer he continued on to the Crow country to try to open a new market for furs.

Crow tradition held that in the distant past the tribe had been one people with the Hidatsas, but had split over a minor disagreement. In the early 1800s, the Crows remained at peace with the Hidatsas and Mandans and often visited them to trade. While he was at the river villages in 1804, Larocque witnessed a symbolic adoption for trade purposes performed between the Mandans and Hidatsas and a group of Crows and Shoshonis.

The next year, when Larocque stayed at a Crow camp on the Bighorn River of southwestern Montana, he witnessed another temporary truce and the custom of the camp circle being an inviolable sanctuary. One day, five men of the enemy Grosventre tribe arrived. "They brought word of peace from their nation," wrote Larocque, "and say they come to trade horses. They were well received by the Indians [Crows] and presents of different articles were made them." Such trading truces were interspersed among months of energetic raiding.[16]

Laroque also witnessed the conclusion of a brief skirmish during his stay with the Crows. A small band of hostile Assiniboins, creeping up on the camp, had the misfortune of having one of the inhabitants spot them. When the Crow shouted out the news of his discovery, all the men grabbed their battle gear, caught and mounted their war horses, and dashed after the enemies. Everyone else except very old people followed closely on the war party's heels. The Assiniboin war party travelled on foot, a common practice in cutting horses. Despite this disadvantage, the Crows ran down and killed only two raiders; the rest got away.

Larocque and his men saw only the gruesome aftermath of the fight. They stood by while the Crows carried out the grisly mutilation of dead bodies, a common practice in plains Indian warfare. In this case — and whenever possible — women and children took part. They skinned the corpses, hacked off the limbs, stabbed the bodies over and over, and tasted the blood. Though Laroque and his fellow Canadians were repulsed, the practice of mutilation gave the Indians what they regarded as the ultimate revenge, because they believed the dead enemy would arrive in the hunting grounds of paradise in this grotesque form.

A celebration and scalp dance followed this seemingly small victory. It began with a stately procession in which women proudly carried their husbands' weapons as well as the fresh, bloody scalps, now stretched over willow hoops. The men recounted their heroic deeds in war. Later, during the dance, the flickering firelight reflected the male dancers as they leaped and whirled wildly, while the women performed a slow, rhythmic shuffle, giving quiet dignity to the otherwise wild proceedings. The celebration continued far into the night, keeping the white traders awake and restless.[17]

In this violent context of war and revenge, the Crows had a reputation as good fighters. Charles MacKenzie, a trader who accompanied Larocque, wrote of the Crow warriors' prowess, especially on horseback. Larocque echoed this sentiment: "They say no equal number of Indians can beat them on horseback, but that on foot they are not capable to cope with those nations who have no horses."[18]

The Crows, however, were greatly outnumbered by their primary rivals, the Blackfeet. War parties invaded the other's territory almost continuously from spring to fall, creating a rivalry that would continue until the waning years of the nineteenth century. The country over which the warriors travelled stretched from the upper Yellowstone to the northern tributaries of the Missouri. Of varied landscape, the country was well watered by streams, rich in game, and dotted with small ranges of hills posted like sentinels east of the Rocky Mountains. The terrain provided good routes for war parties and supplied them with water, wood, food, and cover.

Crow war parties could take one of several routes north, and the Blackfeet used the same routes when travelling south. All the trails were potentially dangerous. Roving enemies, angry grizzly bears, or treacherous crossings of fast-flowing rivers could spell doom for any warrior. Pompeys Pillar, on the Yellowstone River thirty miles downstream from present-day Billings, Montana, was a popular crossing point. From there a Crow party could head generally north, moving quickly across wide open plains to the Musselshell River. After crossing the Musselshell, the warriors could hide in the Big Snowy, Little Snowy, or Judith mountains. From these hills, it was a direct line to the Missouri. The Big River was always difficult to cross, however. Swimming warriors had to hold their clothing and equipment either on their heads or on small rafts. If the war party was on horseback, a man could hold on to the mane or tail of his horse. Once on the north bank, the leader of the war party might decide to raid the Assiniboins and Crees instead of the Blackfeet. If so, the route was straight north through the Bear Paw Mountains into the Milk River country in northern Montana and southern Alberta. To raid the Blackfeet, the leader took his men west.

Another route was to move northwest from Crow country, using the Crazy Mountains as protection and cover, then go north from there. Next came the Judith Basin, famed hunting ground and battle-ground. West of the basin, the Little Belt Mountains might provide a possible haven if the war party sighted enemies. Bearing a little northwest, the warriors would arrive at the Missouri opposite the mouths of the Teton and Marias rivers, where the American Fur Company later built Fort Benton. The two contiguous river valleys extending to the northwest were favorite camping areas for the Piegans.

This journey of 300 or 400 miles was the key to a successful raid. It had to be done secretly and safely so that the war party lost none of its members. Eventually, with some luck or good medicine, the Crows would find an enemy camp, make a plan of attack, and carry it out. After a successful raid the victors again traversed the trail home, this time very rapidly, running captured horses for several days without stopping in order to avoid pursuers. Again, the safety of all the men was a key part to success.

Not only the Crows made these long raids against the Blackfeet. The Crees and Assiniboins, always hungry for horses, attacked from the east. Even the Hidatsas raided the tribes of the Blackfoot confederacy — the Blackfeet, Bloods, Piegans, and Grosventres. The Blackfoot tribes responded in kind, and at the same time they continued to invade the lands of the Shoshonis, Flatheads, and other mountain Indians.

The Blackfoot confederacy, because of its general aggressiveness and its success against many enemies, held the most feared reputation in the Northwest. Alexander Henry maintained that Blackfoot warriors were almost unbeatable. "They are always the aggressors," he wrote; "there never has an instance been known of a native coming to war from the W. side of the mountains. The Crows are the only nation that sometimes ventures northward in search of the Slaves [Blackfeet]." Henry considered the Piegans in particular to have such prowess that they were able to call their Shoshoni enemies "old women, whom they can kill with sticks and stones." Henry exaggerated Blackfoot skill over that of other tribesmen, however, and British-supplied firearms also aided Blackfoot power.[19]

Despite their formidable reputation, the Blackfeet did not dominate intertribal conflict in the Northwest. Though good-sized, the Blackfoot tribes did not have large populations relative to the huge open spaces they inhabited; so it was easy for war parties from smaller tribes to move around at will. And the small tribes also began to gain access to guns, which helped them against their more numerous foe. The North West Company, for example, found many new markets in the mountains despite Blackfoot disapproval. Then, following the Lewis and Clark expedition, American trade in arms and other goods reached the Rocky Mountains.

The British trade began when David Thompson contacted the Kutenais in the winter of 1800-1801 and brought some tribesmen back to the company post: Rocky Mountain House on the North Saskatchewan River in central Alberta. The Kutenais were a small tribe originally pushed off the plains by the Blackfeet; by 1800 they lived on the western slope of the mountains in present-day British Columbia. They were friends with other mountain tribes such as the Flatheads and the Kalispels. The French called the Kalispels Pend d'Oreilles for their pierced and decorated ears. Early in the 1800s, the Blackfeet and the Kutenais made a peace that lasted a number of years. But despite the new friendship, the Blackfeet did not like the Kutenais receiving guns from the British. So, to trade with the Kutenais, Thompson and others circled to the north, staying clear of Blackfoot land to avoid detection.[20]

The spring of 1807 brought Thompson a chance to establish a broader trade. The previous summer, Meriwether Lewis and his men, travelling back from the coast, had killed two Piegans on the Marias River when the Indians tried to steal some guns. According to Thompson, the next year the Piegans moved down closer to the Missouri to exact revenge on any Americans coming upriver. This, said Thompson, allowed him to move more goods directly up through the mountains to the headwaters of the Columbia River in eastern British Columbia, where he set up a new post, Kootenae House, to benefit the Kutenais and other mountain and plateau tribes.[21]

The Blackfoot response to Thompson's efforts was predictable. They broke the long-standing truce with the Kutenais, and a famous Piegan war chief, ironically named Kootenae Appee (Kutenai Man), led an expedition whose purpose, said the tribe's "civil chief," was to "crush the white Men and the Natives on the west side of the Mountains before they become well armed. They [Kutenais] have always been our [Prisoners]," continued the civil chief, "and now they will pretend to equal us. . . ." A large party of 250 men bent on revenge arrived at Kootenae House in the fall of 1808. Bloodshed seemed certain, but

Sioux and Blackfoot warriors skirmishing, as painted by Charles M. Russell. *Courtesy Brown & Bigelow, St. Paul, Minnesota.*

the ever-diplomatic Thompson averted the crisis by distributing presents. Finally, by casually mentioning the presence of a large Kutenai force in the area, he was able to talk the Piegans into returning home.[22]

From Kootenae House, Thompson took guns south to other tribes: the Flatheads in the mountains of northern Montana and the Pend d'Oreilles of northern Idaho. The Shoshonis also received firearms from both British and American traders. Within a few years these weapons enabled the mountain Indians to fight more successfully against their powerful enemies from the plains. In July 1810, for example, 150 Flatheads, armed with twenty guns and several hundred rounds of ammunition supplied by Thompson, made their way confidently to the plains. There they ran into a large force of Piegans. As soon as the Piegans had prepared their war "medicine" — special objects and ceremonies giving spiritual power — they attacked. Their ponies hurtled across the open ground, the warriors whooping with the excitement of combat. But by this time the Flatheads were ready. They had made a rampart of lodgepoles and even used some horses as shields. The angry Piegans made one heroic charge after another, but it proved fruitless against the deadly musket fire from the barricade. For the first time in many years, the Piegans went home defeated by the Flatheads. The proud Piegans had lost seven men killed and thirteen more had been wounded, making this a costly battle for the nomadic band that depended on their limited number of men for hunting and protection.[23]

The Blackfoot suzerainty, begun in the 1700s when they chased the Shoshonis, Flatheads, and Kutenais off the plains, was beginning to be challenged by other tribes as well. In 1810 Alexander Henry, at Rocky Mountain House, noted that in the past the mountain tribes had been easy prey to the Blackfeet. Now, guns had enabled mountain warriors to create a more even military balance, even though the Blackfeet remained the dominating force and were the tribes that most often took the offensive in the Northwest.[24]

The Blackfeet had once seen the English traders as their own private suppliers; now they greatly resented the British commerce that enhanced their enemies' power. The Blackfeet saw this as a conspiracy against them. The traders had already had occasional trouble with the Blackfeet over some of the Crees who worked for the North West Company. Blackfeet sometimes tried to take out their revenge on these employees. But things became more serious after Thompson placated the large war party under Kootenae Appee. After the great Flathead victory, the Piegans headed for Rocky Mountain House to cut off the supply of guns to the mountain tribes. Thompson wrote that "this was the first time the Piegans were in a manner defeated, and they determined to wreak their vengeance on the white man. . . ." Nothing significant happened, however, because the Blackfeet depended too much on the British for arms to go to war with them.[25]

Unable to directly stop the trade in arms, in 1811 the Piegans tried a new approach. They sent a peace delegation to the Flatheads. Being the "frontier" tribe of the Blackfoot confederation, closest to their western enemies, the Piegans had suffered the brunt of the recent raids by armed parties from the mountains. The Flatheads took the Blackfoot request to their allies, and the mountain tribes held a conference. David Thompson, who attended, reported that the Indians decided the Piegans were too tricky to trust with a peace agreement. Besides, the Indians said, the "Piegans have shed too much blood in our country. Now we will shed blood in theirs." Asked for his advice, Thompson told the council that it was better not to make peace with one tribe at a time; a general peace was preferable.

This meeting, which had begun as a peace conference, evolved into a call for war against the Blackfeet. This warlike attitude did not begin on the spur of the moment. Thompson had already noticed how the attitudes of the mountain and plateau Indians changed as soon as they got hold of firearms. They became "Proud of their Guns and iron shod arrows," he wrote, and "they were anxious to try these arms in battle." The year before, Thompson had tried to dissuade three plateau tribes — the Spokane, Kalispel, and Nez Percé — from forming a war party against the Teekanoggin, a small defenseless tribe. He told the plateau tribes that they should help fight the Blackfeet instead. It had not taken long for the mountain and plateau tribes to begin behaving with the same aggressiveness as the Blackfeet.[26]

In less than ten years after the Lewis and Clark expedition, both the Americans and British had become more closely involved in tribal rivalries than ever before. The fur trade strongly affected the fighting, and the white men's dealings with the tribes in order to control trade or end warfare made the situation more complicated. This would continue to be the case as the United States increasingly bent its efforts to stop intertribal raiding.

CHAPTER THREE

Very Impatient of Insult

THE GROWING COMPLEXITY OF WARFARE, 1810-1830

The first sales of guns reflected only the beginning of American and British influence on the tribes. In the two decades after 1810, more and more Americans and British entered this northern theater of tribal warfare. Most were involved in the fur trade; some were government officials; a few were simply travellers. All noticed the Indian conflict, and some tried to influence it, but they were too few in number to have any real impact or success in ending the raiding.

In 1811, one of the first major American fur trading ventures got underway when aggressive businessman John Jacob Astor launched his ambitious plan to establish his new Pacific Fur Company (later the American Fur Company) on the northwest coast. According to Astor's plan, one contingent would sail there; the other would go over land. The leader of the Overland Astorians, as they came to be called, was Wilson Price Hunt, one of Astor's partners. In April 1811, he led sixteen men up the Missouri, accompanied by a Scotsman named John Bradbury. Although the Botanical Society of Liverpool had commissioned Bradbury to do research on American plants, his astute observations of Indians, in addition to his botanical work, soon made him one of the early authorities on plains ethnology.

Two months after Hunt departed, the well-known fur man, Manuel Lisa of the Missouri Fur Company, brought traders upriver. Included in his group was Henry Marie Brackenridge, perhaps the first tourist on the northern plains. A writer and statesman, Brackenridge came up the Missouri simply for pleasure at the invitation of his friend Lisa.

As the Hunt expedition wended its way up the Big River, it encountered increasing evidence of intertribal warfare. Early in the trip, even before reaching the plains, the men were careful to avoid a war party of Sioux and Pottawatomies searching for Osages. The danger was that war parties often decided to attack anyone, especially if the warriors had not succeeded in their original objective. When the traders reached the mouth of the Platte River, they found the Otos and Missouris. Although they had only 200 warriors between them, the two tribes still participated in tribal war, fighting both plains and prairie tribes.

On May 31, Hunt and his men reached what is now South Dakota, where they encountered a camp of Yankton Sioux and two Teton tribes, the Miniconjous and the Brulés. The Sioux intended to stop the traders from selling guns to the Mandans, Hidatsas, and Arikaras. Six hundred mounted warriors ranged along the river bank — an awesome sight that scared the small group of boatmen. The warriors sat ominously on their horses, fully armed, painted, and decorated for war. Because the channel was narrow and the boats had to run in close to the riverbank, Hunt had no choice but to land. Once the men were ashore, however, the Sioux seemed peaceful enough. The two parties held a council at which Hunt supplied the tribesmen with fifteen "carottes," or bundles, of tobacco and some corn. That mollified the Sioux. Then Hunt assured them that his purpose was not to sell arms to their enemies upriver. With that the natives allowed Hunt and his men to continue unharmed.[1]

Several days later, a war party of Mandans, Hidatsas, and Arikaras confronted the traders at a narrow passage where the channel passed around a sandbar. The Indians were heading south, intent on attacking the Sioux, but when they learned they could buy guns from Hunt, they returned to the Arikara village, about ten days' travel, to await the traders. At this point Lisa's party caught up with Hunt's group. Lisa and Hunt were intense rivals, each convinced that the other would turn the Indians against him. They narrowly avoided a fight before deciding to continue on together to the Arikara village.[2]

When the Americans reached the Arikara village, they found that it consisted of rounded earth lodges that stretched for about three-quarters of a mile along the west bank of the Missouri River in central South Dakota. As their keelboats arrived, the traders saw the Arikara women busily paddling "bull boats" loaded with firewood from across the river. These craft, made of buffalo hides stretched over a framework of saplings, could be paddled by one person in the bow. Bradbury noticed that the hills around the village were covered with horses, which, he said, came from the Pawnees, relatives of the Arikaras, and the Poncas, who had travelled all the way to the Southwest to steal them from the Spanish.[3]

During his stay, Bradbury learned that the Arikaras traded with many other tribes, as they had in the past, although some customers had migrated to different areas. The Arapahos and the Cheyennes, for example, now lived together in the vicinity of the Black Hills, 200 miles to the southwest across the flat expanses of present-day South Dakota. The Cheyennes, in particular, made the long journey to trade with the Arikaras despite the presence of their Sioux enemies.

Some Arikaras in the war party that met Hunt apparently respected the treaty made by Lewis and Clark and had stayed at peace with the Mandans and Hidatsas. The Sioux, Crees, and Assiniboins, all well-supplied with British guns, remained the major threats to the Arikaras (as well as to the Hidatsas and Mandans), but these tribes now had guns and ammunition and seemed more aggressive despite the disadvantages of their sedentary way of life. The Arikaras raided west against the Crows; the Mandans and Hidatsas fought the mountain tribes. Bradbury wrote that one small Hidatsa band, the "Ahwhha-ways," who had only fifty warriors, followed the proud Hidatsa military tradition and continually took the offensive in war.[4]

On July 7, while still at the Arikara village, the Americans witnessed a good example of this aggressiveness. A successful war party of 300 Arikaras returned after chasing off a band of Sioux that had been stealing horses and crops for several weeks. The avenging Arikaras had killed seven Sioux at the cost of two of their own men. The women mourned the two dead warriors — they slashed their skin, cut their hair, and dumped dirt and ashes on their heads as signs of grief.

The victory was still important, however. Armed with their guns, clubs, and bows and arrows, the men rode their ponies triumphantly into the village. According to Brackenridge, the warriors who had drunk the enemy's blood painted a red hand across their mouths. Those who had killed a man wore fox tails attached to their moccasin heels. The women divided the scalps to make them seem more numerous, then proudly waved the gruesome trophies in the air during the many hours of dancing that followed. The tribe royally feasted the warriors, and the celebration went on throughout the night.[5]

War played as large a role in this sedentary prairie culture as it did among the nomadic horsemen of the plains. Brackenridge wrote that Arikara parents brought up their young boys to "take blood" naturally. Only through raiding, he continued, could a man attain any prestige. "It is utterly impossible to be a great man amongst them," he wrote, "without being a distinguished warrior, and though respect is paid to birth, it must be accompanied by other merit, to procure much influence."[6]

Hunt and Lisa eyed each other suspiciously throughout their time at the Arikara villages, but they still traded side by side with the Indians. And despite Hunt's earlier assurances to the Sioux, he sold firearms to the river tribes.

From the Arikara settlement Bradbury and Brackenridge, their journeys completed, returned to St. Louis aboard one of Lisa's boats. Hunt continued his cross-country trek. He got horses from Lisa in exchange for his keelboats and from the Arikaras in exchange for guns and ammunition.

The party then struck out westward, following the course of the Grand River. Near the present-day boundary between North and South Dakota the party spent two weeks visiting a band of Cheyennes, whom the traders found very hospitable. According to Hunt, the Cheyennes had only in recent years become a fully nomadic people, but they already possessed a good supply of horses and were accomplished riders. The Sioux were a major enemy. In 1811, the Cheyennes still held a vivid memory of the overwhelming Sioux pressure that had forced them to leave their farming villages east of the Missouri and change to the nomadic plains life.[7]

After leaving the Cheyennes, Hunt and his men continued their journey. First they crossed the rivers that ran diagonally across the middle of the northern plains to intersect the Missouri or the Yellowstone. The Little Missouri came first, then the Powder, and finally the Bighorn, in the heart of Crow country. Here the expedition had some problems. At a Crow village, one of Hunt's interpreters, Edward Rose, a mulatto who had lived with the Crows and much preferred the Indian life, deserted the party to rejoin the tribe. And true to their reputation as notorious horse thieves, the Crows stole some of Hunt's horses. The Crows excused this on the pretext that the Americans were going to sell the animals to the Blackfeet. Despite this lack of hospitality, Rose and his Crow friends helped the Americans find a way through the Bighorn Mountains of northern Wyoming and on to the Rocky Mountains.

The novelist Washington Irving described this encounter in his book *Astoria*. Irving agreed with Alexander Henry that the Crows were a dangerous, warlike tribe. No one, wrote Irving, could match the Crows in stealing horses, "the especial objects of their depredations. . . . Their skill and audacity in stealing them," continued Irving, "are said to be astonishing. This is their glory and delight; an accomplished horse stealer fills up their idea of a hero."[8]

The Hunt party next entered the Rocky Mountains. By now the Shoshonis, Flatheads, and Kutenais often worked in concert against the Blackfeet. With their newly acquired guns they journeyed to the land of the Piegans to hunt, confident in their ability to defend themselves.

The North West Company continued to supply weapons to both sides, even though the Blackfeet threatened to kill traders dealing with the mountain tribes. The traders, for their part, often took the side of their mountain friends. Some of them even joined war parties. Ross Cox, a clerk with the company, wrote about one Irish employee named M'Donald, who often joined war parties because he loved a good fight. M'Donald, however, spurned the Indian practice of charging close to the enemy to demonstrate bravery (and still survive). In a fight in 1814, M'Donald took his gun, ran straight into the Blackfoot ranks, paused to take aim, and fired, killing two Blackfeet. This act of courage earned him the hatred of the Blackfeet but won him great admiration from his Flathead friends. Other outsiders who lived with adopted tribes performed equal feats of daring. The best example was Edward Rose. He led the Crows in numerous daredevil attacks against their enemies.[9]

While the Overland Astorians under Hunt struggled across the continent to finish a trip thought impossible by some of the old Missouri traders, Astor's other party sailed around Cape Horn on the *Tonquin.* In 1811, these men built a fort they named Astoria, where Hunt arrived early in 1812. On June 29, 1812, a party started back to New York to notify Astor of Hunt's arrival and tell him of the supplies needed for the coming year's trade. The leader of this party was Robert Stuart, a 27-year-old Scotsman only recently come to America. Stuart had joined the North West Company when he first migrated to Canada, but then had quit and moved to New York to join Astor's new Pacific Fur Company.[10]

Stuart and his men encountered Indians on a number of occasions, but a run-in with the Crows was nearly disastrous. On a dark night in the fall of 1812, a war party quietly approached the Americans' camp and ran off all the horses. Left without transportation, the party faced a long, trying journey, fraught with danger and food shortages. But through Stuart's leadership, cajolery, persuasion, and even threats, his men overcame the hardships of fatigue, hunger, and Indian threats.

On the journey, Stuart wrote about the various Indians he saw. He echoed some of what other people had observed and provided more precise information. In the mountains Stuart found the Nez Percés and Flatheads "less thievish" than their neighbors, "but of a haughty and imperious disposition, very impatient of insult and revengeful in the extreme. . . ." The Crows, who often invaded Shoshoni territory, held a fearsome reputation with that tribe. The Shoshonis told Stuart that during the previous spring, 1811, at the headwaters of the Missouri River, the Blackfeet had fought a pitched battle with them and killed many Shoshonis, as well as two Canadian traders.

Arriving at the upper reaches of the North Platte River, Stuart discovered newer rivalries heating the cauldron of tribal war. The Arapahos, who had migrated to the western plains before their allies the Cheyennes, were at war with the Crows. The Arapahos were also continuing what had become a long-standing feud with the Utes, who generally lived outside the arena of northern plains conflict. Called "Black Arms" or "Black Men" by other Indians, the dark-complexioned Utes made their home in the Rocky Mountains of present-day Colorado.

In December 1812, the Stuart party camped on the North Platte River, a short distance above present-day Casper, Wyoming. On December 10, a war party of twenty-three tough-looking Arapahos rode up in search of some Crows who had raided an Arapaho camp and "stolen a great many of their Horses, [and] taken some of their women prisoner. . . ." The Arapahos camped with the Astorians and ate voraciously, as was expected in the hospitable largess of plains tribes. The next day the Indians left. After examining their meager food supply, the Americans were very happy to be rid of them. But recognizing that the Arapahos, like other Plains Indians, felt no compunction against stealing anything from people not of their own tribe, the traders thought they had escaped relatively unscathed.[11]

As the Stuart party continued down the Platte River, the first epoch of transcontinental travel came to an end. The War of 1812 began; the British captured Astoria and closed the Northwest to American interests for three years. Yet Stuart and his men had accomplished much. They had traced very nearly the route that would become known as the Oregon Trail, which would run from Independence, Missouri, to the Pacific Coast. It was not long before this trail became one of the major highways for Americans to enter Indian lands and bring their dreaded diseases.

Meanwhile, tribal warfare continued as usual, unabated, as the tribes pursued their slow, westward migration. Increasingly, the Crows lived near the center of the fighting, in the western half of the northern plains. They numbered around 1,400 warriors. But these numbers were fairly small compared to perhaps 3,000 Blackfoot and Grosventre fighters and many more Teton Sioux. In the early 1800s, the Crows were divided into two friendly, but rival, factions. The Mountain Crows stayed mostly south of the Yellowstone around the

War Ground, Beating a Retreat, painted by Alfred Jacob Miller. *Courtesy Public Archives of Canada.*

Bighorn River and the tributarties of the Powder River. The River Crows lived north of the Yellowstone and, in later years, closer to the Missouri.[12]

The Crows believed that their military prowess had originated far in the past when a mythical figure called Child of the Sun came to see them. He led the Crows against the Piegans and the Bannocks, a small mountain tribe, and the Crows were successful any time that Child of the Sun magically lit his special pipe.

After Child of the Sun came another prominent leader, Tattooed Forehead. Although the stories about him appear almost superhuman, he could have been a real person who lived in the late 1700s and early 1800s. He developed his reputation through remarkable feats of sneaking into enemy camps to steal horses, an important act of bravery among the Crows. Tattooed Forehead also liked to disguise himself. On one occasion he dressed like a woman, entered an Assiniboin camp, and smothered a man to death with his bare hands. Another night he pretended to be an idiot and so tricked two men that he was

able to steal their weapons. Whatever the truth, these stories illustrated the great courage necessary to defeat an enemy at close quarters.
The tales also came close to the plains warrior's ideal.[13]

The Crows continued to be blessed with strong leaders. By the
early 1820s, however, two men had grown so influential that the tribe
split over their rivalry. The first was Long Hair. His hair literally
reached the ground (with the help of extra pieces that were glued
on). He entered early manhood without distinction, but spent much
time alone in the hills, fasting and praying for "good medicine," or
spiritual power. Medicine was of the utmost importance to a warrior.
A "medicine bundle," whatever it contained — a collection of pebbles
or the remains of a sacred animal — was what kept the individual
safe in battle and gave him luck. Long Hair's medicine was so powerful
that it helped his reputation and enabled him to become an important
chief.

The reputation of Arapooish, or Rotten Belly, matched that of Long
Hair. The Crows claimed that Arapooish had dreams that told exactly
where an enemy camp could be located, and they believed that his
shield was so sacred it could deflect bullets. The Crows who followed
Long Hair became the Mountain Crows, those who followed
Arapooish, the River Crows.[14]

From about 1800 to 1830, the Crows' major enemies were the
Blackfeet; the Assiniboins were also rivals, and the Sioux and Cheyennes became new opponents as they moved west. As the conflict with
these tribes intensified, the Crows fought several major battles that
resulted in high casualties, even though this phenomenon was becoming less common as intertribal rivalries evolved toward more limited
warfare. In 1816 or 1817, for example, a band of Crows camped on
the Arrow River west of the Bighorn caught and killed thirty Assiniboins who were trying to steal horses. This was a major victory, after
which the Assiniboins apparently were less willing to meet the Crows
in open battle.

The Crows sustained a catastrophe in the early 1820s, however,
when a large war party of Tetons and Cheyennes surprised a Crow
camp. Many men had gone on war parties, and reports given many
years later, obviously with exaggeration, indicated that the Tetons
and Cheyennes killed numerous Crow men still in camp and captured
several hundred women and children. The Crow tribe then built itself
back up by capturing women and children from enemies. This practice
was actually quite common, and it meant that the populations of all
the plains tribes were made up in part with the blood of other peoples.
Even so, casualties sustained in raiding created a slow decline in

numbers that was difficult to rectify in small nomadic societies.[15]

The Crows' widespread wars were another indication of increasingly long-range tribal raiding during the early 1800s. After a slow beginning, firearms from the east and horses from the west and south had become increasingly available. With greater mobility and better arms, northern plains warfare expanded in terms of distances and numbers of opponents. A multitude of rivalries crisscrossed the region, covering hundreds of miles. The Cheyennes roamed between the Missouri and the upper North Platte River. The Arikaras and Hidatsas raided west to the mountains. The Sioux sent their hunting and war parties west and south from their lands near the Missouri River. The Assiniboins and Crees not only fought the Blackfeet and Crows but also raided the Mandans and Hidatsas. The Pawnees, the most powerful prairie people, raided far from their villages against both prairie and plains tribes.

As rivalries became more complex, so did the system of peace making and trade agreements, and sometimes errors led to tragedy. In the early 1820s, for instance, thirty Assiniboins intent on making peace approached a Hidatsa village. Unknown to them, however, only a few days earlier some Assiniboins from another band had ambushed and killed a Hidatsa. His relatives were placing his body on the burial scaffold when the peace delegation arrived. The bitter Hidatsas immediately turned on their visitors with a vengeance, killed twenty of them, and captured three women before the remainder could escape.[16]

Americans observed the increase of warfare in the 1820s because the federal government sent exploration parties there and established Indian agencies. In June 1820, the scientific expedition to explore the central plains, led by Major Stephen H. Long, stopped at the Pawnee villages. The Americans found the four Pawnee tribes strung out along the Platte River and its tributaries in central Nebraska. The villages covered a considerable area and included earth lodges similar to those of the Mandans and other river tribes. But the Pawnee dwellings were larger; they were able to accommodate several families and some of the owners' most valuable horses. Although farmers, the Pawnees also hunted buffalo and avidly participated in the plains intertribal competition.

Edwin James, who served the Long expedition as botanist and geologist, estimated that the Pawnees numbered about 6,000 people, less than 2,000 of whom were warriors. The tribe owned between 6,000 and 8,000 horses.

James described the Pawnees' aggressiveness and the respect they received from the Sioux and other neighboring nations because they were "warlike and powerful." The Pawnees fought the Sioux, Cheyennes, Arapahos, and Crows, as well as river tribes such as the Otos and Omahas. The Pawnees also made long war excursions to the south to fight the southern portions of the Cheyenne and Arapaho tribes and the Comanches and Kiowas.

The Pawnees were not always successful, however. Shortly before the Long expedition reached the Pawnees, Benjamin O'Fallon, who was the new agent for the Indians of the upper Missouri as well as the nephew of the new superintendent of Indian Affairs, William Clark, noted the return of a 93-member Pawnee war party. Members of the Loup tribe, they had suffered heavy losses in a fight with Kiowas, Comanches, and Arapahos far to the southwest, somewhere in present-day Colorado or New Mexico.[17]

Given their military reputation, the Pawnees provided a powerful force on the south side of the northern plains. As Long reported, "Their confidence in their own strength gives them a disposition to dominion over their weaker neighbours." This was true considering the small size of the tribes along the Missouri. Yet the Long expedition found that the small river tribes still remained attached to warfare.

James had a chance to observe the river tribes, especially the Omahas, during the winter of 1819-1820 while the expedition stayed at Council Bluffs above the mouth of the Platte River. James described the Omahas as a small tribe of merely 600 people. They had made some effort to maintain the peace that Lewis and Clark had set up with the Otos, and the Omahas' present chief, Big Elk, had also attempted to establish a policy of fighting only when attacked. To some degree this attitude must have been a facade for obtaining American help against the increasing Sioux threat, because James found that the individual Omaha warrior was still dedicated to raiding.[18]

In these endeavors the Omahas usually set out in small parties led by noted leaders with strong medicine. Sometimes, however, large war parties that included almost all the tribe's 150 warriors struck the Pawnees or another enemy. James described Omaha warfare as being like that of the nomadic plains tribes: Shooting a man from a distance did not prove bravery, only good marksmanship. The ultimate honors went to the man who showed the most courage by attacking an enemy at close quarters; the warrior most admired was one able to capture an enemy or one "who first strikes or even touches the body of a fallen enemy, in the presence of friends of the deceased, who are generally watching their opportunity to revenge his death." This was "counting coup," and a scalp that resulted from such a venture symbolized a brave act.

Warfare among the Omahas carried the same social importance that it did among the other prairie, plains, and mountain tribes. James emphasized the part played by women in intertribal hostilities. A man's wife had the honor of carrying in the victory dance any scalps he had taken. Women generally paid little attention to men who were not successful in combat. "It is to the squaws that many of these excursions are attributable," wrote James, "as those whose husbands have not been successful in war, frequently murmur, saying, 'You have had me for a wife a long time, and have never yet gratified me with the scalp dance.'"[19]

By the 1820s, many Americans had begun to realize how much the Indians emphasized warfare in their cultures. Colonel (later General) Henry Atkinson, commander of the Yellowstone expedition, not only reported the extent of tribal conflict but also recognized its particularly limited nature. "Indeed, there is scarcely a tribe," wrote Atkinson, "but what is at war with some one or more tribes. These wars consist of excursions made by small parties of one nation against another, and amount to the loss of but few lives and the stealing of a few horses."

At this time the United States government was primarily interested in keeping the Indians at peace with Americans in order to protect the fur trade. This was the main object of Atkinson's trip up the Missouri in 1825. Where convenient, however, Atkinson worked at making peace between tribes. In this way he continued a policy begun by Lewis and Clark, which was to become a more important government approach in the future.[20]

Protecting the fur trade also continued to be the major British objective in diplomacy with the Indians. The Treaty of Ghent, which ended the War of 1812, excluded the British from the Missouri River, but they still operated west of the Rocky Mountains. In 1821, the mighty Hudson's Bay Company and the North West Company combined, and three years later George Simpson, governor-general of the Hudson's Bay Territories, travelled to the mountains to rehabilitate the fur trade. He found that intertribal conflict continued to be a major obstacle. The British tried to keep their customers such as the Shoshonis and the Nez Percés from fighting each other. If the Indians had to fight, the traders encouraged them to go to war against the Blackfeet, who were still the major threat to the mountain Indians and the British trade.[21]

Back on the Missouri, tribal war also frustrated the fur traders. From the beginning, the hostility had caused American traders to step lightly, primarily because of Sioux jealousy. Then, in 1823, the Arikaras, or Rees as the mountain men called them, turned on a trading party led by the new entrepreneur out of St. Louis, William Henry Ashley. This resulted in an expedition of soldiers and trappers under Colonel Henry Leavenworth marching to rescue Ashley's beleagured trappers. Along the way Leavenworth recruited Sioux warriors to help fight their old Arikara enemy.

The ensuing engagement at the Arikara villages demonstrated the basic differences in the ways the Americans and the Indians viewed war. During the battle, when the Sioux charged in close to count coup, they got in the way of American cannonfire. Then later, when Leavenworth tried to finish the fight with an attack by the whole force, he found the Sioux had left the battlefield. They were now cleaning the Arikara fields of as much corn as they could carry. The fiasco ended with the Sioux making their own kind of truce with the Arikaras. The Sioux had done some honorable deeds and got some plunder; now it was time to go home. The Arikaras secretly vacated their village at night, and the soldiers were never able to punish them for their attacks on American trappers.[22]

Only twenty years had elapsed between Lewis and Clark's expedition and Leavenworth's debacle at the Arikara village. During that time the Americans witnessed the rise of an intensified and more sophisticated intertribal conflict. All the tribes acquired more horses, and the migrations of the Teton Sioux and the Cheyennes created a larger field of combat. The traders played no small part in these developing rivalries by providing the increasingly important firearms. The fur trade thus became more involved in intertribal conflict, and traders and American officials saw a need to control the fighting in the interests of economic progress.

Accordingly, in 1824 the federal government established the St. Louis Superintendency and the Upper Missouri Agency under the auspices of the War Department. In 1826, the first superintendent, William Clark, developed the policy of ending tribal war by suggesting that each tribe be required to pay for its depredations out of its own resources, that is, money obtained from the government's land purchase. Although this policy was eventually put into effect, in these early years the Indian Office had a chance to control only tribes near the Missouri River. It was almost impossible to stop the nomadic tribes. Agents made treaties like those by Atkinson on his 1825 expedition, but seldom did the truces last very long.[23]

The ability of the tribes to roam freely through the plains began to change in the 1830s as American immigration increased. Although he was unaware of it, General Atkinson helped signal this change with his report for the 1825 expedition. He described the northern plains as part of the planned "Permanent Indian Frontier," the home of the eastern tribes. Few soldiers would be needed to man the line of posts along the eastern boundary. Ironically, when Atkinson submitted his report, he enclosed Ashley's trading report that showed South Pass in present-day Wyoming as an easy route for wagon travel west. This route would be a key passageway for later migrations west.[24]

Americans did not use the northern plains much in the early years of the century, but in the next several decades, with the South Pass route through the mountains, the area became heavily travelled by fur trappers, missionaries, travellers, and settlers going west. Inevitably, tribal warfare would become mixed up with this sizable migration that occurred just as intertribal conflict was entering its golden age, when the nomadic horseman ruled the plains in his search for glory.

CHAPTER FOUR

Their Name Is A Terror

WARFARE IN BLACKFOOT AND CROW COUNTRY, 1830-1850

On a summer morning in 1832, a camp of eighty Piegan lodges filed out along the flatland bordering the Musselshell River in central Montana. Women guided the horses dragging the heavily laden travois. Children and dogs loped through the column. And armed warriors guarded the caravan closely, for this was the most dangerous possible position for a nomadic band. With the young, old, and helpless strung out in the open, the band was vulnerable to attack and difficult to defend. Suddenly, several hundred Crow warriors broke from cover. They whooped wildly and galloped headlong for the caravan's rear. Bullets and arrows filled the clear, crisp air as the frantic Piegans scattered over the plain, desperately looking for cover or escape. But it was hopeless. The Crows, led by their famous chief, Rotten Belly, overran the badly outnumbered Piegan warriors and killed almost all. Then they rounded up more than 200 women and children and marched them off to a life of captivity or adoption into the Crow tribe.

The ambush was a severe blow to the proud Piegans and helped mark the beginning of an era of mounting intertribal warfare. An attack of this type was one of the few instances within the limited nature of tribal conflict in which an enemy inflicted a large number of casualties. Massacres of entire bands were unusual; otherwise, the survival of the nomadic people would have been difficult. But as raiding intensified during the 1830s and 1840s, the attrition rate increasingly drained populations.

The few massacres like the Piegan slaughter kept the revenge cycle spinning endlessly. The year after that victory, the Crows themselves suffered a similar defeat at the hands of the Cheyennes on the Platte River. In revenge, Rotten Belly, who had masterminded the victory over the Piegans, led a victorious attack on the Cheyennes that avenged the humiliation.

Rotten Belly, or Arapooish, epitomized the ideal plains warrior. He had risen to renown partly because he belonged to an important family and was rich in horses, but his prestige rested mainly on bravery and strong medicine. Although he was tall and handsome, according to some Crows, he was "not an agreeable man, but rather of a quiet, surly disposition. He spoke little, but that in a tone of command." Warriors followed him and deferred to him because of his "decision, action, and an utter disregard for the safety of his person."[1]

Aside from Rotten Belly's victory over the Piegans, the year 1832 marked the beginning of greater white migration into the plains, a development that paralleled the intensified tribal raiding. That year, the steamboat *Yellowstone* arrived on the Missouri, thus opening the northern plains to the most advanced form of transportation. It was a momentous occasion. The American Fur Company and other fur trading organizations could greatly develop their trade, and more Americans than ever before entered the northern plains.

The artist George Catlin was one of the earliest to take advantage of the new mode of travel. He arrived at Fort Union, at the present-day boundary of North Dakota and Montana, on the first voyage of the *Yellowstone*. Catlin was a dark-complexioned man with a shock of black hair and the piercing blue eyes of an outdoorsman. He was handsome, despite a long tomahawk scar down his left cheek, the result of a boyhood accident. He cut a rather dashing figure when he arrived at Fort Union ready to start work on his avowed project of portraying the red man's true culture.

Catlin sympathized with the Indians, even to the point of identifying with them. His intent was always to paint them realistically. Other visitors to the northern plains in the next two decades reinforced Catlin's efforts to create objective Indian paintings. The resulting pictures, as well as descriptions of the peculiar brand of warfare, were an important contribution to plains ethnology.

The disparate activities of Rotten Belly and Catlin signalled the beginning of an era during which tribal warfare reached a high degree of cultural sophistication, while at the same time the white man observed it in greater detail and attempted to control and end it. The 1830s and 1840s witnessed the first significant American expansion into and across the plains after the tentative approach of the early 1800s. The fur trade, dominated by the American Fur Company, reached its peak. Hundreds of its employees ascended the Missouri, and many of them became well acquainted with Indian life. Travellers, whether artists, writers, amateur naturalists, missionaries, or civil servants, could now make the journey in the comparative luxury of a steamboat. By the 1840s, as expansionism seized the imagination of the American people and their government, numerous pioneers bound for Oregon or California were crossing the northern plains.

At the same time that these newcomers entered the plains, life for the plains warrior was improving. Buffalo, the staff of life, was plentiful, and a good hunter could produce enough meat in a few hours to feed his family for months. Women did the rest of the daily labor, which freed men to spend their time at war. The supply of firearms, knives, and iron for arrowheads increased with the booming fur trade. Pony herds grew because of improved breeding methods, purchases from the mountain tribes, and the perennial horse cutting raids on enemy villages.

As white Americans came to the plains in greater numbers, however, the huge buffalo herds continued to migrate farther west. The nomadic tribes moved westward with the herds, taking their rivalries with them. Traders, travellers, and government officials found that as warfare spread, all the tribes involved expanded their raiding territory. The conflict divided itself rather naturally into four very general areas, or theaters, of war. Although some tribes fought in a number of these areas, the four sections covered fairly distinct terrain and reflected specific rivalries.

In the southeast corner of the northern plains — present-day eastern Nebraska and southeastern South Dakota — combat centered on a number of sedentary horticultural tribes. The Pawnees lived along the lower Platte River and the Loup tributary. Below them, near the mouth of the Platte, were the Otos, Omahas, and other small tribes. As time passed and the Sioux migration swelled, these sedentary tribes increasingly became the objects of raids by the "Sioux alliance." The southern Teton Sioux — Oglalas and Brulés — along with their Miniconjou relatives to the north — the Yanktons and Yanktonais from east of the Missouri — and the Northern Cheyennes and Northern Arapahos together comprised a powerful force that the smaller prairie tribes could not stop.

The second arena of war was farther up the Missouri. It centered on the mouth of the Knife River in present-day North Dakota, where the three river tribes — the Mandans, Hidatsas, and Arikaras — formed the hub for trade and warfare among the surrounding tribes. Here also were the Sioux. The northern Teton Sioux — Hunkpapas, Blackfoot Sioux, and Sans Arcs — raided from the west and south, often helped by the Miniconjous and the Two Kettles. The Yanktonai

Teton Sioux War Dance, painted by George Catlin in the 1830s. *Courtesy National Museum of American Art, Smithsonian Institution.*

Sioux attacked from the east and north. Assiniboin and Cree war parties descended on the three river tribes from the northwest (and often battled the Sioux as well). By the 1830s and 1840s the violence had grown so intense that raids and skirmishes often continued for days at a time.

While intertribal raiding was heavy in these eastern theaters close to the Missouri, war in the western theaters matched that in the east and became more pronounced as the century wore on. The northwest sector of war surrounded the land of the Piegans, where the plains met the mountains in northern Montana and southern Alberta. The Blackfoot tribes constantly raided the Flatheads and Shoshonis in the mountains, the Assiniboins and Crees to the east, and the Crows to the south. At the same time, the Assiniboins, Crows, and others attacked the Blackfeet in their own land.

The Crow land, generally south of the upper Yellowstone River, comprised the fourth, or southwestern, region of warfare. The Crows, in the middle of the area, fought all the surrounding tribes: Blackfeet, Assiniboins, Sioux, Cheyennes, Arapahos, Pawnees, and Shoshonis. The Crows were at the center of the most varied and complex of the combat zones. During the 1840s, the general westward movement of Indians and buffalo herds led several observers to predict that one major battleground would emerge where the tribes would fight over the remaining food supply. Edwin Thompson Denig, a fur trader, and Father Pierre De Smet, the well-known Belgian Jesuit, believed that the last home of the buffalo, where the tribes would meet, would be the land between the lower Yellowstone and the Missouri rivers. Colonel J. J. Abert, the army's chief of topographical engineers, held similar views but believed the upper North Platte River would be the center of the last buffalo range. He recommended that the army build a fort in that location (later Fort Laramie) to watch over the last intertribal struggle.[2]

Of the four combat areas, the northwest received considerable attention from the many Canadian and American fur men who traded in the area. Traders testified to the massive number of Blackfoot raids against the mountain tribes. John Work, an employee of the Hudson's Bay Company, completed two journals in which he described this conflict. From 1830 to 1832, as a chief trader, he visited the Shoshonis in the Snake and Salmon river country of present-day Idaho and the Flathead and Blackfoot lands of present-day Montana. Hardly a day went by, regardless of the season, when a Blackfoot war party did not make its presence felt. During one ten-day period in 1831, even though it was December, Work saw five Blackfoot parties leading captured horses. The Blackfeet also followed the traders to steal their horses. Most war parties consisted of Bloods and Grosventres of the Prairie; their harassment of the mountain Indians was constant, although the Shoshonis and Flatheads had several victories to their credit.

Many others echoed Work's comments. Traders in the mountains were at the mercy of Blackfoot war parties because of the commerce with the mountain tribes. The famous Battle of Pierre's Hole, west of the Teton Mountains of western Wyoming, resulted from Blackfoot jealousy over American trade with the mountain tribes. In this fight, a large body of Grosventres, whom many mountain men regarded as the most aggressive warriors of the Blackfoot confederacy, attacked a group of Rocky Mountain Fur Company trappers and their Flathead and Nez Percés friends. The mountain men and their Indian associates quickly took cover in a thickly wooded area and poured deadly gunfire into the ranks of the attackers, killing twenty-six Grosventres and eventually forcing the enemy to retire from the field.

In spite of some defeats, Blackfoot aggressiveness was such that the confederation's warriors gained a reputation in the 1830s and

1840s as the most hostile and warlike fighters in the Northwest. Captain Benjamin Bonneville's 1832 and 1833 trading expeditions, for example, constantly encountered evidence of Blackfoot raids. Bonneville was an ambitious man who managed to obtain leave from the United States Army for several years in order to try to make a quick fortune in the fur business. During his trapping and travels Bonneville had so many encounters with the Blackfeet that he came to see them as the "most dangerous banditti of the mountains. . . ."

This opinion was typical among the traders. Alfred Jacob Miller summarized the attitude well in 1837. The Blackfeet, he wrote, possessed "the worst reputation for war and aggression of all the Indian tribes of the North-West. Their name is a terror to most of the Indian tribes, and they are so strong in numbers, so determined in their vengeance that indiscriminate slaughter follows victory." Miller acquired this view from the fur trading rendezvous of American trappers and mountain Indians.

The many theories of Blackfoot power and its threat to the mountain tribes, however, were mixed with some contradictory views. Using their new guns, Flatheads and Shoshonis began to take the offensive. Despite their small numbers, these tribes did not at all dislike fighting. On one occasion, the Flatheads and Nez Percés responded to Bonneville's proposition to go to the Blackfeet with a peace proposal by saying that they could not trust their enemy, and that war "keeps the eyes of the chiefs always open, and makes the limbs of the young men strong and supple."

Bonneville himself emphasized the limited character of Blackfoot warfare. He pointed out that if a war party lost but one man, it "casts a shade over the glory of their achievements. Hence the Indian is often less fierce and reckless in general battle, than he is in a private brawl; and chiefs are checked in their boldest undertakings by the fear of sacrificing their warriors." This statement came close to explaining the essence of intertribal conflict. Tribal war's limited nature, quite different from the battles of technologically advanced cultures, helped explain why large tribes did not annihilate smaller, more helpless bands. Within this context the fierce Blackfoot reputation did not mean one-sided massacres.[3]

In the 1840s, Jesuit missionaries became involved in the wars between the Blackfeet and the mountain tribes, but in a different way than the fur traders. In 1840, a group of missionaries led by Father Pierre De Smet, a man whose round face was lit by a benign yet humorous expression, created St. Mary's Mission in the Flatheads' Bitterroot Valley near present-day Missoula, Montana. His purpose was to bring Christianity to the Indians. In the next few years De Smet and his associates, Father Gregory Mengarini and Father Nicholas Point, converted Flatheads, Pend d'Oreilles, Kutenais, and Nez Percés. Eventually, De Smet's priests even converted people in the Small Robe band of Piegans. The Small Robes were an independent but prominent band that often hunted in the same area as the Flatheads, the land around Three Forks, Montana, where the Jefferson, Madison, and Gallatin rivers meet to form the Missouri. The Small Robes and the Flatheads became friends and allies despite the long years of antipathy between them.

While the priests worked hard at converting the Indians, they also attempted to stop the raiding. In the fall of 1846, Father De Smet brought together 2,000 representatives from various mountain and Blackfoot tribes for a council on the Musselshell River. Rather than intertribal peace and conversion to Christianity, one suspects that the gathering attracted the Indians because some Christian Indians had recently enjoyed military success. Earlier in the year, the Crows had dealt a crushing blow to the Small Robe band, but the remnants of that people, along with their Flathead friends, had gained revenge by killing fourteen Crows. In that battle, the Small Robes had lost only one man, a non-Christian. That was significant. Surrounding tribes interpreted the victory as the result of the new "medicine" brought by the priests, whom they called the Black Robes. So did De Smet, though viewing it from a Christian position: "Indeed, I look upon this miraculous escape of our Christian warriors, in this fierce contest as further evidence of the peculiar protection of heaven. . . ."

Interestingly, De Smet did not think that his views contradicted the council's purposes — conversion and intertribal peace. After several days of preaching, baptizing, and translating a Catholic chant into Blackfoot, De Smet felt he had established an important truce between old enemies. He returned east, leaving Father Point to continue the missionary work in Blackfoot country. In the next months Point had some success with baptism, though his church members were mostly children. Point's problem was that he found that the warriors who embraced Christianity simply wanted it as a war medicine. Point complained in his letters to De Smet that the warriors would stop their wars with the mountain tribes only if Point could make them great men by a method as equally successful as war.

Point understood the central problem in establishing intertribal peace. First, he tried to expand the peace by including a group of Pend d'Oreilles, but the Piegans plundered their old enemies' camp. Next, Point tried to extend the peace to the Crows. He encouraged a delegation of Blackfeet to broach the matter with the American Fur Company traders at Fort Alexander (at the time, this was the Crow trading post located on the Yellowstone at the mouth of Rosebud River). Nothing came of this, however, and Point felt that the traders were to blame. He wrote that "many traders thought that such a peace would be detrimental to commerce."[4]

Whether or not that was the traders' attitude, the incident did reveal that the Jesuits and the fur men had very different views on how to deal with the Indians. While the traders influenced war with their supplies of guns and tried to control raiding if it interfered with business, the priests tried to spread Christianity and end war for religious purposes.

Ironically for the Jesuits, their greatest impact, aside from converting the Indians, was to increase the warriors' military fortunes. During the 1840s, the Christian Flatheads, Pend d'Oreilles, and Kutenais enjoyed several remarkable victories over large Blackfoot war parties. De Smet documented four of these engagements himself. Each time the Blackfeet retreated, with large losses of fifteen or twenty men. De Smet wrote that the Flatheads had "acquired such reputation for valor, that notwithstanding their inferior numbers, they are feared much more than they on their side dread their bitterest enemies." He went on to claim that "in battle one Flathead or Kalispel [Pend d'Oreille] is worth five of his enemies."

The Blackfeet attributed their enemies' success to the new medicine — the white man's religion. Father De Smet agreed. He described incidents when the Flatheads used prayer before they went to war, demonstrating a firm reliance on their new faith. Like many white men before them, the priests tended to favor the smaller, weaker tribes against the more powerful ones.

Tribal war carried on despite the efforts of the Jesuits, and in the late 1840s, the priests closed St. Mary's Mission in part because of increased Blackfoot raids. In the final analysis, De Smet and his two associates did little to end the age-old tradition of war; they only added a new dimension.[5]

Even with their occasional victories, however, the mountain tribes were too small to have much impact on the numerous Blackfeet. Only the Assiniboins and Plains Crees posed any major threat to the Blackfoot confederacy in the early 1800s.

The Plains Crees became culturally distinct from the eastern portion of the tribe, which lived in the lake country of south-central Canada. As the Plains Crees migrated west, they became an integral part of the nomadic culture. They were a little more practical than the Assiniboins and other Plains Indians, however. Though they held bravery in close combat in high esteem, they regarded horses, the source of wealth, as the prime motive in warfare. "The unceasing hostility between the Plains Cree and their enemies," according to anthropologist David G. Mandelbaum, "was not due to any dispute over territory or struggle for trade advantages, but was largely the result of the continual raiding and counter raiding for horses."

In the second half of the 1800s, conflict over land changed somewhat with a massive Sioux invasion, but the Crees did not emphasize risking life as much as other tribes. They did not, for example, have a society like the Sioux "Crazy Dogs," who vowed, in certain circumstances, not to retreat from the enemy no matter what the consequences. With their desire to build wealth by capturing horses, the Crees attacked their primary enemy, the Blackfeet. "Most war parties were directed against the Blood, Blackfoot, and Piegan," wrote Mandelbaum, and the "heaviest losses suffered by the tribe were inflicted by these people."[6]

The Assiniboins, in their wars with the Blackfeet, were even more zealous and extravagant than their Cree allies. Observers noted the Assiniboins' almost fanatical willingness to take chances to obtain glory or horses. Father De Smet described the Assiniboins' antipathy toward the Blackfoot confederacy, although he did not realize that as recently as the middle 1700s the two enemies had often acted in concert. The Assiniboins, he maintained, "entertained a mortal hatred against the Blackfeet; this detestation had been transmitted from father to son, and augmented by continual aggressions and reprisals." The Cree tribe, De Smet added, was "one of the most formidable enemies of the Blackfeet, and continually encroaches upon the territory of its adversaries. The preceding year they carried off more than 200 horses."[7]

In 1833, the Assiniboins and Crees dealt the Blackfeet a major defeat right in front of Fort McKenzie, the American Fur Company's post on the Missouri about fifty miles downriver from present-day Great Falls, Montana. The battle occurred at dawn on August 28. All was quiet in the twenty Piegan lodges pitched in front of the fort. Then, with a suddenness possible only in Indian warfare, 500 Assiniboins and 100 Crees, some mounted, others on foot, burst from the willows bordering the river and fell upon the sleeping Piegans. The startled traders inside the fort at first thought they were under attack and fired on the assailants. But when they understood the situation, David Mitchell, head trader for the post, halted the shooting. He understood the need for the traders to remain neutral in tribal conflict. But some employees continued to fire at the attackers, helping the Piegans defend themselves.

Meanwhile, before the eyes of the fort's horrified inhabitants, the attackers ripped open lodge covers and shot, stabbed, clubbed, and scalped the occupants. The Assiniboins and Crees killed seven Piegans and wounded twenty before the survivors could reach the refuge of the fort's walls. Mitchell had "linen and balsam" handed out to wrap wounds. Indians young and old sat stoically as traders dug the bullets out of their flesh and dressed the wounds. All the while, Indian women continually gave off their high wails of mourning.

The battle was not yet over, however. The attackers retreated to the cover along the river bank as the traders and Blackfeet from nearby camps rallied for a counterattack. Prince Maximilian of Wied, who was there, described the approaching warriors: "They came galloping in groups of from three to twenty together, their horses covered with foam, and they themselves in their finest apparel, with all kinds of ornaments and arms, bows and quivers on their backs, guns in their hands, furnished with their medicines, with feathers on their heads, some had splendid crowns of black and white eagle feathers, and a large hood of feathers hanging down behind, sitting on fine panther skins lined with red; the upper part of their bodies partly naked, with a long strip of wolf skin thrown across the shoulder, and carrying shields adorned with feathers and pieces of colored cloth. A truly original sight!"

The Blackfoot reinforcements came up more for show than for action, however. None of the warriors were foolish enough to follow the enemy into the thick willows. They knew they would die without even a chance for heroic action, and that was antithetical to the ideals of tribal warfare. Thus, the Assiniboins' and Crees' victory was complete, even though they left one of their number dead upon the field. All they had to do was hide in the willows and wait for a chance to escape. The next day, they slipped away and ran for the protection of the distant Bear Paw Mountains, about 100 miles to the northeast. The Piegans followed and killed one, but that was slight recompense.

The Blackfoot warriors left much of the revenge to the women and children, who mutilated the one dead Assiniboin at the fort to such an extent the corpse hardly resembled a human body. Some traders recoiled in horror. Prince Maximilian tried to obtain the dead man's skull for his scientific collection, but he was too late to save it from complete destruction.

The traders expected the Assiniboins to attack the fort again because the fur men had helped the Blackfeet. The battle had also broken a truce between the two sets of enemies which Kenneth McKenzie, head of the American Fur Company on the upper Missouri, had negotiated the year before. Breaking the truce so suddenly was typical of intertribal relations, but the Americans' part in the matter obviously aggravated the situation. The Assiniboins had become jealous of the Blackfoot trade. It was enough that the Americans had opened trade with the Assiniboins' Blackfoot enemies, but now the Americans had even supported the Blackfeet in war. That was too much of an insult.[8]

Although the expected attack did not materialize in this case, such resentment occasionally led tribes to threaten fur posts. The chief danger was usually the loss of stolen stock from stealing or isolated raids. Attacking a fort was generally out of the question, however, because the dictates of tribal warfare made high casualties unacceptable. Despite this, in the spring of 1834, the Crows under Rotten Belly actually laid siege to Fort McKenzie. Like the Assiniboins, the Crows worried about this new post in Blackfoot country. Although the Crows had their own post, Fort Cass on the Yellowstone, they did not like to see their enemies getting any extra help. The Crows believed that Blackfoot war parties received ammunition from Fort McKenzie (which lay on the route to Crow country), then sold captured horses to the fort's employees on their way back home from raids against the Crows.

Rotten Belly, now forty-five years old and at the height of his power, persuaded his 200 warriors to follow a strategy antithetical to their way of war. For several weeks, his warriors cut off the post from outside help, from its own animals, and from fresh provisions. Eventually, Alexander Culbertson, the post trader, fired the cannon and prepared a contingent of men to sally out against the Crows. At this, the Crows decamped. Neither they nor the traders really desired a confrontation that would destroy their years of friendship.

Although Rotten Belly's siege was not a success, it indicated the impact of the trading posts on intertribal conflict. Rotten Belly saw the failure as a stain on his reputation, however. A short time after, he was killed in a suicidal charge on an enemy position. The Crows explained that he chose death instead of watching his power slip away after his loss of prestige following the Fort McKenzie affair.

The Crows were important trading partners for a number of fur companies during the trade's busy years, and they jealously guarded the posts in their own country. The American Fur Company changed the location of its trading post in the Yellowstone country four times between 1832 and 1850 in part because of Crow objections to hostile Blackfeet lurking in the vicinity.[9]

The jealousy over trading posts, as with other things in intertribal conflict, was ambiguous and contradictory. Often the forts served as neutral ground. Fort Union, at the fork of the Missouri and Yellowstone rivers, was especially important in this regard. The American Fur Company constructed it during 1828 and 1829 out of square-hewn cottonwood logs. The fort encompassed a large area, 220 by 240 feet. It was the best-built post on the Missouri, and, with the exception of Bent's Fort on the Arkansas, perhaps the best built in the West. Fort Union, the headquarters for the American Fur Company's upper Missouri and Yellowstone trade, was strategically located on the southern border of the Assiniboin territory, but also served other nearby tribes such as the Plains Crees, Plains Ojibwas, Blackfeet, and Crows.

Fort Union was George Catlin's destination when he went upriver in 1832. Here, and later at Fort Clark near the Mandan villages, Catlin learned all he could about Indian cultures. With an artist's eye he noted the specifics of tribal war, and his portraits included such details as medicine bundles, body painting, warpaint, and graphic decorations on warshirts.

During Catlin's stay at Fort Union, a Cree band and a Blackfoot band camped nearby and managed to get along well. Of course, it was the only way to buy the traders' desirable goods: ". . . according to a regulation of the fort," wrote Catlin, "their [Indians'] arms and weapons were all locked up by [Kenneth] M'Kenzie in his 'arsenal' for the purpose of preserving the peace. . . ." Catlin was amazed at the Indians' ability to socialize amiably even though they had only recently been making every effort to kill each other.

On one occasion Catlin did a portrait of a well-known Blackfoot chief named Buffalo Bull's Back Fat, a dignified man of middle age. He sat quietly for hours dressed in his best warshirt, leggings, and honorable decorations. During the entire time, according to Catlin, "his enemies, the Crows and the Knisteneaux [Crees], Assiniboins, and Ojibbeways; a number of distinguished personages of each tribe, have laid all day around the sides of my room; reciting to each other the battles they have fought, and pointing to scalp-locks, worn as proof of their victories and attached to the seams of their shirts and leggings."[10]

Fort Union's important location for trade and peaceful coexistence also made it the central point from which spread the most terrible of the white man's "gifts" to the Indian — smallpox. In 1837, infected clothing aboard the steamboat *Yellowstone* created one of the worst epidemics to affect the American Indian. As the boat worked its way upriver to Fort Union, the smallpox spread from tribe to tribe and

Buffalo Bull's Back Fat, a Blackfoot chief. He sat for several hours, surrounded by erstwhile enemies, to have this portrait painted by George Catlin. *Courtesy National Museum of American Art, Smithsonian Institution.*

was especially disastrous to the Mandans, Hidatsas, and Arikaras near Fort Clark.

When the steamboat arrived at Fort Union, traders tried to keep the Indians away and contain the disease at the fort. Many of the tribesmen, however, unfamiliar with the potential devastation, insisted on coming in to trade. The results were appalling. Among the nearby nomadic tribes, the Blackfeet and the Assiniboins suffered the greatest. Each lost more than half their population! This terrible disaster, measured in military terms, weakened many tribes already short on manpower. In the next decades the Blackfeet were able to rebuild much of their former population, but the Assiniboins did not gain back as much, and the decrease in population contributed to their decline in the 1840s.[11]

The Crows did not suffer greatly from this particular epidemic, but their day was coming. During the 1830s and 1840s, smallpox, influenza, and cholera killed hundreds of them. The tribe declined from around 800 lodges, or 6,400 people, to something like 450 lodges, or 3,600 people. As the century progressed, this decline continued, particularly as more tribes entered Crow territory and fighting increased.[12]

The Crows were the focal point of fighting in the southwest theater of warfare even though their warlike reputation seemed to contradict their relatively small size. Many observers regarded them as prodigious fighters. Undoubtedly, some of their reputation came from the stories of Americans who lived with the tribe. Edward Rose dwelled with the Crows in the early 1800s; the trader Robert Meldrum lived with them in the 1830s; and the well-known mountain man Jim Beckwourth became an honorary member of the tribe. In between the many stories commemorating his own prowess, Beckwourth commented on the Crows' ability both as horsemen and horse thieves. They lived for war, he said — "the excitement of war suits them."

Many fur traders also commented on the Crows' abilities. Echoing the words of Beckwourth, Captain Bonneville noted that the Crows were the most notorious warriors of the area, being "roving, warlike, crafty, and predatory. . . ." Warren Ferris, an astute observer working for the American Fur Company, saw the Crows as the best horse thieves of all the tribes. Their herds illustrated this. Estimates put the size at fifteen ponies per lodge, while the Piegans averaged only ten and the Assiniboins just two. Only the mountain and plateau tribes such as the Flatheads and Nez Percés, who were expert raisers and breeders of horses, owned more horses than the Crows.

The Crows had a high regard for their own fighting abilities. This, however, was typical plains tribalism, which viewed outsiders as inferior and even less than human. "There is more personal ambition and rivalry existing among this tribe than any other I became acquainted with — each trying to excel the other in merit, whilst engaged in some dangerous adventure," wrote Zenas Leonard, a member of Bonneville's trapping party.

Like all tribes, the Crows carried on a sophisticated competition based on individual actions that required close contact in fighting the enemy. For a warrior, "counting coup," or touching an enemy, was the most daring exploit. As Ferris described it, the greatest war honor "belongs not to him who shot down the enemy, but to him who first rushed upon him and struck him on the head." A total of four Crows could count coup on one enemy. The most honor went to the first one and descended in order from there. Other favorable war exploits were to snatch a weapon from the hand of an opponent, rescue a comrade, cut out a horse picketed inside an enemy camp, and organize and lead a war party. Other tribes recognized basically the same feats, though sometimes with different emphases. Taking a weapon from an enemy was the most important exploit for Blackfeet; counting coup was next. Good medicine, which was essential in achieving all these deeds, was worth a high price to a young man anxious for success.[13]

With such a set of standards the Crows set out in all directions against enemies who operated under similar rules. The Crows' spirited defense against so many enemies provided much of their warlike reputation. Only to the west was the rivalry less intense. As often as not, the Crows maintained peace with the Nez Percés and Flatheads; the rivalry with the eastern Shoshonis also declined. An old story held that the Crows, in helping to drive the Shoshonis off the plains in the late eighteenth century, killed 300 of them in a three-day battle in which a Crow chief made the sun stand still. This might have been a reference to the mythical Crow figure Child of the Sun.

By the 1830s and 1840s, with plenty of other rivals, Crow-Shoshoni conflicts became intermittent. In 1837, while visiting a trappers' rendezvous, Alfred Jacob Miller found a number of Crow war parties in the mountains looking for Shoshoni horses. While there, Miller made several romanticized portraits of Crow chiefs. One was of Chief Big Bowl, who allowed only a profile. The side of his face that he did not want painted had a small bag hanging from the ear. This was his medicine, and he feared that if Miller put it in a picture, that side of the chief would be "sick in battle."

Four years after Miller painted the Crow chief, an old mountain man named William Hamilton found the Crows again in the mountains. But now the Crows were peacefully visiting the Shoshonis under the famous Chief Washakie. The two tribes were camped on Stinking Water Creek near South Pass in Wyoming, engrossed in one of their favorite pastimes — racing horses for high stakes.[14]

The Crows had more enemies to the south and east. In the 1820s and 1830s, the Arikaras left the Missouri and wandered west. They roamed at will, but sometimes stayed with their Pawnee relatives. They appeared to fight everyone, both white and red, including the Crows.

The Pawnees also made the long trip from the Platte River to attack the Crows. The solitary expedition of Black Chief, a Skidi Pawnee leader, was an unusual example. In 1832, having lost the respect of his tribe, Black Chief set off on the warpath in order to reestablish his status. He ended up at a Crow village 200 miles away. According to the story, at nightfall Black Chief quietly entered a lodge on the edge of camp and quickly stabbed to death two men, a woman, and a child. Intertribal warfare did not respect enemies' age or sex. Black Chief scalped his victims, then stole a horse outside and escaped. He made it safely back to his own village and, after recounting his tale, was restored to a place of honor. Indians usually did not doubt a man's war stories. It was something that warriors did not lie about, and, if they were tempted, usually enough witnesses were present to discourage falsehood.[15]

The Crows' major enemies to the south and east, however, were not the Arikaras and Pawnees, but the Sioux, Northern Cheyennes, and Northern Arapahos. During the 1820s and 1830s the Sioux alliance began to form. The Cheyennes began to act more in concert with their old Sioux enemies, forgetting some of the old hostility, although the Arapahos remained more leery of Sioux friendship. In later years the three tribes formed a more solid alliance.

Although some Arapahos and Cheyennes moved south to the Arkansas and South Platte rivers in the 1820s and 1830s, the northern branches continued to live in the neighborhood of the Black Hills and the upper North Platte River of eastern Wyoming. The Arapahos carried on an especially intense rivalry with the Utes of western Colorado and also fought the Shoshonis, Crows, and Pawnees. The Arapahos remained firm friends with their relatives far to the north, the Grosventres of the Prairie, with whom they had formed one tribe before moving south in the late 1700s.

The Cheyennes had the same enemies as their Arapaho allies, but concentrated more on the Crows, Shoshonis, and Pawnees. With numerous possibilities for raiding in and around Crow territory, the Arapaho and Cheyenne war parties crisscrossed the low mountains, the plains, and the vast basins that run through central and eastern Wyoming from the Laramie River to the Powder River. Beginning in the 1840s, the Oglala Sioux often joined them to hunt and fight the Shoshonis and Crows.[16]

Like the Cheyennes, the Sioux were becoming permanent rivals of the Crows. In the 1830s and 1840s, the seven Teton Sioux tribes pushed farther south and west from the Missouri and began to challenge the Crows' traditional control of the Powder River country south of the Yellowstone, in eastern Wyoming and southeastern Montana. The tempting Crow horse herds also lay directly west and northwest of these tribes. The Sioux were often successful in taking horses and fighting battles, and their numbers inevitably pressed the Crows back into the Bighorn country. But as often as not, the Crows were victorious in individual battles.

In 1848 Father De Smet described a Crow triumph that also illustrated how a victory sometimes led to the loser's humiliation, a peculiar event that coincided with the concept of limited war. The Oglalas had invaded Crow territory and attacked the tribe, but in one engagement the Crows had routed the Oglalas, killing ten or twelve. Then, wrote De Smet, the Crows "employed a mode of repulsion which covered the tribe that experienced its effects with immortal disgrace: they pursued the Ogallalas with rods and clubs. This, according to them, signifies 'that their adversaries were worth neither the lead nor the powder that would be expended in killing them.'" In tribal war, once a party met defeat, retreat of any kind was the only answer, the losers concluding that their medicine was not working properly.

As if this defeat was not enough, Red Fish, the Oglala leader, had his daughter captured. Seeing De Smet at Fort Pierre, Red Fish asked him to help ransom her. Recognizing conversion possibilities, De Smet replied that Red Fish must first work for the blessing of heaven by trying to convert the Oglalas. As it turned out, the girl escaped, but the Oglalas believed it was due to the white man's medicine.[17]

As the years passed, the Crows' enemies to the north remained the Assiniboins and Crees. The Assiniboins were particularly aggressive in raiding the Crows to supplement their own scanty pony herds.

The trader who knew the most about the Assiniboins was Edwin Denig. He worked at Fort Union from 1837 to 1856, eventually rising to the position of chief clerk and finally to "bourgeois," or head of the trading post. He was a small man with stern features and a beard that covered his chin and jaws, and he was reputed to be difficult with his employees and stingy with everyone. His associates also knew him as a hard drinker who often went through several gallons of rye whiskey during the cold winter months. (That, of course, was not at all uncommon at the lonely trading posts.)

Although he had his detractors, some individuals found Denig generous and helpful to travellers, especially when he shared his knowledge of the plants and animals and Indians of the region. Denig married an Assiniboin named Deer Little Woman. They stayed together for life and even formally married in St. Louis. This was uncommon among most traders, who had temporary Indian "wives." In the 1850s, Denig wrote down his knowledge of the Indians of the area, which was later published as *Five Indian Tribes of the Upper Missouri*.

In writing about the Assiniboins, Denig noted that they captured many horses from the Crows as well as the Blackfeet and Grosventres of the Prairie. But in any battles that resulted, the Assiniboins often came out second best. Their losses, together with the terrible devastation wrought by the smallpox epidemic of 1837, made them consider peace more seriously than other tribes. "When overtures of peace were made in 1844 by the Crows," wrote Denig, "the other [Assiniboin tribe] readily accepted the proposal. In a few years these two nations became good friends, often camped and hunted together, the Crows giving the others a good many horses, hunting in their company and furnishing them with hides and meat." For many Assiniboins and River Crows, this peace continued during the 1800s, but like most Indian truces it could not be kept inviolate. Raiding between various tribal groups continued through the century at irregular intervals.

The peace benefitted the Crows because of their declining population and their many enemies. It enabled them to turn more attention to their primary enemies, the Blackfeet to the northwest. Denig theorized that horse raids were at the heart of the long and bloody conflict between the two. "Scarcely a week passes but large numbers [of horses] are swept off by the war parties on both sides," wrote Denig. "In these depredations men are killed which calls for revenge by the losing tribe. During a single summer or winter several hundred animals in this way change owners."

This constant quest for horses was a central factor in all intertribal conflict on the northern plains. But intimately tied to it was the prestige that came from the risk taken in stealing the horses, just as glory came from the risk of counting coup in battle. Fighting over hunting territory also increased as the tribes gradually pressed closer together in search of the decreasing buffalo herds. This was much more of a factor in the wars of migrating Sioux than in the Blackfoot-Crow conflict, however.[18]

Deer Little Woman, the Assiniboin wife of Edwin Thompson Denig. Unlike most such marriages, their union endured for life. *Courtesy Smithsonian Institution National Anthropological Archives, Bureau of American Ethnology Collection.*

Despite the constant warfare and the cycle of revenge described by Denig, the tribes still enjoyed periodic peace. Some rivalries were more serious than others, however, as in the case of the Crows and Blackfeet. According to Denig, "the Crows are solicitous for peace with all tribes except the Blackfeet, with whom they wish to be at war as long as one of them remains."

In 1838 Joshua Pilcher, the Upper Missouri Indian agent, reported that "no peace has ever been known to exist between them [Crows] and the Blackfeet, and as they frequently roam over the same region of country many bloody conflicts ensue between the parties."

Although Pilcher exaggerated, the confrontations between the two tribes were more frequent and intense than most intertribal warfare. Most of the battles recorded occurred in Crow territory against invading Blackfeet war parties, who generally ended up the losers. This generalization, however, may have resulted from many observers' favoritism toward the friendly Crows as opposed to the Blackfeet, who were often hostile to white Americans.

In their struggles against the Blackfeet, certainly, the Crows had many successful war leaders — even women. One of them was a captured Grosventre raised from childhood and adopted into the tribe. She gained such respect as she grew up that the Crows called her Woman Chief. Although it was unusual, though not unknown, for women to become warriors, Woman Chief was one. At an early age she took part in the games and duties of a boy and grew up to become a successful warrior, even reaching the exalted position of a war party leader. She was particularly successful in her raids against the Blackfeet. Ironically, while on a peace mission she was killed by her former people, the Grosventres.

In 1846, the Crows reached the height of their success in the wars against the Blackfeet when they almost destroyed the Small Robe band of Piegans, who had recently become Christians and friends and allies of the Flatheads. Father De Smet was shocked to learn of his new converts' demise. "The year 1846," he wrote, "will be a memorable epoch in the sad annals of the Blackfeet nation." In addition to previous defeats by the Flatheads and Crees, De Smet mourned, "The Crows have struck them a mortal blow — fifty families, the entire band of the Little Robe, were lately massacred, and 160 women and children have been led into captivity." Actually, the whole band was not annihilated, and the Crows usually adopted captives into the tribe instead of killing or enslaving them. Nevertheless, it was a hard blow to the Blackfeet. Certainly, they had their victories, especially in the mountains, but they also suffered many casualties.[19]

Considering the number of times the Crows defeated their more numerous foes, it is interesting that so many observers believed the Blackfeet and Sioux would eventually annihilate them. But that is what Catlin, Bonneville, Denig, and others thought. In retrospect, one suspects that this may have been some kind of common belief that was passed from one person to another.[20]

Throughout the nineteenth century, a number of such theories debated the fate of the small tribes faced with powerful adversaries. Certainly, small tribes, when suffering the same number of casualties, declined more rapidly than larger tribes. The white man's diseases made this decline much more rapid and serious than warfare itself. At the same time, Indians tended to belittle or exaggerate tribal losses depending on what benefitted the individual's status or the tribe's prestige or hopes for American aid. In the long run it was difficult to foretell the destruction of any of the tribes. Tribal warfare's methods and motives worked against such destruction. Not only this, other factors were to have greater impacts on the livelihood of the tribes and their culture: white American migration that forced the tribes into smaller areas, disease, and the decrease in the buffalo herds.

While the characteristics of intertribal conflict tended to preclude the destruction of the small western tribes, that did not seem to be true on the eastern plains. There, on the edge of the prairie, the small sedentary tribes did not have the mobility of the less powerful tribes in the western plains and mountains. In the 1830s and 1840s, the massive Sioux migration west gathered momentum and appeared likely to smother the farming peoples living along the banks of the major rivers.

CHAPTER FIVE

War Is the Breath
of Their Nostrils

THE SIOUX ADVANCE ON THE EASTERN PLAINS, 1830-1850

While raiding in the West intensified during the 1830s and 1840s, the small tribes there had the advantage of mobility and a plentiful supply of buffalo. On the eastern plains, however, the buffalo decreased rapidly as the Teton and Yanktonai Sioux flooded the area and white settlement edged west. This made the small sedentary tribes vulnerable. For the first time Mandans, Hidatsas, and Arikaras, as well as the Omahas and Pawnees, faced serious Sioux threats, even in terms of the characteristic limits of intertribal conflict. Because the Sioux dominated this region, the United States greatly expanded its policy of ending tribal war.

Many Americans doubted the long-term viability of the Arikaras, Hidatsas, and Mandans. As with the Crows in the West, enemies surrounded these three small river tribes. In spite of the traditional, periodic truces for trading, this northeast theater of war became an increasingly dangerous area filled with circulating war parties. Various Sioux tribes, the Assiniboins and Crees, and the Northern Cheyennes raided the river tribes. Gradually, the Mandans, Hidatsas, and Arikaras found it more convenient to live closer together for mutual protection.

For a time, the Arikaras were a stumbling block to this movement toward more cooperation. Very few of them stayed true to the peace treaty set up by Lewis and Clark in 1804, and when the Arikaras left the Missouri in 1823 to roam the plains, they went on the warpath against almost everyone. But when the Arikaras returned to the Missouri in 1837, they seemed ready for more decorous behavior. They even went so far as to ask the Mandans and Hidatsas to join them at

71

their village near the Knife River, adjacent to the American Fur Company's Fort Clark. The Mandans and Hidatsas, seeing the benefit of another ally in their current warfare, enthusiastically welcomed their old rivals and let them move in. Old conflicts cropped up, however. The "Rees" proved themselves less than congenial. They stole Mandan women and quarreled with the Hidatsas. Difficulties continued for several years, and not until the 1850s did the three tribes contract a permanent alliance.[1]

Before the Arikaras' return, the Hidatsas and Mandans had continued their old wars much as before. In the early 1830s, both George Catlin and Prince Maximilian found them still aggressive, though on the defensive much of the time. As in past years, the Hidatsas were still the primary aggressors. Said Catlin: "There is no tribe in the western wilds, perhaps, who are better entitled to the style of warlike, than the Minatarees [Hidatsas]; for they, unlike the Mandans, are continually carrying war into their enemies's countries; oftentimes drawing the poor Mandans into unnecessary broils. . . ." The Hidatsas, according to Prince Maximilian, occasionally raided as far away as the Blackfoot and Pawnee lands.

The Mandans, though not as aggressive as the Hidatsas, still had their share of brave fighters. Four Bears, one of the principal chiefs, represented the epitome of the stalwart Mandan warrior. Both Catlin and Prince Maximilian heard him tell stories of his prowess. Catlin painted a portrait of him dressed in a splendid warshirt with small wooden knives sewn on to mark the number of men he had killed along with painted horse tracks to illustrate captured ponies. He was a tall, distinguished man, and his bravery was unquestioned.

Four Bears accomplished one of these feats the same year he talked to Catlin. He had entered an Arikara lodge at night and sat down to eat from a pot of stew by the fire. The inhabitants had already repaired to their beds of buffalo robes for the night and thought he was just a casual visitor. Apparently, the man who headed this family had killed Four Bears' brother a few months before. When all was quiet, and after eating his fill, Four Bears casually rose from the fire, seized the man's lance, stabbed him to death, and slipped silently into the night.[2]

Despite such moments of what the Indians considered glory, the river tribes were at the mercy of debilitating outside forces. In 1837, the same year the Arikaras returned to the Missouri, disaster struck. Coming up the Missouri on its ill-fated voyage, the *Yellowstone* stopped first at Fort Clark and, unaware, left an infectious cargo of smallpox. Medicine men, with their magic and sweat lodges, were helpless, and

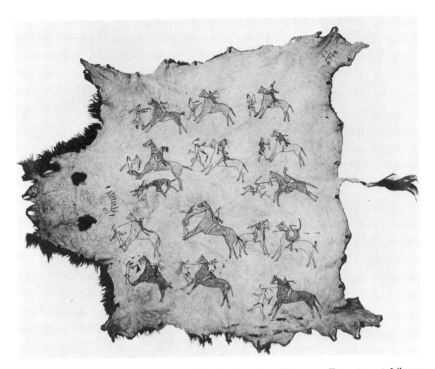

Sioux Buffalo Robe. Photograph by H. S. Rice. *Courtesy Department Library Services, American Museum of Natural History.*

the disease decimated the three river tribes. Joshua Pilcher, the agent at Fort Clark, estimated that 1,200 Arikaras, 1,300 Hidatsas, and 1,500 Mandans died. The count was less than that among the Blackfeet and Assiniboins the same year, but the key was that the small tribes lost larger percentages of their populations. The Mandans suffered the worst; only about fifty people survived the disaster.

Francois Antoine Chardon, a Fort Clark trader, described how warriors stabbed themselves and then jumped into the Missouri River rather than succumb to the unheroic death of smallpox. Four Bears blamed the whites when he caught the disease. Lying on his deathbed, his handsome face scarred by unsightly pustules, he bemoaned this death, so degrading in comparison to dying in battle. "I do not fear Death my friends," he said. "You know it, but to die with my face rotten, that even the Wolves will shrink with horror at seeing me, and say to themselves, that is 4 Bears the Friend of the Whites. . . ."[3]

After the epidemic the three tribes became more closely tied together, left as they were with their diminishing numbers amidst Assiniboin and Sioux war parties. As before, the enemies of the river tribes tried to dominate them in war, but also as before, these sedentary people still had one advantage — their enemies' desire for corn and squash. However, one ambitious Assiniboin chief known as Tchatka, or Left Handed, made a plan for the ultimate "coup," or victory, to finish off the Mandans after their losses from smallpox. Tchatka was an anamoly in the traditional warrior societies of the plains. He was not a talented fighter — in fact some people accused him of being a coward — but he was able to attain great control over his people by his ability to find weak enemy bands to attack and thus provide easy victories. He also secretly and mysteriously poisoned any Assiniboin who opposed his power, thus gaining a reputation for magic.

Tchatka's plan was to trick the Mandans by setting up a peace council and then kill them when they were off guard. The two tribes held the council a short distance from the Mandan village, but the Assiniboins did not know that the Arikaras had returned to the Missouri. The Mandans, suspicious of their visitors' intentions, at the last minute called for help from their new allies. The Arikaras made a surprise attack and routed the Assiniboins, killing twenty of them.

Despite this incident, warfare between the Assiniboins and the farming tribes generally declined in the 1830s and 1840s. In 1844, the same year the Assiniboins halted their wars with the Crows, they made peace with the Hidatsas. None of these treaties were completely permanent, but in any case the Assiniboins, hurt by smallpox, Blackfoot raids, and increasing Sioux pressure, were becoming less of a power than they had been in earlier days.

The Assiniboins' gradual decline, however, had its roots in earlier developments. After the Blackfeet moved west in the 1700s, the Assiniboins had, by the early 1800s, ended up in the area where the present borders of North Dakota, Saskatchewan, and Montana meet. Besides the debilitating impact of smallpox, the Assiniboins had another problem — they were not able to acquire as much wealth as other tribes. Many observers found the Assiniboins to be the poorest of the plains tribes. In 1830 they averaged just two horses per lodge and only one gun for every ten lodges.

Edwin Denig pointed out that by mid-century the Assiniboins were on the losing end with both the Blackfeet and the Sioux. Denig considered the Assiniboins a lazy tribe that failed to care for its horses or obtain firearms. "The consequences of this negligence," he wrote, "is that at war they get killed and at home starve half the time. They do not seem to keep up with the age of advancements in the same degree as other nations who have had fewer opportunities. . . ." Despite this decline, the Assiniboins' reputation carried on: "They are considered good warriors, are famous for a sudden rush on enemies, for their horse stealing qualifications and, when brought to a stand, are known to fight with almost unequaled desperation." The Assiniboins' spirit and pride remained intact, and they continued to fight both the Blackfeet to the west and the three river tribes to the east.[4]

By the 1830s and particularly by the 1840s, however, the Sioux rather than the Assiniboins had become the major opponents of the river tribes. When Prince Maximilian visited Fort Clark in 1833 and 1834, Toussaint Charbonneau, the interpreter for Lewis and Clark, was still there living with the Indians (though Sacagawea had long since left him). The old man supplied the prince with a quantity of information from the past thirty years. The Sioux, he said, had often camped near the villages for long periods of time during which they harassed and, at times, almost put the Mandans and Hidatsas under siege. It was the old man's opinion, however, that the two tribes often triumphed when they sallied out from the poles and brush surrounding their villages and confronted their adversaries.

In these years the Yanktons and in particular the Yanktonais were the major Sioux opponents of the Mandans, Hidatsas, and Arikaras. The Yanktons lived east of the Missouri from the southeast corner of present-day South Dakota upriver to around the site of the town of Pierre. North of them, the Yanktonais made their camps along the Coteau du Missouri, the high divide between the Missouri and James rivers.

Chardon reported frequent Yanktonai invasions of Mandan and Hidatsa territory. The fighting, as usual, was not so intense that there could be no truces. In September 1833, for example, the Yanktonais, after one failed negotiation, effected a treaty with the Hidatsas and Mandans. Feasting and rejoicing lasted a month, but by December the Yanktonais had broken the peace on four separate occasions. Then, in the following months, the Yanktonais continued to make it dangerous for the sedentary tribes, especially when the river people crossed the Missouri in their bull boats to hunt, raid, or gather firewood.[5]

The Teton Sioux raided the three tribes from the south. The Brulés, one of the largest of the seven Teton tribes, sometimes joined these raids from their lands in southern South Dakota and northern Nebraska. The Brulés had fought the Arikaras when the latter roamed as nomads, and now they continued to attack them, the Arikaras, as well as the Mandans and Hidatsas, in their villages far to the north. But the major objects of Brulé raids were the sedentary tribes farther south, the Omahas and the Pawnees in particular.

Another opponent of the three river tribes were the Miniconjous. They numbered only about 1,800 people, which was far less than the Brulés or Oglalas, each of whom had around 3,000 people. But the Miniconjou men were reputed to be great warriors, and the tribe, being centrally located, fought most of the Sioux' opponents.

Chief One Horn, identified by a small shell hanging around his neck, was a primary Miniconjou leader in the 1830s. He made a strong impression on George Catlin when the artist painted his portrait at Fort Pierre, the American Fur Company post at present-day Pierre, South Dakota. Catlin described One Horn as middle-aged, of medium height, and of "noble countenance." Four years later, Catlin learned of the man's bizarre death. When his favorite wife died, the chief went out of his mind. He soon "dashed off at full speed upon the prairies, repeating the most solemn oath 'that he would slay the first living thing that fell in his way, be it man or beast, friend or foe.'" He found and wounded a lone buffalo bull; then, ignoring the animal's wild rage and slashing horns, he attacked the bull using only his knife. Before long, both of them lay dead.[6]

After One Horn's death, the Miniconjous had fewer good leaders and grew increasingly hostile. Their wars against the three river tribes continued until 1846 when the Miniconjous made a peace with the Arikaras in order to trade hides for corn. This treaty also enabled the Miniconjous to move into new hunting lands west of the Mandans, Hidatsas, and Arikaras, lands in the Little Missouri River country near the present-day border between North Dakota and Montana. This was an important Sioux migration into prime buffalo hunting country at a time when the herds along the Missouri were decreasing. The three tribes making up the "northern" Teton Sioux — the Hunkpapas, Blackfoot Sioux, and Sans Arcs (meaning No Bow) — joined the Miniconjous in using this new land, which became important for hunting as well as raiding the nearby Assiniboins.

The Hunkpapas, Blackfoot Sioux, and Sans Arcs were smaller tribes than the "southern" Teton Sioux, the Oglalas and the Brulés, but they were still known for their warlike behavior. They lived separately but their camps remained close to one another. They roamed along the Moreau, Grand, Cannonball, and Heart rivers in the alternating flat and rolling plains west of the Missouri River where North Dakota

One Horn, chief of the Miniconjou Sioux, who took his name from the shell given him by his father and worn around his neck. Painted by George Catlin. *Courtesy National Museum of American Art, Smithsonian Institution.*

and South Dakota now meet. Although these tribes were probably the last of the western Sioux to migrate across the Missouri, they already were gaining notoriety among Americans.

The northern Sioux stayed at peace with the Arikaras long enough to maintain the benefits of trade, but they warred often against the Mandans and Hidatsas. Oftentimes, the small Two Kettle tribe joined the northern tribes in their raids. Living to the south of the northern Sioux, they fought the three river tribes but stayed at peace with the whites. According to Edwin Denig, these Sioux warriors were often found "lying around the borders of the farming villages waiting a favorable opportunity to pounce upon some solitary hunter or woman in quest of fuel in the adjacent woods."[7]

As they moved west, the Teton and Yanktonai Sioux swiftly became the major force on the eastern plains, but their power was greatest in the southeastern theater of war. This arena included the horticultural prairie peoples of present-day southern South Dakota and Nebraska — the Poncas near the mouth of the Niobrara, the Omahas south of them on the Missouri, the Otos and Missouris at the mouth of the Platte, and the Pawnees along the Platte and its Loup tributary in northern Nebraska.

These prairie tribes only bordered the plains. Like the Mandans, Hidatsas, and Arikaras (now almost surrounded by Sioux), they lived most of the year in permanent earth-lodge villages where they raised corn and squash, and they spent time hunting buffalo on territory the Sioux intended to acquire. All these village people except the Pawnees were small tribes, numbering around 1,500 people or less; the Pawnee nation totalled around 4,000 people. The Pawnees had decreased in number since the Pike and Long expeditions and were continuing to lose people as various diseases spread among them from the nearby Oregon Trail.

Besides the tribes of eastern Nebraska, across the Missouri there were other, non-plains tribes peripherally involved in the northern plains wars. Santees (or Eastern Sioux), Sacs and Foxes, Potawatomies, and Iowas lived near the Missouri. Even several hundred Delawares inhabited the area (they and their ancestors had been pushing west from the Susquehannah Valley of Pennsylvania since the 1700s, always staying ahead of the rapacious effects of the American frontier). These tribes of eastern South Dakota, Minnesota, and Iowa fought the prairie peoples west of the river. But for the Poncas, Omahas, Otos and Missouris, and Pawnees west of the Missouri River, the Teton Sioux were by far the major opponents. The Oglalas and Brulés were the primary raiders, the Omahas and the Pawnees their main victims.

The Poncas, hounded constantly by the Sioux, finally left their homes on the Missouri and roamed the plains during part of the 1830s and 1840s. At that point they found it safer to become allies with their Sioux enemies. In this way they could remain undisturbed and fight their old Pawnee foes with Sioux help.

By the 1830s and 1840s these conflicts on both sides of the Missouri had become so intense that the United States government became more involved in trying to stop them. The army built more forts to pacify the country — Fort Leavenworth, Fort Atkinson, and others on the Missouri River and eventually Fort Kearny and Fort Laramie on the Platte River. The army also added the Council Bluffs Agency and the Upper Platte and Upper Arkansas agencies to the St. Louis Superintendency. In these early years, however, the Indian Office could not control the nomadic tribes. It had more influence on the permanently placed horticultural peoples.

Given this situation, the government had to concentrate on the rivalry among the river tribes. Coming in from the outside, the Delawares further complicated this already complex system of military competition. The American government gave the Delawares permission to hunt on land claimed by the Pawnees, who then, of course, fought the Delawares to keep them out of the area. But the Delawares, after years of war, were a tough lot; so this was no easy job for the Pawnees. In fact, the Delawares became so aggressive toward many tribes, including the Sioux, that in 1841 Superintendent of Indian Affairs David D. Mitchell, a former trader with the American Fur Company, took action. He told his agent to inform the Delawares that their annuity payments would be halted if they made more forays against the Sioux. If things got too bad, the agent was to notify Colonel Kearny at Fort Leavenworth for help in stopping war parties.

While this was happening, the Indian Office had to face other confrontations. The declining but still powerful Pawnees raided the Omahas and threatened the small Oto and Missouri tribes living in southeastern Nebraska. The Poncas, with their new Sioux allies, in turn attacked the Pawnees. It took a while, but the government successfully ended these conflicts in part because the tribes did not move around and were easier to control.[8]

These squabbles also became less important in the late 1830s and 1840s because of the growing Sioux threat. The Oglalas, Brulés, and Miniconjous, in their migration south into lucrative hunting grounds of the Platte River Valley, began to harass the villages of the river people without mercy. In 1846, the aspiring young historian Francis Parkman vividly described the Sioux bands' warlike spirit. Traveling west from his New England home, intent on finding adventure despite his poor health, Parkman managed to spend some time with an Oglala band under Chief Whirlwind. Impressed with Sioux military attitudes and ability, Parkman depicted them in a dramatized and exaggerated but fairly accurate style. "War is the breath of their nostrils," he wrote. "Against most of the neighboring tribes they cherish a rancorous hatred, transmitted from father to son, and inflamed by constant aggression and retaliation. Many times a year, in every village, the Great Spirit is called upon, fasts are made, the war-parade is celebrated, and the warriors go out by handfuls at a time against the enemy."[9]

This hostile aggressiveness was often directed against the prairie peoples. In 1819, for example, Edwin James described the Omahas as outnumbered by their enemies though still actively involved in war. By the 1830s, however, the Omahas found themselves in a hazardous position. Their numbers were declining due to smallpox and numerous wars. Their population had shrunk to about 1,500 people, and they often fell prey to Sioux war parties. With the establishment of the Council Bluffs Agency in 1836, the Omahas had nearby protection, but it was not enough. By the 1840s the situation worsened, and the tribe asked the United States government for help.[10]

American manpower and the control policy were hardly adequate for help of this sort, however. On January 4, 1847, for example, Superintendent Thomas Harvey reported that the Sioux had killed seventy-three Omahas in an attack on a small village. The trouble in reacting to this emergency, said Harvey, was that the policy of stopping intertribal warfare unfairly held back the Omahas. "The instructions from your department are that the agents shall use all their influence to prevent Indians going to war." Therefore, Harvey concluded, since the Omahas were permanently settled in the area, they were hampered in making a united effort against the Sioux, while the Sioux raided them at will. In 1848, Council Bluffs Agent John Miller reported that in the last two years the Sioux had killed about 200 Omahas, Pawnees, and Otos, most of the casualties being Omahas.

The Omahas claimed that they were not going to be able to exist for long because it was difficult to hunt without fear of Sioux attack. These words paralleled the "ultimate destruction" theories that Denig and others held about the future of the Crows, Mandans, and others. Nonetheless, although the Omahas were in greater danger than most other small tribes, intertribal conflict was never capable of destroying this tribe or any other.[11]

During the 1830s and 1840s, and for years after, the Tetons' primary target was the still powerful but declining Pawnee nation, made up of the Skidi, Tapage, Grand, and Republican tribes. Here were worthy opponents. The warriors of the Sioux alliance — Miniconjous, Oglalas, and Brulés — joined by the Northern Cheyennes and Northern Arapahos, swarmed south in great numbers to raid the earth-lodge villages.

In 1848, the Pawnees became part of the new agency of the Upper Platte and Upper Arkansas. Formed at the end of the Mexican War, the agency resulted as part of the organization of the new lands acquired from Mexico, and Thomas Fitzpatrick, the retired mountain man and trader, became the agent. The Indians respected Fitzpatrick, whom they called Broken Hand because a rifle explosion had crippled one of his hands. A tall, spare man, Fitzpatrick had been in the West for two decades and was a knowledgeable and discerning observer of the Indians. He attributed the intensifying Sioux-Pawnee rivalry to the competition over the Pawnees' Platte and Kansas river hunting grounds.

This serious rivalry endured for decades with few of the usual truces. The competition, similar in savagery to that between the Crows and the Blackfeet, was fought more over hunting territory than horse stealing.

Northern plains warfare did not usually include the torture of captives, although mistreating and beating prisoners and mutilating the dead were common. Torture was more the practice of eastern woodland cultures such as the Iroquois and a few western tribes such as the Apaches. But the Pawnees did conduct human sacrifice, which was a direct and insulting challenge to their enemies.

The Pawnees practiced the Morning Star Ceremony, which was devoted to their most important deity. In some ways it was reminiscent of ancient Mayan and Aztec practices, as well as some of the Mound Building cultures of the eastern United States. To carry out this ceremony, which was a fertility rite, each year the Pawnees took a young captive girl who was believed to be a virgin and for a number of months treated her with the utmost care and respect. Then, on the day of the spring ceremony, the Pawnee priests took her up to a scaffold, tied her, and cut out her heart, offering it to the morning star god. Afterward, they placed her body out on the plains as an additional sacrifice.

Nothing could have inspired more bitterness among the Pawnees' enemies than this ceremony. A movement to abolish the Morning Star Ceremony began in the early 1800s, but it took a while to be successful because of the ritual's deep-seated religious significance.

In 1832, Upper Missouri Agent John Dougherty, acting on government policy, attempted to save a young Cheyenne girl from her fate at the hands of the Loup, or Skidi, Pawnees, but some warriors abruptly grabbed her away from Dougherty and killed her anyway.

About the same time a young Skidi leader named Petalasharo tried to end the ceremony, which had held on longest in his tribe. He rescued a Comanche girl and carried her off to her own country and freedom. The fact that no supernatural catastrophe befell him led the tribe to consider that it could safely discontinue the important sacrifice, although some of the more involved medicine men still practiced it secretly. Later on in the century, another chief, also named Petalasharo, managed to break up the ritual permanently. Other tribes' hatred of the Morning Star Ceremony, reinforced by the intense competition for land and military glory, remained long after the Pawnees had ended the sacrifice.[12]

One reason the Pawnees ended the gruesome rite was to please the Americans, whom they were beginning to rely upon as allies. Though active in war, the Pawnees had the disadvantage of permanent settlements that had to be guarded from large enemy forces. In an 1833 treaty, the Pawnees sold the fertile land south of the Platte River to the United States and moved north of the river to the territory between the Platte and its Loup River tributary in central Nebraska. As part compensation, the government was supposed to give them aid, including guns, to help them defend themselves against raiding Sioux.

But the Pawnees needed more help than the Americans made available. Faced with the Sioux alliance, the tribe experienced major problems in the late 1830s and the 1840s. In 1838, smallpox hit both the Pawnees and the Oglala Sioux, but the village Indians, being sedentary and close to the Platte River Trail, suffered the most. In 1839, in retaliation for a previous Pawnee attack, the Sioux killed between eighty and one hundred of them, a serious defeat. In 1843, Sioux destroyed a new Pawnee village, and in 1847, 700 Sioux attacked a small Pawnee town, killing eighty-three people. The Pawnees retaliated, but they were less successful than the Sioux.

Major battles with large casualties were unusual in most parts of the plains, but the Pawnees' permanent villages gave attackers an advantage and sometimes allowed the worst to happen. For example, early in the morning of June 27, in the 1843 attack, between 300 and 500 mounted Sioux suddenly appeared before a small, new Pawnee village near present-day Omaha. Greatly outnumbering the Pawnees, the Sioux made a series of charges into the village, captured horses, and set fire to lodges. Thoroughly defeated, the Pawnees vacated the village, having lost about seventy people, with others wounded or captured. Yet this defeat, like most of the battles, was not as one-sided as it appeared. The Sioux lost forty men and many more were badly wounded. The large attacks on villages usually continued to illustrate the typically limited nature of plains warfare. Only extremely uneven odds produced crushing defeats in intertribal conflict.

Over a period of years, however, the Pawnees' aggregate losses exceeded those typical of tribal war. Many villages could not be defended against the sizable Sioux, Cheyenne, and Arapaho war parties. In 1847, Superintendent Harvey reported that the Pawnees were in such desperate straits that they had moved south of the Platte River again in order to get farther away from their enemies. Harvey told the commissioner that he had assured the Pawnees that American troops would arrive in the tribe's territory the next spring to provide protection. How desperate the Pawnees' situation was is hard to gauge, but the American aid was never enough to offset the Sioux attacks. Unfortunately, the Pawnees' situation got nothing but worse as the century wore on.[13]

The government's policy of ending tribal conflict and protecting the vulnerable prairie tribes did not advance far during the 1830s and 1840s. Indian agents, with the help of a few troops, had some influence on the tribes living near the Missouri River, the major area of American forts, settlement, and travel. These tribes had treaties with the United States and received annual supplies of goods, or annuities, in payment for land sales. This meant that the government could easily call them to council and even deduct from their annuities the cost of the goods they stole from an enemy.

This control over the river tribes was offset by the near impossibility of influencing the nomadic peoples. In 1844, Upper Missouri Agent Andrew Drips noted this problem in regard to the Pawnees, just as Superintendent Harvey would describe the difficulties of the Omahas in 1847. After watching a Sioux war party ride casually into Fort Pierre with fresh Pawnee scalps, Drips wrote that it was "impossible to prevent these Indians from going to war." He felt helpless. Despite such pessimism, the government did make an effort. The army dispatched a few troops and planned forts, and officials of the Indian Office held councils at which they distributed presents.[14]

The problem only seemed to grow larger, however, as more westward moving Americans inadvertently became involved. In 1838, Upper Missouri Agent Pilcher complained that "war parties from one tribe against another are incessantly in motion, and owing to the great number of whites that are now in the habit of traversing this great Northwestern region for various purposes, it is a matter of no surprise when one of them falls a victim of his own wanderings, and a trait of character inseparable from wild savages."[15]

By the end of the 1830s and 1840s, as plains warfare reached new heights, traders, missionaries, and government officials had all failed to control it to any significant degree. The various failures only proved to Americans the mounting need to control what they saw as a crisis situation. By midcentury most white men, no matter what their interests in the northern plains, believed that only a formal agreement could place permanent control on tribal warfare as well as guard against Indian hostility toward whites.

Without an agreement of some sort, the Blackfoot confederacy and the Sioux alliance were too aggressive and powerful for the government to maintain stability on the northern plains, just as the Comanche-Kiowa alliance had prevented stability on the southern plains. The situation seemed more crucial when considered within the larger policy of establishing trails and forts to protect the many Americans coming into and across the region during the 1840s. These attitudes led eventually to the first large Indian council on the plains at Fort Laramie, but even as the government moved in that direction it still had little understanding of tribal warfare and the direction it was taking.

CHAPTER SIX

Disregard Their Treaty Obligations

EARLY TREATIES AND THE SIOUX ADVANCE, 1851-1865

Late in the summer of 1851, 10,000 Indians slowly gathered on the open, windy plains near Fort Laramie in present-day Wyoming. As each band arrived, it began a flurry of activity until brown, smoke-stained tipis and hundreds of grazing horses carpeted the undulating plain. As with any large Indian gathering, the mood was festive. Women set up their lodges, children scampered playfully among the drying racks of meat, and men sat in the shade of the tipis talking and repairing their weapons. The rival tribes of the northern plains — Sioux, Cheyennes, Arapahos, Crows, Shoshonis, Arikaras, Hidatsas, and Assiniboins — had arrived for a peace council.

This gathering, arranged and administered by Superintendent David D. Mitchell and Agent Thomas Fitzpatrick with the help of Father Pierre De Smet, resulted from American concerns that dated back at least a decade. Increasing travel across the plains had inevitably created conflicts, but intertribal warfare was also a major issue, and Edwin Denig, Father De Smet, and Colonel J. J. Abert had warned of a final battle over the buffalo. For some time Indian agents had advocated a major council to solve the problems of intertribal conflict. In answer to these concerns, Mitchell, in his 1849 report to Commissioner of Indian Affairs Orlando Brown, suggested assembling the tribes in order to settle their boundaries and stop the warfare, which, said Mitchell, "was one of the greatest calamities with which they are afflicted. . . ."

Brown presented the problem to Secretary of the Interior Thomas Ewing. "It is to tribal and intestine wars," he maintained, "as much if not more than to any other causes, that the decline and misery of the Indian race are justly to be attributed." Brown continued to suggest naive solutions such as forcing the Indians to pay for their depredations out of annuities, bringing them to trial, or punishing them by death or hard labor. With these methods, he thought the government could bring the warfare's "lamentable and dreadful consequences" to an end.[1]

Mitchell and Fitzpatrick organized the 1851 meeting, and the Indians gathered at Fort Laramie. Despite hostilities based on countless horse raids and revenge killings, the rival tribes easily slipped into a spirit of camaraderie. As if they were old friends, they visited, feasted, danced, and exchanged gifts. Many people spent entire days and nights in this easy boisterous company much favored by the northern plains Indians.

Even the Shoshonis, who had lost two men killed and scalped by the Cheyennes on the way to the council, allowed the Cheyennes to mollify their anger through the proper ceremony. It started with the customary smoking of the calumet, or peace pipe; then the two tribes feasted (leaving out the usual dog stew because, unlike their plains brethren, the Shoshonis did not relish boiled dog). The Cheyennes gave gifts of blankets, knives, tobacco, and red and blue cloth in order to cover the "price of blood." They also returned the two scalps with a conciliatory assurance to the men's relatives that the Cheyennes had not celebrated a scalp dance over the grisly trophies. Ceremonial adoptions followed, along with the usual exchange of gifts and eloquent orations to strengthen this new amity.[2]

As with most Indian councils, the Fort Laramie gathering interspersed the social with the formal. The meetings, attended by chiefs dressed in their finery, consisted of many elaborate orations, an art form at which plains Indians excelled. These flowery, metaphorical speeches continued for hours, unbroken except by whispering breezes and buzzing insects. After some haggling, all the representatives signed the document that became known as the Treaty of Fort Laramie.

The treaty marked a beginning of the government's new Indian policy, one now operating under the Interior Department instead of the War Department. In the treaty, the Indians agreed to allow settlers to travel the Oregon Trail and the government to construct forts along the way to protect Oregon pioneers and California goldseekers. Many federal officials believed the treaty would solve the problem of intertribal conflict because the tribes agreed "to abstain in future from all hostilities whatever against each other, to maintain good faith and friendship in all their mutual intercourse, and to make an effective and lasting peace." The treaty also set tribal boundaries according to

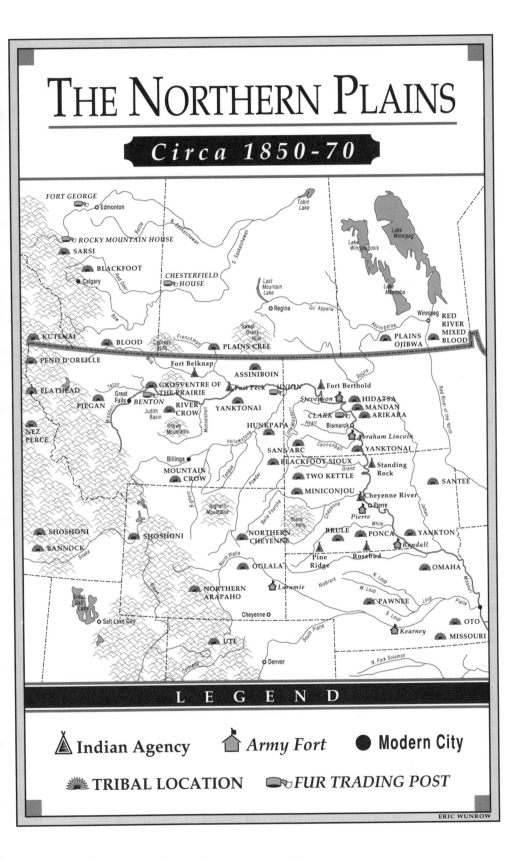

THE NORTHERN PLAINS

Circa 1850-70

those that the respective tribes generally claimed, although it ignored the fact that parts of the lands claimed by the Sioux were only recently conquered. (The Sioux had taken territory from the Arikaras, Hidatsas, and Mandans, from the Crows, and from the Pawnees.)

Despite the treaty's apparent inequities, the council ended on a convivial note. Following the accepted convention, Indian Office officials distributed presents to demonstrate their good will. Then the Indians drifted away across the arid plains to continue their nomadic warlike existence while the government representatives congratulated themselves on the tangible outcome of the proceedings — a signed document. Events were soon to prove that the red man's view of peace treaties was much different from the white man's. Initially, agents and Indians both reported examples of compliance with the treaty, but inevitably the agreement followed the path of most intertribal truces. Peace, the absence of raiding, always provided but an interlude in the warriors' search for glory.[3]

The first and most obvious defect of the Laramie council was that it had not included the Pawnees, Omahas, Poncas, Otos, and Missouris of the southeast corner of the plains in present-day Nebraska. Therefore, the Sioux, Cheyennes, and Arapahos had no "legal" restraints on their attacks against these prairie peoples, though such restraints would not have ended their wars anyway. The Sioux were outraged that the Omahas, Pawnees, and others had sold part of their lands to the United States, land that the Sioux intended for their own hunting. The Sioux and their allies had shown their bitterness when Superintendent Mitchell tried to escort the Pawnees to Fort Laramie. While waiting for him, however, the Pawnees had received word from the Sioux and Cheyennes, as reported by Fort Kearny commander Captain H. W. Wharton, to come to the council, "but they [Sioux and Cheyennes] would destroy them on the way back." The Pawnees decided not to attend.

On his way back east from the council, Mitchell stopped by Fort Kearny to meet with the Pawnees. Father De Smet and a delegation of Sioux, Cheyennes, and Arapahos accompanied him. The two white men tried to reconcile the enemies. Chief Big Fatty of the Skidi tribe spoke for the Pawnees when he said that after sending many successful war parties against his enemies, he and his men were ready to "bury the hatchet." A few of the visitors accepted the Pawnee calumet, but the Cheyenne chief Ride on the Cloud spoke for the majority of the warriors when he said they would not consider peace with the Pawnees. This negative stand did not put a damper on the feast that followed, but it demonstrated how these wars would seemingly continue forever.[4]

The fact that some tribes were left out of the treaty was not the major problem. Rather, problems arose when warriors began to ignore the treaty and raiding resumed among all the tribes. Roving bands of warriors, usually fighting other Indians, still endangered whites on the Emigrant Trail even though the Laramie Treaty supposedly protected the thoroughfare. The situation seemed little different than from what it had been before the treaty, as seen in the Fort Kearny commanders' reports before and after the council. In 1849, for example, Lieutenant Colonel Benjamin Bonneville, no longer the colorful young captain pursuing an extravagant trapping spree through the West but now an overweight officer whose puffy face reflected the dissipation of the officer's sedentary life at remote army posts, hinted at the army's superior handling of the Indians as opposed to the Interior Department's approach. He wrote that because of the Indian disturbances, "it is to be hoped that the Agents of the various tribes around here will keep these people at peace with each other — or put this matter into the hands of the Military."[5]

Captain Wharton, commanding Fort Kearny the year after the Laramie Treaty, still wrote of tribal war dangers along the Oregon Trail. The Sioux and Cheyennes, he said, were "constantly lying in wait for the Pawnees, scalping and killing them, while out in small parties hunting. . . ." Shoshoni and Crow war parties threatened the trail's upper portions near eastern Wyoming. In 1857, Upper Platte Agent Thomas Twiss complained to his superior that "their numerous War parties in the vicinity of the Emigrant Road, and even crossing it, in their attacks upon each other are becoming not only annoying, but extremely dangerous to the Whites." Behind the sparse, obtuse language of government communications, the situation showed that federal representatives certainly were not in control and were at a loss as to how to contain the warfare that threatened not only peaceful tribes, but also the emigrants.

The tribes also resumed their rivalries in other parts of the northern plains. The Teton Sioux, particularly the northern tribes, continued their old habit of alternately raiding and trading with the Hidatsas, Mandans, and Arikaras. These Sioux tribes, with the help of the Yanktonais, also continued their invasion of lands west of the three river tribes and close to the Assiniboins.

The old wars with the Crows did not cease, but recommenced in force, according to Sioux "winter counts." These were the annual

"For Supremacy" by Charles M. Russell. However dramatic, this painting is not a particularly accurate depiction of intertribal fighting. *Courtesy Amon Carter Museum, Fort Worth, Texas.*

records kept by various men in nomadic bands. Using tanned buffalo hides, the artist represented each year with a drawing illustrating an important event of that twelve-month period. Sometimes a whole year centered around one major battle. Substantiated by Americans' writings, winter counts recorded Sioux attempts at peace with the Crows in 1852 but showed confrontations occurring again in the following two years. Then, in 1856, one Sioux winter count portrayed a big fight in which the Crows fought a large war party of Hunkpapas intent on stealing horses.[7]

Indian agent reports showed the Sioux guilty of perpetrating the most depredations after the treaty, but this had been typical for the past ten or twenty years given their superior numbers and their westward and southward migration. But other tribes by no means stayed inactive after the council at Fort Laramie. In 1858, the Arikaras did rather well stealing Sioux horses; the Assiniboins sent war parties against the Arikaras, Mandans, and Hidatsas; and the Crows continued to travel long distances to fight the Arikaras and other enemies.[8]

In spite of the Laramie Treaty's obvious weaknesses, the United States government held to the panacea of the "grand council." Such would always be the case because large gatherings appeared to hold the word of many Indians and reinforced a certain democratic ideal. American officials commonly tried to make this a reality when they rather arbitrarily chose a "head chief," and he, along with others, signed a document.

Not surprisingly, soon after the Fort Laramie meeting the Indian Office discovered a need for another all-inclusive council. The Blackfeet were not part of the gathering on the Platte, yet for years frontiersmen had considered them the most savage of Indians. To end Blackfoot hostility toward white Americans and to resolve the bitter intertribal conflict in the Northwest, the Indian Office planned a new council. As with the Laramie meeting, intertribal raiding also brought about this gathering because the Blackfoot wars with the mountain and plains tribes continued with the usual ferocity, disrupting life in the Northwest.

The Indian Office's perception of the Blackfeet also helped cause the council. Upper Missouri Agent Alfred J. Vaughan, a man fond of exaggeration, reported that in their many conflicts the Blackfeet were undermining the Laramie Treaty among some of its adherents. In his annual report of 1853, Vaughan naively maintained that the tribes under his jurisdiction "have no wish to violate the treaty they have entered into with the government; but constantly annoyed as they are by the Blackfeet, they are compelled to act on the defensive, as instinct teaches that self preservation is the first law of nature." Vaughan even placed the Assinboins within this category of peace-loving tribes. The Crows, he wrote, were afraid to come to Fort Union for their annuities promised by the treaty because of the chance of running into Blackfoot war parties. Commissioner of Indian Affairs George Manypenny passed this view on to Secretary of the Interior Robert McClelland, thus reinforcing the general belief that the Blackfeet were more warlike than other tribes.[9]

In addition to the problems of tribal warfare, American expansionism played a more important role in this northwest council than in the one at Fort Laramie. By 1854, the federal government's Pacific surveys scoured the West, looking for the best railroad route to the Pacific Coast. Any route needed the assurance of peaceful Indians. The survey exploring the northern route, led by Isaac I. Stevens, was the most elaborate of the explorations. It passed through the northern part of the plains near the U.S.-Canadian border and through the heart of the Blackfoot lands.

Stevens, a small man with the energy to meet any challenge, was the governor of the huge new Washington Territory. As such, he was also ex-officio superintendent of Indian Affairs and was responsible for dealing with the tribes to attain both intertribal peace and a railroad right-of-way. Because Stevens was very eager for his route to be accepted, he made extraordinary efforts to assure the success of the exploration. Undaunted by the magnitude of his responsibilities or the reputation of the Blackfeet, Stevens methodically approached all the tribes in his territory, endeavoring to convince them of the need for a grand council.

Stevens was practical enough to seek the help of a person who knew as much about the Blackfeet as any white man — Alexander Culbertson. A trader with the American Fur Company, Culbertson had worked with the Blackfeet for more than two decades. He made Stevens' preliminary dealings with the tribes of the Blackfoot confederacy successful by interpreting, following the etiquette expected in Indian conferences, and taking advantage of his personal acquaintances among the Indians.

Culbertson's wife was as much help as he was to the new governor. Born into the Blood tribe of the Blackfeet and named Medicine Snake Woman, she had become a personage of some note among whites of the upper Missouri. She was a cultured woman and had had her children educated in white schools, but she maintained a connection with her people and their way of life. In this regard, Mrs. Culbertson shocked the famous naturalist John James Audubon while on a buffalo hunt near Fort Union in 1843. After the men had killed a buffalo, the good-looking, refined woman requested that her husband break open the skull so she could eat the still-warm brains, a delicacy among the Indians. They also relished the vitamin and mineral-rich organs, as well as other less palatable items such as raw testicles, intestines, and the soft gristle of the nose. While some of her customs may have caused some queasiness in various circles, Medicine Snake Woman's ability to operate in two such different societies made it possible for her to pave the way for Stevens's meetings with the Blackfeet.[10]

With this kind of help, Stevens found the Blackfeet willing to attend a large council, although they were not especially optimistic about its outcome. Chief Low Horn of the Piegans brought up an age-old difficulty common to all bands: The chiefs and older men were willing to establish peace, but they could not restrain the younger men. The latter pursued war as the only method of becoming chiefs and important men themselves.

Low Horn's views and those of the warrior societies supported these ambitions. These "men's clubs" organized the warrior's social life and raiding activities. The societies were age-graded; so as a man grew older and more adept at war or eventually retired from war, he graduated to a higher group or his club moved up all together. In most tribes the active life of raiding started around fifteen or sixteen years of age and continued on to the late thirties, or longer if the man had no son to carry on in his place.

The military societies provided a key element in the competitive nature of warfare because they usually made up their own war parties and tried to exceed the military accomplishments of rival societies. Everything else was also competitive, whether it involved groups vying to see who defended the camp best or who killed the most buffalo. Among the Crows the Lumpwood and Fox societies even competed, half in sport and half seriously, in kidnapping wives.[11]

Taking the information he received, Governor Stevens still followed the traditional American approach to Indian diplomacy and worked for a large council as the solution to the widespread intertribal raiding. He sent Culbertson to Washington, D.C., to urge the Indian Office to approve a major conference. Then, even after he learned that Secretary of War Jefferson Davis would never allow the approval of the northern railroad route because of his southern bias, Stevens still continued to work for a council that would make a safer passageway west. Yet he became irritated when he was not chosen as the senior peace commissioner. That honor went to Alfred Cumming, Superintendent of Indian Affairs in St. Louis. In the Indian Office, position and connections often counted for more than expertise.

Finally, the conference convened on October 16, 1855, at the point where the Judith River flowed into the Missouri in north-central Montana. The four tribes of the Blackfoot confederacy attended, joined by the Flatheads and Pend d'Oreilles from the mountains and the Nez Percés from the plateau beyond the mountains. One Cree, Chief Broken Arm, representing both the Crees and Assiniboins, brought tobacco as a token of friendship. Stevens and Alfred Cumming, the senior peace commissioner, expected the Crows and Shoshonis to come, but they did not show up.

The peace commissioners carried out the negotiations according to Indian Commissioner Manypenny's instructions. The principal objective was to establish "permanent relations of amity with all of the most numerous and warlike tribes in that remote region of country, both between the Indians and the United States, and between the tribes as among themselves." The terse directive did little justice to the richness of the spectacle taking place in this remote location —

the massing of the tribesmen and their counterparts representing the United States government. The solemn black frock coats of the peace commissioners were in stark contrast to the warriors resplendent in all their best military finery.

The Judith Treaty that resulted from the council included many of the same provisions as the Fort Laramie agreement. It defined tribal lands: Blackfoot territory reached from the mountains to the Milk River in north-central Montana and south to the Musselshell River to border the Crows. The Blackfeet agreed to allow Americans to pass through Blackfoot land; in return the nation would receive annuities. If a raid occurred, the offenders were to pay the victimized tribe damages out of their own tribal annuity fund.

The greatest disagreement of the conference concerned the use of hunting grounds. Chief Alexander and a famous war leader, Chief Big Canoe, both of the Pend d'Oreille tribe, complained that they were not able to hunt north of the Musselshell. As some of the original residents on the plains, the Pend d'Oreilles insisted on their rights to hunt on their ancient buffalo lands. At length, the tribes agreed on a common hunting territory located between the Missouri River and the lower Yellowstone River. This region, however, was already becoming the scene of increasing struggles of war parties and hunting bands.

Although the Judith council broke up with sonorous words from various leaders, some chiefs were more realistic about the chance for peace. Seen From Afar, head chief of the Bloods, wanted to maintain peace, but admitted, "The Crows are not here to smoke the pipe with us and I am afraid our young men will not be persuaded that they ought not to war against the Crows. We, however, will try our best to keep our young men at home."[12]

Seen From Afar's words were prophetic. The Blackfoot wars with the mountain tribes declined, but this had been the trend for a number of years. It was due in part to the increasing Piegan desire for peace, which had begun with the Small Robe band and the efforts of the Jesuit priests. After the treaty the mountain Indians still encountered hostility when they came to the plains to hunt, not only from the Blackfeet, but also from the Crows, Assiniboins, and Plains Crees. The Crows often clashed with the Flatheads when the Flatheads came to hunt buffalo or steal Crow horses. In the fall of 1860, for example, the Crees and Assiniboins struck Chief Alexander's band while it was hunting along the Milk River in north-central Montana. An overwhelming force surprised the Pend d'Oreille camp at daybreak. The inhabitants of the camp escaped only with their lives and had to flee the 200 miles home on foot. The relations between mountain and plains Indians were continuing much as they had in the past.[13]

In retrospect, the Judith Treaty had little impact on intertribal conflict. Traders at Fort Benton, Fort Sarpy, and Fort Union kept fairly regular accounts. One trader, James Chambers, took detailed notes at one time or another from each of the three forts. The records showed no significant decline in the number of war parties that passed by or stopped at the posts. Piegans, Bloods, Grosventres, Assiniboins, Crees, Sioux, and Crows steadily sent raids through the area. From October 4, 1854, to September 27, 1855, forty-eight Blackfoot war parties passed by Fort Benton. And this was only a small portion of the confederation's total military efforts during the year, not to speak of the warriors from other tribes operating in that area.[14]

It was no wonder that by 1858, Agent A. H. Redfield wrote that the Indians of the upper Missouri "almost entirely disregard their treaty obligations, are involved in continual predatory wars upon each other and that, indeed they frequently steal from and rob, and not infrequently kill, white people also. . . ." In the same year, acting Commissioner Charles Mix suggested the need for a new treaty and effective military forces to protect whites and cause the Indians to "cease hostilities with one another. . . ."

Government officials still had not learned the ineffectiveness of large councils, but they had discovered that intertribal conflict could have a very detrimental impact on the white population and had learned how difficult it was to stop Indian raiding. When the Civil War began in 1861, the difficulty increased. With almost all military effort directed toward the war, the Union could spare few supplies and men to control raiding plains Indians.[15]

During the 1850s, along with the failure of the Laramie and Judith treaties, the Indian Office's inability to stop warfare was most evident in the intense fighting of the southeastern theater. For several decades the Teton Sioux had gradually encroached on the Platte River hunting grounds in Nebraska, Colorado, and Wyoming. In past years the Cheyennes and Arapahos and the eastern border tribes — the Pawnees, Poncas, Omahas, Otos, and Missouris — had hunted on this land. Now the buffalo were scarcer as a result of the fur trade, increased Indian hunting, and emigrants' hunting along the Oregon Trail. Fewer buffalo helped to intensify an already active tribal warfare in the southeastern arena.

Complicating the situation, in 1854 the United States, in an attempt to solve the mounting problems coming from white migration and tribal war, signed a series of treaties with the tribes on the west side of the Missouri in eastern Nebraska. Farmers were pushing into the Kansas and Nebraska territories, and these treaties were part of the policy to move the prairie tribes out of that region, usually to the Indian Territory (present-day Oklahoma). This in turn was part of the overall government policy to make the central plains of Nebraska and Kansas free for settlement and transportation development. The Fort Laramie Treaty had begun the process by delineating all land belonging to the attending tribes as lying north of the Platte River, away from the major transportation routes. In 1854, Congress passed the Kansas-Nebraska Act in order to help develop the area, prepare for a railroad, and, it was hoped, solve the problem of the extension of slavery.

The Otos and Missouris in their treaty managed to keep a small reservation on the Big Blue River south of the Platte, but the Omahas had to move north from the vicinity of present-day Omaha to a reservation just south of present-day Sioux City, Iowa. This took them out of the way of the proposed transportation routes between the 37th and 42nd parallels. Through Article VII of the Omaha treaty, the federal government enticed the tribe to move by promising to "protect them from the Sioux and all other hostile tribes, as long as the President may deem such protection necessary. . . ." Future years would show that the government often did not deem protection necessary, thus leaving the small tribes to fend for themselves.16

Four years after these land sale agreements, the Poncas sold most of their land in the southeast corner of present-day South Dakota to the United States. According to the Sioux, the Yankton tribe had originally given some of this land to the Poncas, and the Tetons saw it as treachery to sell land to the white man, especially since the Poncas had been their allies in recent years. Two Brulé chiefs, Medicine Cup and White Black Bear, told the Ponca agent that the Poncas "injured them by the treaty recently made." To the Sioux, this was just cause for commencing a full-scale war.

Raids, especially by the Brulés began right away and increased steadily. In 1859, a large group of Brulés, Oglalas, and Northern Cheyennes caught a Ponca hunting party on the Elk Horn River in northeast Nebraska, killed several men, captured some children, and destroyed the camp supplies. For protection the Poncas formed alliances with the Omahas and the Poncas' old enemies, the Pawnees.

The Ponca Agency at the mouth of the Niobrara River near Fort Randall afforded some protection. Between 1859 and 1862, Ponca agents I. Shaw Gregory and J. B. Hoffman asked for muskets and small cannons. Apparently, the army felt it could not spare the weapons, but, like most agents, Gregory and Hoffman vociferously asserted the rights and necessities of their Indians. According to the treaty, the government had to pay for damages done by the Poncas' enemies, and in 1863 it finally paid the Poncas more than $11,000 in compensation for 100 horses stolen by the Sioux in 1860. Sometimes the agents were able to prevail upon the Yanktons or the Lower Brulés who lived close to the Missouri, to return stolen horses, because the Sioux war with the Poncas was rather intermittent. But often the cost came out of the federal government's pocket, when Congress would approve it.[17]

At the same time, the United States also had to protect the Omahas and pay for damages as provided for in the 1854 treaty. Protection was a long time in coming, but in 1864 the Indian department built a blockhouse at the agency for a cost of slightly more than $400. By 1865, eleven years after the treaty, the Omahas had accumulated a list of depredations by the Brulés, Northern Cheyennes, and Santee Sioux. The list included twenty-two lives lost, 152 horses stolen, plus more other property taken or destroyed. The agent calculated that the federal government owed the Omahas $13,120.

Meanwhile, the Winnebago tribe had joined the Omahas. After the eastern Sioux uprising known as the Minnesota War of 1862, the United States unceremoniously moved the Winnebagoes from Minnesota to land west of the Missouri even though they were enemies of the Sioux. There they suffered from Teton Sioux raids but finally found a haven with the Omahas. The two tribes survived the Sioux and today their two reservations stand side by side a short way downriver from Sioux City, Iowa.[18]

Sioux warfare against the border tribes grew in proportion as one traveled west, the general direction of migration by both the buffalo and the Teton Sioux. The Sioux showed no mercy when the prairie people hunted on land the Sioux now considered their own. The Pawnees were the primary victims in these wars. The earth-lodge villages were closer to the Oglala and Upper Brulé camps along the White River and the Miniconjou, Cheyenne, and Arapaho tribes farther north and west, respectively. The border tribes living close to the Missouri, at the coaxing of the Indian Office, began to stay at home and farm and to hunt less often on the plains. But the Pawnees continued their buffalo hunts and therefore challenged the Sioux' recent claim to the hunting grounds of the Platte River Valley.

The four confederated Pawnee bands had already ceded their lands south of the Platte River to the United States in 1833. The Sioux, Cheyennes, and Arapahos had then invaded the remaining Pawnee holdings to the north of the river. In an 1848 treaty, the Pawnees sold more land along the Platte River to the United States so that the government could better protect the Emigrant Trail. But the Pawnees, occupying a reservation just to the north of the Platte along the Loup River, were still well within range of the Sioux alliance. Raids continued unabated throughout the 1850s, and in 1857 the United States made a new treaty guaranteeing the Pawnees protection in their new homes. As with other border tribes, troops and weapons were sometimes available to protect the Pawnees, though intermittently and often too late to be of use.[19]

During the 1850s and early 1860s, the Pawnees slowly declined in power as the Sioux rose to new and dominant heights. Pawnee losses in some fights were disastrous, and the white man's diseases that filtered into Pawnee villages from the Oregon Trail took their toll. This meant that the nation constantly lost people. The few calamitous battles were not the most common type of confrontation, however, and most intertribal conflict still consisted of large extensive displays of bravado with little destruction.

Though few in number, massacres occurred when a small camp or hunting party fell prey to a vastly superior force. Inconclusive battles with few casualties, often fought outside Pawnee villages, were more typical. At dawn on any given day, several hundred Sioux, Cheyennes, and Arapahos might appear suddenly on the rise that fronted a sleeping earth-lodge village along the Loup River. The hostiles sat stoically on their horses in all the barbaric splendor of painted plains warriors. Lances glittered in the early sunlight and feathers fluttered in the breeze. The war party might immediately achieve its objective of gaining war honors if it caught a few Pawnees outside the village. Women getting water from the river often became unlucky victims. To count coup was the most important war honor, no matter on whom it was counted — man, woman, or child. Likewise, fair odds in the European sense had nothing to do with proving one's courage as long as the warrior took a risk by attacking an enemy at close quarters.

The Pawnees reacted to all these incursions. Warriors quickly ran for their weapons and horses and rode out to meet the enemy. Meanwhile, the invaders waited quietly until the two sides came to meet almost formally, facing each other across several hundred yards of open ground much as they had in Saukamappe's days in the early 1700s. Harangues of bravado followed, accompanied by sporadic firing. The warriors hurled insults back and forth, and called the other side's women ugly. The men accompanied the jeers with derisive, insulting hand and arm gestures popular with soldiers in all cultures at all times.

Occasionally, a determined young man might dash into gunshot range, then swing to the side of his mount for protection and ride dangerously close to, or even through, the enemy ranks. This often signalled the two sides to charge. They collided violently. War clubs smashed on shields and coup sticks whistled through the air as men struggled against their opponents. Often, however, the clash ended quickly and the warriors reformed their lines to look for an advantage enabling them to overcome the opposing side. Such confrontations usually ended in few casualties unless one side retreated or was greatly outnumbered, at which time a massacre might occur. Whatever the overall results, the important thing was for individuals to achieve personal war honors no matter how many of their opponents they actually killed.[20]

Despite the Pawnees' dwindling power, the plains tribes continued to respect them as fighters. In tribal warfare, men usually increased their status the more challenging their enemies. Two young Cheyennes, Left Hand and Stands on a Hill, provide a case in point. They became "suicide warriors" and decided to die in battle against the Pawnees, whom they considered worthy opponents. Suicide warriors were not common, though there were examples of them among tribes such as the Sioux, the Crows, and the Comanches to the south, as well as the Cheyennes. These men wanted to die, whether because of injury, sickness, disappointment in love, or some other reason. They were different from various tribes' Crazy Dogs, who vowed never to retreat from the enemy but whose vows ended at the raiding season's close or on certain other occasions.

Around 1850, Left Hand and Stands on a Hill rode out to a Pawnee village, followed by their Cheyenne band, which camped nearby. Their people watched while the young men deliberately charged the earth lodges until the Pawnees shot them off their horses and cut them to pieces. Afterward, the Cheyennes retrieved what was left of the bodies to mourn the dead warriors and prepare them for the afterlife.[21]

By 1859, the Cheyennes and their allies were actively raiding the main Pawnee village adjacent to the agency near the mouth of the Loup River in eastern Nebraska. Here, the agent dispersed the annuities that were payment for the Pawnee land sales, tried to "civilize" the Pawnees, and, increasingly, tried to provide the protection promised by treaties. To gain this aid, the Pawnees made numerous pleas for arms, ammunition, and troop protection from Fort Kearny, 100 miles to the east.

Pawnee Agent J. L. Gillis reported a typical battle near the agency and the village in 1860. It began at sunrise when a force of 200 or 300 Sioux, Cheyennes, and Arapahos surprised and killed two women. The Pawnee men quickly rushed to fight, and two opposing lines formed. After the preliminary skirmishing, Gillis tried to stop the fight by riding between the two battle lines. Seeing himself as somewhat of a hero, Gillis claimed that he was in more danger than the Indians because they were too far from each other to do any damage. He convinced the Sioux, Cheyennes, and Arapahos to leave, but they assured him they would return to "wipe out" the Pawnees. Sure enough, about two weeks later, when most of the Pawnees went on a summer hunt leaving the sick and crippled behind, the same enemy war party promptly reappeared at the now helpless village, killed one woman, destroyed the corn crop, and burned some of the earth lodges. Gillis hid the survivors in a cave nearby.

Gillis attempted to get help from the army throughout the summer, and finally in September a detachment of dragoons came to stay at the agency. The soldiers helped by chasing away a few war parties, but the raiding did not stop. In October 1860, much to Gillis' disgust, the army recalled the troops to Fort Kearny. The agent's attempt to procure arms for the Pawnees ran afoul of the army because General Alfred Sully, an experienced officer, found out that the Pawnees were also making offensive raids against the Sioux.

By this time the government was caught up in its own conflicting bureaucracy. The army had withdrawn from the reservation but would not turn over any firearms to the Indians. The commissioner of Indian Affairs would not approve issuing the Pawnees weapons because he said it was the army's duty to protect the tribe. Federal officials, especially army officers, were skeptical about giving arms to Indians for fear they might be used against frontiersmen. Many agents like Gillis, however, demanded guns so that their Indian charges could defend themselves against raiders. Given all the different views, arguments flourished and a unified policy was a long time in developing.[22]

Eventually, the United States supplied the Pawnees with some Sharps rifles, a more practical way to follow treaty obligations than sending troops. Then in July 1861, agency employees built a "rampart of sod" to protect the village near the agency. Yet raiding did not slow, and at one point the Sioux burned the grass in the area where the Pawnees had reasonably safe hunting so the buffalo herds would not come close to the village.

After the Sioux uprising in Minnesota in 1862, many Teton Sioux became more hostile to whites; this prompted the Pawnee agents to show more concern for the safety of agency employees. While American preoccupation with the Minnesota War and the Civil War meant less military protection for the Pawnees, ironically, the Pawnees began to see their future safety as lying with the whites. Many warriors jumped at the chance to join the new Pawnee Scouts, formed in 1864. This allowed them to seek revenge on Sioux and Cheyenne enemies. In years to come, the Pawnee Scouts became invaluable allies in fighting the hostile tribes.[23]

Four hundred miles north of the Pawnee villages, the Mandans, Hidatsas, and Arikaras continued their usual trade/war relationship with the northern Tetons and the Yanktonais. In particular, the numerous Yanktonais added weight to the westward Sioux migration that menaced the three tribes of the upper Missouri. During the 1840s and 1850s the Red River "half breeds" invaded the Yanktonai land north and east of the Missouri River. The so-called half breeds, or mixed bloods, were mostly Métis, or people of mixed French and Cree or Ojibwa ancestry. They traveled from their settlements along the Red River in the area south of present-day Winnipeg, Manitoba, to hunt buffalo. They destroyed thousands of the animals in order to sell the hides to the Hudson's Bay Company.

The Yankton and Yanktonai Sioux, their livelihood threatened by the mixed bloods, struck out at the invaders. Because of American concern for the welfare of Indians south of the border, in 1856 Colonel C. F. Smith led an expedition into the Red River country to warn the mixed bloods to stay in Canada. But the government was helpless. Indian, white, and Métis hunting, as well as white settlement, eliminated the buffalo herds. So the Yanktonais gradually moved westward, taking with them their rivalry both with the Métis and the three river tribes.

The Sioux pressure, increasing during the 1850s, placed the three river tribes in a tenuous position even though their relations with the Sioux continued to vacillate between war and peaceful trade. One observer, Lieutenant Gouverneur Warren, interpreted the relationship in terms of the type of bondage that traders noted in the late 1790s. In 1857, Warren was leading a surveying party through parts of Nebraska. An ambitious young officer of twenty-seven with a reputation for bravery under fire, Warren had a lively career ahead of him, which would include heroism at Little Round Top during the Battle of Gettysburg. He was a small man with a sallow complexion and black hair. He was also an efficient and even self-righteous officer and in his descriptions of Plains Indians demonstrated a strong belief in his own expertise.

Warren believed, like some of the eighteenth-century traders, that the river tribes survived only because the Sioux needed to keep them around for trading. From a conversation with the Hunkpapa chief Bear Rib, Warren reached the conclusion that the Sioux would never desire peace. The chief said no entreaties or gifts from the whites would change Sioux habits. "War with them," he said, "was not only a necessity but a pastime."[24]

Faced with the great Sioux migration westward, the Hidatsa, Mandan, and Arikara tribes gradually moved farther upriver as they had done in the past. This put them closer to their Assiniboin enemies, but it was better than being near the enveloping Sioux. In the early 1850s, the Hidatsas moved eighty or ninety miles upriver to Fort Berthold, built in 1845 as the successor to Fort Clark. Located near the mouth of the Little Missouri River, it was seventy miles east of the present-day Montana border. In the late 1850s, the Arikaras and what was left of the Mandan tribe joined them. Finally, these tribes became permanent allies and were known as the Three Confederated Tribes.

But the Sioux were also moving into that area. In 1864 and 1865, the Three Tribes obtained the military protection their agents had long been asking for. Two army expeditions, one led by General Alfred Sully, the other by General Henry H. Sibley, came up the Missouri to look for any hostile Teton Sioux and to hunt down those fleeing Santee Sioux who had been involved in the Minnesota uprising. The expeditions were not particularly successful. All they managed to do was to make the Hunkpapas and other northern Tetons even more hostile than before. For a time the Three Tribes had some military protection, but this ended when the soldiers left in 1865.[25]

The unrelenting pressure the Sioux put on the Three Tribes, while not nearly as dangerous as the Sioux pressure on the Pawnees, gave further proof that the Sioux' all-encompassing march had begun to alter the impact of intertribal conflict on the northern plains. Sioux raids on the Omahas, Pawnees, and Three Tribes had begun to have a truly detrimental impact upon populations and lifestyles. But to the west, in the Crow and Blackfoot land, tribal competition more closely followed its traditional characteristics of limited warfare.

There, the Sioux pushed the Crows from land along the Powder River and around the Black Hills of northeastern Wyoming that the Crows had dominated in the early 1800s. However, the Crows were not inundated with Sioux war parties and still took the offensive much of the time.

Plenty Coups, an important Crow leader of the late 1800s, remembered those days of his youth during the middle part of the century. A handsome warrior with a moon-shaped face of Oriental caste surmounted by the forelock of hair brushed straight up in the Crow style, Plenty Coups said that many enemies surrounded the tribe, but the Crows always fought back to protect their country, which now centered on the Bighorn and Little Bighorn rivers. Plenty Coups recalled the major enemies, the "Lacota, the Striped-feathered-arrows [Cheyennes], and Tattoed-breasts [Arapahos], . . ." but also others such as the "Flatheads, Assiniboines, and Hairy-noses [Grosventres of the Prairie]." Without hesitation, Plenty Coups named as his bravest opponents not the numerous Sioux but "the Striped-feathered-arrows and next are the Flatheads. A Flathead will not run. He will drop his robe [die where he stands]."[26]

The Crows, like other tribes, paid little attention to the Laramie Treaty when they did not feel like it. By 1858, Agent Thomas Twiss of the Upper Platte Agency even complained that Crow harassment made it difficult for the Oglalas, Brulés, Cheyennes, and Arapahos of his agency to remain true to the treaty. During the next years, the Crows continued to give the Oglalas, Brulés, Miniconjous, Cheyennes, and Arapahos considerable trouble.

In a council on September 18, 1858, these tribes complained that while hunting in the Yellowstone country, "the Crow Tribe of Indians show hostile feelings toward us when we hunt there; Oftentimes Scaring away the game, and stealing our horses." Agent Twiss, representing the aggrieved Indians, did not take into consideration the Sioux expansion into Crow lands or the power of Sioux raiding, but reported in 1860 that the Crows "are constantly sending out war parties against the Sioux & Cheyenne Tribes of this Agency." Like many men in his position, Twiss saw only the viewpoint of the Indians under his jurisdiction. Even so, despite earlier prophecies, the Crows hardly seemed on the point of extinction. They also raided their other enemies, even going as far away as the Arikara villages. Their main enemy, however, continued to be the Blackfoot tribes.[27]

When considering the sheer volume of warring and the number of enemies, the Blackfeet had to rank among the leaders of tribal military efforts. This was true both before and after the Judith Treaty and continued into the 1860s, when the Blackfeet reached the height of their power.

Plenty Coups, an important Crow chief in the late 1800s. Note the hair brushed straight up in typical Crow style. *Courtesy Smithsonian Institution National Anthropological Archives, Bureau of American Ethnology Collection.*

On December 28, 1853, Indian Peace Commissioner James Doty reported that since October 1, an estimated 500 Piegans had gone to war. Another 800 to 1,000 Blackfeet, Bloods, and Grosventres had passed Fort Benton on their way to fight other tribes. The confederation still fought the mountain tribes but seemed to be shifting more attention to their plains foes, the Crows, Crees, and Assiniboins. After the Judith Treaty, the Blackfeet easily justified fighting the plains tribes because these tribes had not been properly represented at the council.[28]

The Assiniboins, however, continued on in the weakened condition that had led them to seek peace treaties in the 1840s. By the mid-1850s, the northern Tetons and Yanktonais were beginning to be more of a threat to the Assiniboins in the area of present-day southeastern Saskatchewan and western North Dakota. Edwin Denig noted that declining buffalo herds in the East during this time had caused the Sioux migration. The result was that the Sioux and Assiniboins came into conflict more often. "Every year," said Denig, "the battles between the Sioux and the Assiniboines become more frequent, but as the latter are on the alert no great damage has as yet resulted. A few killed on both sides or some horses taken off generally determines the success of these collisions." This was the beginning, however, of greater conflicts to come.[29]

In this northwest theater of war an important transition in alliances occurred in the early 1860s, a change that would significantly influence intertribal warfare in its remaining days. It began one night in 1861 when a stealthy Pend d'Oreille war party captured some Grosventre horses. To confuse their pursuers, the Pend d'Oreilles deliberately left some of the horses near a Piegan camp on the Marias River. Practical jokes like this were typical of Plains Indian culture. War parties often played jokes on their enemies to make them appear ludicrous. In this case, however, the result was more monumental than the jesters could have hoped for. When pursuing Grosventres came upon the horses, they believed the Piegans were the culprits and attacked the camp of their allies. Later the Piegans retaliated, and peace was never renewed between the former friends. The Grosventres then began to develop a close friendship with their former enemies, the River Crows, who lived north of the Mountain Crows across the Yellowstone River in central Montana. Soon the River Crows and Grosventres were living on the upper Missouri, hunting together, and even intermarrying on occasion. As allies, they fought the Blackfeet as well as the increasing numbers of Sioux on the upper Missouri.[30]

In 1866, the Piegans scored a major victory over these two newly joined allies. A large party of Grosventres and River Crows discovered a band of Piegans camped near the Cypress Hills, located in the southeast corner of present-day Alberta. They planned a surprise attack and expected an easy victory, but the Piegans, alert to the situation, secretly prepared an ambush. The Crows and Grosventres, totally unaware, approached openly in formal order. So confident were they that they brought their women to sing songs of encouragement during the battle. The Piegans fell on them with a fury born from resentment of slights by an old ally as well as the thirst to gain revenge for a recently slain, popular chief. The Crows and Grosventres, shocked at this unexpected turn of events and the obvious failure of their medicine, immediately fled. The Piegans ran them down, and the trail of retreat was strewn with abandoned weapons, battle finery, dead horses, and the mutilated bodies of the optimistic contestants. It was one of the greatest Piegan victories, in which they supposedly killed 300 of the enemy.[31]

In the 1850s and 1860s, the Yanktonai Sioux further complicated this situation of shifting alliances on the upper Missouri. They not only joined the Tetons in the invasion of the land west of the Three Tribes, but also intruded on the Assiniboin lands that stretched from the present-day border between North Dakota and Montana all the way to the Milk River. Partly as a result of the encroachment, the Assiniboin tribe split. The Lower Assiniboins, or Canoe Band, found it easier to make peace with the Yanktonais and eventually shared a reservation with some of them. The rest of the tribe, the Upper Assiniboins, became more friendly with the River Crows and made peace with their old Grosventre enemies.

The splits in the Assiniboin tribe and in the Blackfoot confederacy, together with the addition of new tribes in the area, provided new competitive intertribal rivalries. These factors fueled a bitter tribal war on the upper Missouri in later years, one that was difficult for the army and the Indian Office to control. At the time, the United States showed little interest in restraining this warfare in the northwestern theater. Relatively few Americans were living on the upper Missouri at this time; so tribal raiding had little of the impact that it did along the Oregon Trail or along the Missouri River farther east.[32]

The Teton and Yanktonai Sioux, meanwhile, were in position for further encroachments on the upper Missouri as well as an invasion into Crow land and beyond into the mountain country of the Shoshonis. From 1850 to 1865, the Sioux migration intensified. They threatened the border tribes to the east and south as never before. In

The Cheyenne chief Dull Knife after he retired from the warpath. *Courtesy Smithsonian Institution National Anthropological Archives, Bureau of American Ethnology Collection.*

the years to come, most of the other northern plains tribes would feel the effects of some 8,000 Sioux warriors raiding into every corner of the region. The characteristics of intertribal war were not changing, but the migrations caused by hunting needs were having a greater impact. This factor would become more important after the Civil War, when Americans quickly overran their last frontier, the Great Plains, and found themselves competing with the nomadic tribes for the same habitat and hunting grounds.

The government's ability to control tribal war had not developed to a great extent; the Civil War meant that even less effort was extended in the direction of controlling intertribal rivalries. After the war, the government would gradually make greater efforts to control the warring plains warriors, but adding to the government's problems would be an increasing hostility of the Sioux alliance toward white Americans, facing officials with much greater difficulties than intertribal warfare alone.

The alliance's leaders in the fight against the engulfing American frontier movement had grown up, proven themselves as warriors, and become leaders of their people in the 1850s and early 1860s. Dull Knife and Little Wolf were popular Northern Cheyenne leaders. Representing the Oglalas was Red Cloud, with the dour face of an old but wise man, and his rival the lithe young Crazy Horse, the quiet but lionized leader of the hostile Oglalas. Sitting Bull of the Hunkpapas was the most famous chief. A stocky, unprepossessing man, he nonetheless was gifted with a charismatic manner that caused hundreds of warriors to follow his path as the most irreconcilable chief in all the Teton Sioux tribes. These men and other Indian leaders of the 1860s and 1870s wars had been trained not in warfare against white Americans, but in the heyday of intertribal conflict. In most cases, hostile chiefs saw whites as simply alternative tribal enemies. Few of them realized that the ultimate threats were the Americans' numbers, diseases, and technology. In the plains culture's last days of glory, individual fighting and raiding, no matter who the opponent, continued to be the basis of a man's position in Indian society.

CHAPTER SEVEN

Scourge of the Missouri

WARFARE IN THE AGE OF SIOUX SUZERAINTY, 1865-1877

After the Civil War, the Indian leaders who emerged in the heyday of tribal conflict raised the Sioux alliance to its height of military glory. The alliance members — Tetons, Yanktonais, Cheyennes, and Arapahos — moved into all sections of the northern plains, crowded the older inhabitants into corners, and even forced some tribes out of the area completely. This type of domination had seldom occurred before. The Iroquois confederation had ruled much of the Northeast in colonial days; the Apaches had controlled the southern plains in the seventeenth century and were succeeded by the Comanches in the late eighteenth century; and the Shoshonis had enjoyed a degree of sovereignty on the northern plains in the 1700s before their enemies drove them into the mountains. Now, the Sioux alliance dominated much of the northern plains.

Numerical superiority was a key factor. By 1865, the Tetons, Yanktonais, Cheyennes, and Arapahos had a total population of almost 20,000 people, about 5,000 of them warriors. The fighting men alone outnumbered the entire populations of some tribes. Given the limited grazing land and hunting grounds, the tribes of the alliance could not often operate as one force in one area, but numerous groups sometimes camped together for short periods of time, then traveled in large war parties that were both militarily powerful and psychologically fearsome. Due to this disproportionate advantage in numbers, warfare became considerably more dangerous for some of the smaller tribes.[1]

Inevitably, as miners, cattlemen, farmers, and travellers flocked to conquer the last American frontier, intertribal warfare became intertwined with Sioux hostility toward the westward-moving settlers. The United States Army represented a numerous and dangerous opponent, but the Indians usually treated the army simply as another tribal enemy. In terms of motives and tactics, fighting the army remained the same as intertribal combat. But with the vast American migration, as with previous powerful Indian forces, Sioux dominance became a transitory thing. The white population from the East that had helped cause the Sioux migration soon followed it and then enveloped it.[2]

The widespread Sioux hostility toward whites, beginning around 1865, reflected several developments. The Minnesota War of 1862, fought by the eastern Sioux, helped create hostile feelings among many of their Teton brethren, especially the northern tribes. The Sibley and Sully expeditions against the Sioux along the upper Missouri in 1864 greatly aggravated those feelings. Meanwhile, the Rocky Mountain gold strikes of the 1860s vastly increased travel on the overland trails. This traffic multiplied after the Civil War and raised the ire of those tribes hunting along the routes that crossed the plains. To add to this, in November 1864, several hundred volunteer soldiers attacked a peaceful camp of Southern Cheyennes and Southern Arapahos near the Arkansas River in Colorado Territory. The Sand Creek Massacre further proved to the Indians the Americans' perfidy.

After Sand Creek, some of the Southern Cheyennes and Southern Arapahos fled north. En route, they raided stage stations and even attacked the town of Julesburg in northeastern Colorado. By February 1865, they had reached the upper North Platte and Powder River country. Oglalas and Brulés were already in the area, hunting and raiding their usual enemies, the Crows and the Shoshonis. Now the refugees from the south joined the Sioux in war. The primary target became the Americans, and the motive was revenge for Sand Creek. Thus began three years of war, variously labelled the Powder River War (1865-1868) or Red Cloud's War (1866-1868). Although the Indians fought primarily against the army in order to challenge the Americans on the upper North Platte and keep them out of the Powder River country, the war provides excellent examples of the methods used in intertribal fighting. Not only did the Sioux alliance fight its Indian enemies at the same time as the whites, but the hostiles employed their usual tactics against the United States Army.

One of the best accounts of the early war was left by George Bent, the mixed-blood son of William Bent, builder of Bent's Fort, and Owl Woman of the Southern Cheyennes. Educated as a youth at a Missouri academy, Bent fought for a short time with the Confederate Army. Afterward, he returned to Colorado, where he lived with his mother's people because of discrimination and even threats from white Coloradans. What could have been worse than a mixed blood and a former

Confederate? Wounded at Sand Creek, Bent accompanied the hostile Southern Cheyennes to the northern plains.

Characterized by the square jaw of his white father and the high cheekbones of his Indian mother, Bent was a literate man who was able to function in both the white and Indian worlds. He was fair-minded and objective in his observations, providing us with a clear view of the war that developed during the late 1860s in present-day Wyoming.

Bent remembered the huge Indian gathering that he joined in the spring of 1865. Scattered along the bottomland of the Powder River, the countless lodges included Oglalas under Red Cloud, Northern Arapahos, Northern Cheyennes, and Southern Cheyennes. Both camaraderie and the desire for revenge brought them together; visiting, celebrating, and dancing commenced immediately. This was the essence of tribal gatherings, or powwows — large circles of tipis swarmed with barking dogs, small children played among racks of drying meat, and people of all ages laughed, played, gambled, and renewed old acquaintances.

Naturally, such a huge encampment attracted horse raiders, and one night nine Crows silently made off with some ponies. The camp discovered the loss the next morning, and within a few minutes several mounted parties had galloped off in hot pursuit. They followed a clear trail going west toward the Tongue River. The leading pursuers caught the Crows near the river and a brief but violent skirmish ensued. The Sioux and Cheyennes killed and scalped four Crows; the rest of the raiders abandoned the stolen horses, scattered or made for cover, and disappeared.

The victors divided each of the gory scalps in half to make the battle seem greater, and "for three long weeks," wrote Bent, "the scalps of those unfortunate Crow men were danced through all the camps, almost without a pause, and the beating of the drums made such a racket that the buffalo herds left our vicinity." The northern Plains Indians, said Bent, danced much more than the southern Indians, "and the way they kept up the dancing, drumming, and singing beat anything I have ever seen." The less ceremonial and more stoical nature of southern Indians such as the Comanches and Kiowas, however, did not make them better fighters. Bent maintained that those tribes made their great raids into Mexico, killing "poor peons" and running off horses, "but they would not stand up and fight like the tribes farther north. They were great raiders and full of tricks, but not much account in a real fight."[3]

By summer, the large camp on the Powder River had grown to

1,000 lodges, with representatives from the Cheyenne, Arapaho, Oglala, Brulé, Miniconjou, and San Arc tribes. In July, the men, anxious for action after weeks of easy camp life, prepared for a major offensive. They planned to attack the army station at the Platte River Bridge, located at present-day Casper, Wyoming.

The Indians formed a huge war party of 3,000 men. Before setting out, they made an old-style procession, the men on horseback, painted for war, with their feathers fluttering in the breeze and their lances, rifle barrels, and tomahawks glittering in the sunlight. The "pipeholders," or most distinguished war leaders, clad in impressively detailed warshirts and carrying their brightly decorated shields, led the way as the huge force grandly paraded around the entire encampment. Then, through dust clouds raised by hundreds of horses, the mighty force disappeared in the distance, following the course of the Powder River. It was a large but disciplined war party, as members of the warrior societies chosen for the occasion performed their duty of preventing any young men from spoiling the surprise by breaking away from the group to go and be the first to engage the enemy.

When the large war party quietly reached the hills overlooking the Platte Bridge, it stopped to prepare for battle. This did not entail building fortifications or planning strategy, but achieving individual spiritual readiness. A man's most important objective before a battle was to make sure his medicine, or spiritual power, was in working order. This necessitated preparing himself according to his medicine vision, an experience that every young man avidly sought before he became a warrior. If a man could not experience a powerful or successful dream, he would buy a "proven" medicine from an old and successful warrior. Before battle, the combatant followed a precise ceremony which usually included prayers and such things as dressing and painting himself in accordance with his medicine. Finally, he would sling over his shoulder his "medicine bundle," which included sacred objects, take up his shield and weapons, and only then feel ready for any challenge.

Once prepared, the warriors won two small victories near the Platte Bridge Station, victories that resulted from typical Plains Indian fighting. First, the Sioux used a small group of "decoy" warriors as tempting bait to lure the unwary into a trap. The decoy tactic usually failed because it was an obvious ploy and, too often, as almost happened in this case, young men ruined the surprise by trying to get in ahead of time to count first coup. But this time the ruse succeeded. The Indians lured a small detachment under Lieutenant Caspar Collins away from the safety of the station, then swarms of mounted warriors ambushed the troops once they were too far from the station to get reinforcements.

Lieutenant Collins at first escaped the ambush, but then he charged back into the fray to help some of his troops. He did not emerge alive from the swirling mass of men and horses. Shot fatally, he lost control of his horse and the animal bolted through the crowd of fighting men, its master lifeless in the saddle with an arrow protruding from his forehead. The Indians considered Collins a courageous opponent, someone who in even the most hateful intertribal rivalries always received respect. Nearly all of Collins's men were killed with him.

Very shortly after the Collins fight, farther upriver the Indians caught a small wagon train of soldiers whom Collins's unit had been trying to rescue. The detachment tried to defend itself. The soldiers circled the wagons and used them as a barricade from which they fired at the attackers. But the hundreds of warriors soon overran and slaughtered the small force. In tribal warfare, attacks like this one against a fortified enemy only occurred if the warriors were sure of a large victory. A resulting massacre, like that at the wagon train, made it worth a few Indian casualties.

In terms of Indian warfare, both of these brief, limited engagements were worthwhile because individuals had accomplished heroic deeds and achieved a great victory. The war party had attained sufficient glory for one day. So the Indians left the army post alone and returned to the Powder River encampment at the mouth of Crazy Woman Creek. However, warriors thrived on many small raids and fights; so very soon after, smaller war parties scattered indiscriminately throughout the area around the big camp, most of them planning to raid the Shoshonis or Crows.

Because it was the middle of summer, it was also the time to "make medicine" as tribal groups. The Cheyennes held their Medicine Arrows ceremony, and the Sioux performed a Sun Dance, a most important ceremony used by many of the plains tribes (it had originated with the Arapahos). Young men willingly suffered the torture of having their chest muscles torn as they pulled away from the ropes that held them bound to a center pole. In this way, they fullfilled earlier vows they had made to spiritual forces for good luck in war. Through this ceremony an entire tribe also renewed itself spiritually and hoped for a profitable and safe year ahead.[4]

After the religious ceremonies, the large camp dwindled as bands broke off to find better grazing and hunting grounds, and small raiding parties scattered in all directions. Tribal enemies were abundant. But the army also provided nearby targets because, in the summer of

1865, General Patrick Connor led a three-pronged expedition into the Powder River country. Connor had gained popularity as an Indian fighter in Utah, and he had some success in his portion of this campaign, but it was due in large part to his Omaha and Pawnee scouts, who scored a victory over some Cheyennes and discovered an Arapaho camp that the troops destroyed.

Colonel Nelson Cole and Lieutenant Colonel Samuel Walker led the other two columns, which joined each other in September on the Powder River. Their part of the expedition was a failure. The Sioux and Cheyennes constantly harassed the troops, stole horses, and cut off any small troop detachment. A number of confrontations took place during which the soldiers, with their superior firepower from rifles and cannons, drove off the attackers. The warriors appeared threatening in their daredevil charges at the troops, but, using their individual tactics, the Indians did not present a serious danger to the large body of troops. In reality, the attacks were more demonstrations of horsemanship and courage, the riders always breaking away before actually colliding with the solid line of well-armed troops.

A good example was the daring ride of Roman Nose, the most admired Southern Cheyenne war leader. He led the Dog Soldiers, a military society that became almost a subtribe because of its uncompromising hostility to the whites. Roman Nose supposedly possessed an invincible medicine, and on September 5, 1865, he sought to demonstrate it. First, he led an unsuccessful charge of 1,000 Indians against massed troops. Then, by himself, he rode the whole length of the troops' line. The soldiers shot his horse from under him, but Roman Nose emerged untouched after catapulting to the ground. It was an exciting and rewarding day for the Indians, even though there were very few white casualties. Roman Nose had proved himself superior in courage among comrades who also achieved war honors. Afterwards, the Cheyennes called the engagement Roman Nose's Fight.[5]

The conflicts elicited by Connor's Powder River expedition graphically illustrated the rapidly growing Sioux antagonism toward whites. This hostility, against the backdrop of the ever-present intertribal warfare and the beginnings of the largest westward movement in American history, led the government to seek a reconciliation with the plains tribesmen through the Northwestern Treaty Commission. In 1865 and 1866, its six members, headed by Dakota Territorial Governor Newton Edmunds, met with the Teton and Yanktonai Sioux tribes. Included in the treaties negotiated in the fall of 1865 were peace agreements between both the Sioux and the government as well as the Sioux and their tribal enemies. The United States government was to arbitrate conflicts between the tribes.[6]

Although these treaties were no more successful than earlier agreements, the commission's report demonstrated that its members, at least, had learned something of tribal conflict. The commissioners emphasized the social importance of war to the Indians, the extensive time spent in raiding, and the ceremonies and celebrations connected with it. The continual cycle of raids, scalp dances, alliances, and temporary truces, the report read, was the Indians' "understanding of peace and war, never conceiving of a universal peace, or a united general war." The idea of a general peace seemed to the Indians "quite preposterous, and they accepted this clause of our treaties with great misgivings as to its success." The tribes were willing to try the idea of peace, but believed it would be difficult to maintain. "War seems necessary to Indians, as the only occasion for distinction. . . ."

Little seemed to have changed since Lewis and Clark had appeared on the Missouri sixty years earlier. But now, as the treaty commissioners made clear, tribal war had a significant connection with the Sioux hostility to whites. After seeing the arms, legs, and other portions of human anatomy remaining from the mutilation following a fight near Fort Berthold, the commission reported, "Their hostilities against each other are carried on with the same cruelties evinced toward white victums." The report continued, with some American optimism, "Indeed there seems to be less inherent hostility towards whites than their own species. . . ."[7]

In the late 1860s, after the Northwest Treaty Commission had finished its work, the Sioux once again relentlessly pursued their wars with the Three Tribes of the upper Missouri and especially with the Pawnees on the Loup River. In addition, the Oglalas, Miniconjous, and Brulés, with the help of their Northern Cheyenne and Northern Arapaho allies, were extending themselves even farther west. They now dominated the Powder River country and were pushing beyond that to increase their hunting and raiding in the Shoshoni lands of south-central Wyoming; this included the upper waters of the North Platte, Wind, and Sweetwater rivers.

At this point the Sioux alliance's control of the Powder River country led the hostiles into a conflict with whites over use of the Bozeman Trail, a road that ran north from the Oregon Trail through eastern Wyoming to the Montana gold mining camps. The successful defense of the valued Powder River hunting grounds was known as Red Cloud's War; it was the culminating flourish of the general conflict that began in 1865. To the government and the army, this appeared to be a great Sioux war to protect their land. And it was — but the Sioux had only recently conquered this land from other tribes and now defended the territory both from other tribes and from the advance of white settlers. The Sioux and Cheyennes fought the Shoshonis and Crows in particular, because these tribes still contested the control of the lands where they had hunted long before the Sioux arrived.

After the army fortified the Bozeman Trail in 1866, using forts Reno, Phil Kearny, and C. F. Smith, the tribes harassed the soldiers unmercifully, constantly attacking small parties sent out to mow hay fields, collect firewood, or cut logs for lumber. It was remarkable that the Sioux leaders, especially Red Cloud, were able to keep hundreds of warriors in one area for a number of months, considering the independence of the average plains warrior. Yet it was not a siege in the commonly accepted meaning of the word. Mostly, the hostiles attacked small parties of soldiers; in between times, the warriors hanging around the forts took off on excursions to capture horses from the Crows or Shoshonis.

Some Indian leaders, such as Red Cloud and Crazy Horse, had unusual foresight. They recognized the permanence of the white man's threat and the need to change military tactics to combat it. They tried to convince their warriors to fight in a more organized and unified way like the soldiers in order to achieve more total victories. The Sioux chiefs even invited some Crows to their camp and suggested an alliance to help drive out the whites, an offer the Crows refused. But despite their advanced and grandiose plans, Crazy Horse, Red Cloud, and others found it difficult to completely step out of their traditional ways of war. Crazy Horse, for instance, varied his campaign against Fort Phil Kearny with periodic expeditions against the Crows and Shoshonis. On the whole, the warfare was as relaxed as tribal contests always were. A Cheyenne named White Elk in later years recalled how he and two friends had set off from one of the camps in the area to raid the Shoshonis, only to fall in with some Sioux acquaintances. Then, after accompanying the Sioux to their camp, the three Cheyennes spontaneously decided to join in the ambush of Captain William Fetterman's command.[8]

The Fetterman Massacre of December 21, 1866, was also a battle typical of intertribal conflict. That morning several Sioux appeared a short distance away from Fort Phil Kearny near present-day Sheridan, Wyoming. Working as decoys, they moved slowly away from the fort, appearing to have trouble moving very quickly because of difficulty with their horses. At the same time, other Indians attacked the wagon train bringing firewood to the fort, an almost daily fight. Captain William J. Fetterman, an ambitious officer who believed he could defeat any number of Indians with only a few troopers, led the relief column of eighty men. But not stopping simply to rescue the wood train, he continued after the small group of Indians led by Crazy Horse. The soldiers followed the decoys all the way into an ambush by hundreds of Sioux and Cheyennes.

The fight did not last long. The Indians lost some men, but they killed all the soldiers. Of course, there never would have been a battle without the element of surprise and the Indians' tremendous numerical superiority. Afterward, the jubilant victors systematically mutilated the bodies of the soldiers. They cut off heads and limbs, slit open bodies, and cut out organs. Next, the warriors arranged the bodies, portions of bodies, and organs in supposedly humorous ways, one of the most popular being to cut off a man's private parts and stuff them in his mouth. The Indians wanted to achieve the greatest possible revenge and play the best practical jokes since they believed a body would arrive in the afterlife in the same form as it had left life.[9]

Red Cloud's War ended in 1868. The United States closed the Bozeman Trail and agreed in the Fort Laramie Treaty of that year that the Sioux could continue to use the Powder River for hunting. This new agreement was part of a larger series of treaties with all Sioux tribes, Northern Cheyennes, Northern Arapahos, Crows, the Three Tribes, Shoshonis, and Bannocks, a small mountain tribe living close to the Shoshonis. A new Peace Commission drew up the agreements. In theory, the treaties made peace on the plains, stopped intertribal raiding, and continued the policy of "concentration," which actually had begun in a small way with the Fort Laramie Treaty of 1851. The idea was to concentrate all tribes either north of the Platte or south of the Arkansas, eventually confining them on reservations, thus leaving the central plains open and safe for travel and development.

Both military men and civilians made up the commission. Nathaniel G. Taylor, the stout new commissioner of Indian Affairs, headed the group. A former congressman from Tennessee and a man of "apparent" piety, Taylor seemed a fitting representative of the Interior Department's policy of "civilizing" the Indian through education, religion, and agriculture. The new concentration of the plains tribes onto reservations would aid in this goal by removing Indians from the negative influences of white society. Samuel F. Tappan, another of the three civilian members of the commission, was a well-known crusader for humanitarian issues. He had already gained some notor-

Negotiating the Treaty of Fort Laramie, April 1868. The government agreed
to withdraw its soldiers from the forts on the Bozeman Trail. The treaty
began, "From this day forward, all wars between the parties to this agreement
shall forever cease." *Courtesy Smithsonian Institution National Anthropological
Archives, Bureau of American Ethnology Collection.*

iety in the West as an "Indian lover" for his critical investigation of
Colonel John Chivington after the Sand Creek Massacre.

Three generals joined the commission, the most conspicuous being
the famous William Tecumseh Sherman, now commander of the Division of the Missouri. Sherman, the hard-bitten Civil War veteran
with short hair and a scruffy beard, went along with the concentration
idea. But as commander of the whole frontier east of the Contintental
Divide, he differed from the Indian Office representatives on how
best to deal with the Indians. Sherman's view was to keep them
unarmed, disciplined, and penned up out of trouble on reservations.[10]

For weeks on end, the various treaty councils met. The old processes, now familiar to both parties, continued as they had in countless previous consultations. The Indians came in their best buckskin war-shirts and leggings, gaily decorated with colorfully dyed porcupine quills and bordered with small black wisps of scalp locks. They often arrived in a whirlwind of charging horses. After this mock battle charge, the chiefs sat themselves solemnly on the ground with their warriors behind them — men of chiseled visage in stark constrast to their conspicuous finery, a lifetime spent on the plains etched on every face.

Facing them, the seven commissioners sat on small army stools. An old army tent stretched above them, its sides rolled up to catch any kind of breeze in the sweltering heat of the open plains. Most probably, the commissioners sweated profusely in their heavy blue woolen uniforms or black frock coats. With their clean fingernails, trimmed beards, tight collars, and, for some, indoor complexions, the American officials were hardly at ease in the company of the barbaric, though majestic, plains warriors.

All of the treaties that resulted from the meetings were similar. The documents set up large reservations that were, in general, the lands the tribes already held. The United States tacitly recognized the nine-teenth-century Sioux military advances into the lands of the Three Tribes, the Poncas, the Assiniboins, the Crows, and the Pawnees by setting aside the Great Sioux Reserve west of the Missouri River, as well as designating the Powder River country for Sioux hunting land. In essence, the commission saw the power of the Sioux and recognized their unstoppable movement to the south and west. It was almost a mirror image of the Americans' unremitting conquest and develop-ment of their own frontier, which was now poised at the edge of Sioux territory. But in this case the land did not seem usable by Americans. How could they possibly farm the waterless sea of sod and grass? The Sioux could keep it.

Each of the treaties established a general peace. No Indians were to commit depredations on "whites, Negroes, or other Indians." The punishment was that the offending tribe would deliver up the guilty warriors and pay the cost of any damages out of the annuity fund that the treaty provided.[11]

The treaties of 1868, however, did little to change the situation or the practice of intertribal conflict. By the late 1860s the Omahas, Win-nebagoes, and Otos and Missouris enjoyed some peace, as the Sioux directed their efforts more to the west and south. But the Sioux con-tinued their intensive raids on the Pawnees and Poncas. Sometimes the Sioux followed the Pawnees and Poncas to the hunting grounds and waited until a hunt began. Then the Sioux had the chance to destroy the small hunting parties. At times the Pawnees and Poncas hunted together, but often returned with little meat to show for their efforts. The Sioux' constriction of their lifestyle was beginning to move far beyond the usual results of tribal warfare.

By now the Pawnees increasingly relied on the power of the whites to protect their interests. This was demonstrated in 1869 by a number of Pawnee chiefs who wanted to visit Washington, D.C., and air their grievances about the Sioux attacks. But in the main, Pawnee warriors relied for their revenge on membership in the elite unit of the Pawnee Scouts. In 1864, Captain, later Major, Frank North organized the Scouts at the suggestion of General Samuel R. Curtis. The Pawnees were so anxious to get a chance to fight the Sioux that in less than an hour after he made his offer, North had enlisted 100 warriors for one year. The army issued the Pawnees old-fashioned muzzle-loading muskets, and only later provided horses. The manual of arms, thought by the army to be indispensable to soldiers, was given up in the Pawnee "battalion" because the Pawnees knew almost no English.

The scouts proved to be of tremendous value. At first, the army used them to protect the crews building the Union Pacific Railroad across Nebraska. Unlike regular troops, the Pawnee reaction to a Sioux raid was immediate. The scouts were often able to run down a war party and could effectively find hostile camps. As the Sioux war increased in the 1870s, the Pawnee battalion frequently moved quickly around to different locations by train, further confusing and frustrating the hostiles. The effectiveness of the scouts, however, came from the Pawnees' long warrior traditions and also from the army's leaders. Major North, and later his brother, Captain Luther North, proved to be good officers. They were courageous and often led the scouts in battle, not being content with ordering their men to the front.[12]

North of the Pawnee conflict, the Three Tribes — the Mandans, Hidatsas, and Arikaras — still lived in the midst of their Sioux enemies. The move to Fort Berthold did not get them out of reach of the Sioux since that nation continued to move steadily west and northwest along the Missouri River. In 1869, the Three Tribes informed their agent that they needed guns from the Great White Father to defend their fields against the Sioux and so plant enough to feed themselves. "The Sioux are better armed," they said, "and kill our women while they are working, and we have no arms to keep them away." Unfortunately, the government had adopted a rule that restricted the practice of turning over guns to Indians because the weapons might be used against white Americans. Finally, after much red tape, the army provided the Three Tribes with some guns for defending their exposed position.[13]

In the western part of the northern plains the Sioux encroachment was much greater. They continued to mount major expeditions against the Crows and to hold Crow land west of the Powder River. The Crows complained of this occupation to the Peace Commission, but the 1868 treaties contained no recognition of it.[14]

The Sioux, Northern Cheyennes, and Northern Arapahos also penetrated deep into the Shoshoni country of central Wyoming. Because of this, in 1867 Shoshoni Agent Luther Mann suggested that the tribe be established on a reservation in the Wind River Valley, a good place for hunting and defense. He went on to suggest that perhaps the Shoshonis could provide some unofficial protection for the miners working on the Sweetwater River near South Pass. This idea, appealing to frontiersmen, did not become official federal policy, although the government did create the reservation in the Wind River country. In addition, the Indian Office made a peace between the Shoshonis and the Crows and, for a time, between the Shoshonis and their old enemies the Arapahos. The treaty with the Arapahos did not last long, however, and the raids by the Sioux and their allies did not end.[15]

The Sioux also infiltrated the upper Missouri in increasing numbers. The Santees, Yanktonais, and Hunkpapas, in particular, roamed from the territory of the Three Tribes around Fort Berthold all the way up the river into north-central Montana.

In the 1860s the Hunkpapas had begun to acquire the warlike reputation that remained with them through the glorious days of their great chief Sitting Bull. They threatened all tribes within their reach, even the Blackfeet. In addition, most Hunkpapas became perpetual enemies of all whites. They and the recently migrated Santees often harassed Fort Buford at the mouth of the Yellowstone, as well as encampments in the surrounding country. In 1869 Lieutenant Colonel Henry A. Morrow, commander of the fort, labelled the Hunkpapas "the scourge of the Missouri . . . their numbers permit them to encroach with impunity on their neighbors, and they therefore roam at will. . . ."[16]

Despite the rising Sioux influence, in the late 1860s the Blackfoot tribes still dominated the northwestern arena. Year after year, they harassed the mountain tribesmen who still hunted on the plains, often catching small parties undefended and chasing them home, inflicting losses in lives and equipment. Pend d'Oreille hunting bands, for instance, lost twenty people in 1866 and five more in 1869. Each time the Blackfeet also stole horses, meat, and supplies.

The mountain tribes, who often had to hunt as far south as the Yellowstone and beyond when white settlement pushed herds away from the Missouri, also ran into trouble with the Sioux and Northern Cheyennes. None of this stopped the determined Flathead and Pend d'Oreille hunters, despite their agent's prediction in 1865 that hunting and fighting on the plains would soon end because his Indians spent more time farming.

The Flatheads and Pend d'Oreilles did not see the situation in exactly the same light as the Indian Office, apparently, because they refused to stop going to the plains, farming or no farming. Big Canoe, the feisty old Pend d'Oreille warrior who always spoke his mind, explained that his people not only were still deeply involved in fighting the Blackfeet but also intended to keep hunting on the plains. Big Canoe also resented the fact that the United States did not systematically help the tribes that had always been its friends: "Why is it that the Government arms our enemies the 'Bloods,' 'Piegans,' and 'Blackfeet'? they kill us, and the whites, with these same arms and ammunition on all occasions: — Why don't the Government furnish us arms and ammunition? we are the friends of the white man!"[17]

In addition to their old wars with the mountain Indians, the Blackfeet continued to fight their other traditional rivals. The Crows, particularly the River Crows, were a major target along with their new Grosventre friends. The Blackfeet still fought the Assiniboins and Crees, but they fought their last major battle in 1870 near the present town of Lethbridge in south-central Alberta, although minor raiding continued for many more years. On occasion the Blackfeet clashed with the Plains Ojibwas, a small branch of the large Ojibwa, or Chippewa, tribe of the Great Lakes area that had migrated to the northern plains and lived near the Crees. Blackfoot conflict with the intruding Sioux became common only in the 1870s and later. Blackfoot warriors who had reached manhood and fought during the 1860s and 1870s in later years recalled how the tribe had faced all these enemies. One Piegan named Mountain Chief claimed to have counted coup against a total of eight tribes.[18]

The long years of Blackfoot dominance in the Northwest came to a rather abrupt end in the years 1869-1870. First, another smallpox epidemic hit the tribes in 1869. More than 1,000 Piegans died as did more than 600 people in both the Blood and Blackfoot tribes. Then in 1870, an army detachment under Major Eugene M. Baker set out to punish Piegan warriors who had been raiding the whites. The men of Mountain Chief's band were guilty, and Major Baker, setting off in January 1870, was under strict orders not to bother the other, more peaceful, bands. Four cavalry companies and one infantry company marched to the Marias River, where they expected to find the guilty Piegans. The temperature was twenty degrees below zero, and an icy wind howled through the village. While the Piegans huddled close by their lodge fires, the army attacked. Unfortunately, this was not Mountain Chief's village but a friendly band under Chief Heavy Runner. In the massacre that resulted, the soldiers killed 173 Indians, many of them women and children.

This tragic event, along with the smallpox epidemic, led the Blackfeet to recognize the overwhelming, if indiscriminate, power of the United States; Blackfoot warriors no longer fought whites. Intertribal conflict continued for many years, but the events of 1869 and 1870 essentially broke the confederacy's previous power. It no longer held the degree of suzerainty over its neighbors that it had in the past.[19]

As the 1860s ended and Blackfoot power declined, the United States government began to define a more precise Indian policy. With the blessing of President Ulysses S. Grant, the Interior Department instituted the new Indian peace policy of 1869. The reservations, with agents picked by various churches, became the key vehicles for introducing a humanitarian idealism to Indian affairs. In theory, reservations would separate the Indians from any corrupt influences of white society, while agency employees would teach them farming, Christianity, and the positive aspects of American life. Although few warriors took to the farming life and agency farmers did most of the plowing, planting, and harvesting, the reservation did tend to slow down the warriors' raiding ways.

Actually, the nomads' entire lifestyle gradually changed because as increasing numbers of people chose to live off of government annuities rather than hunt the steadily decreasing buffalo herds. Separate agencies within the large Sioux reservation provided annuities for various tribes, and each of these tribes included factions both friendly and hostile to white Americans. Although the friendly Sioux continued intertribal raiding, the distribution of food and the regimen of the reservations tended to limit their actions.

Though small, this was the real beginning in the decline of intertribal conflict, but the usual wars between the tribes did not significantly decrease until 1877. After most of the hostiles had surrendered in that year, the northern plains reservations began to control Indian movement more closely. But during the late 1860s and the 1870s the threat of the Sioux appeared almost overwhelming as they continued to move inexorably southwest, west, and northwest into almost all corners of the northern plains.

It was not that intertribal conflict had increased more than in the past, except in new areas to which the Sioux now migrated, but that other factors complicated the old competition. More whites inhabited the northern plains, creating greater pressure on the Indians' way of life. The buffalo herds declined and brought larger concentrations of Indians closer to the remaining herds. Americans not only viewed the hostile Sioux as a serious threat, but also feared the intermittent raids of other, normally friendly tribes. The amount of intertribal raiding appeared to be very great, in part because of the number of government employees making reports that included the daily happenings around the army posts and the Indian agencies.

Responding to the situation, the government stepped up its efforts to curtail intertribal war at the same time that it mounted campaigns against the hostile Sioux, Cheyennes, and Arapahos. Indian Office efforts to aid friendly tribes and carry out the peace policy's goals sometimes seemed counter to the army's efforts against hostiles and intertribal raiders. As a result, government dealings with tribal war in the 1860s and 1870s often appeared ambivalent and contradictory.

The Poncas' and Pawnees' situation was the biggest problem for federal officials in applying the rather ambiguous Indian policy. Sioux, Cheyenne, and Arapaho raids were in large part responsible for the government moving the Poncas and Pawnees out of the northern plains to the Indian Territory in the 1870s. The concentrated raids of the Sioux alliance created havoc in themselves, but the Indian Office made things much worse with its continual demands that the Poncas and Pawnees not retaliate and its requests that they not hunt on the western plains, where many of the battles took place. This policy contributed nothing to the two tribes but created feelings of frustration and helplessness.

Although the policy to end the Pawnees' and Poncas' involvement in tribal conflict became more defined, it was not efficient or even palatable to everyone. On the whole, army officers scorned the Interior Department's idealistic goal of "civilizing" the Indians — still the basic Indian department motive in trying to stop tribal war. But the government's overall problem continued to be that, while officials could influence the sedentary peoples on the edge of the plains, they still could not control the nomadic peoples who roamed at will and easily supported themselves by hunting the buffalo.

With the beginning of President Grant's peace policy, the Indian department pressured the Pawnees even more to stay at home, farm, and avoid the pleasures of the hunt so that the tribe would confront the Sioux less often. But Sioux raids on Pawnee villages continued. At one point in 1871, the Pawnee agent warned that employees would soon quit their jobs and abandon the agency if the government did not provide more protection. In January 1873, Agent Barclay White reported that the Pawnees had lost 191 horses over a period of several months.[20]

In response to the growing problem, the Indian Office continued to control the Pawnees on the one hand and gave explicit instructions to Sioux agents to detain war parties on the other. The army provided troops to carry out this order, but it was impossible to control warriors who had free access to hundreds of square miles of country. The government attempted treaties, but the Sioux always turned them down. In 1871 the Upper Brulés almost agreed to a treaty, but in the end said they could not sign because they could not speak for the Lower Brulés or the Northern Sioux.[21]

Yet another disaster struck the Pawnees in the summer of 1873. A Pawnee hunting party consisting of 250 men, 150 women, and 50 children was hunting a herd of buffalo on the Republican River of southwestern Nebraska. Without warning, several hundred Sioux, hidden behind a rise, charged the Pawnees while they were scattered over the area butchering their kill. Several men of the rear guard quickly fell to Sioux arrows and bullets, while the rest of the men rushed the women and children to a nearby ravine from which the Pawnees were able to fire effectively at the Sioux.

Unfortunately, word had spread like wildfire through the nearby Oglala and Brulé hunting camps. Soon 800 to 1,000 young men thirsting for blood galloped onto the scene. In their overwhelming numbers, they were able to charge recklessly along the very edges of the ravine and shoot directly down into the Pawnees huddled at the bottom. As men, women, and children died from a hail of Sioux bullets, the Pawnees panicked. Warriors cut loose the fresh buffalo meat from the pack horses, got everyone on these extra mounts, and made a dash to escape. But the Sioux were on them immediately and chased them for ten miles before a detachment of the Third Cavalry appeared. Various agencies had sent word to the army about Sioux plans for an offensive on the Pawnee hunting grounds, and the troops, commanded by Major Gerald Russell, had made a forced march to intercept the war parties. At the sight of the soldiers the Sioux left the field.

The ravine was a charnel house. Twenty men, thirty-nine women, and ten children lay dead. The Sioux had mutilated the bodies and thrown some of them on a bonfire made of Pawnee lodge poles. Broken camp equipment, packs, and dead horses were strewn everywhere. The Sioux had also captured eleven women and children, rounded up 100 Pawnee horses, and stolen the meat and hides of 800 buffalo from the summer hunt.

Although the government compensated the Pawnees, this massacre on top of those in the past, along with years of government control that benefitted their enemies, helped break the Pawnees' spirit. And things did not improve. The same year, a naive Brulé agent reported to the commissioner that it would be all right to hand over 250 guns to the Brulés because they had learned their lesson by being chastised after the Pawnee affair and such a thing would not happen again. Of course, the raids did not slow down at all. Agents such as this one, always taking the side of the Indians under their jurisdiction, made it difficult for the Indian department to carry out its policy. Whether an agent was honest or was making money by cheating the Indians, his agency was the source of his income and provided a groundwork for advancement. Therefore, his loyalty to "his" tribe was assured, and he tried to show the Indians of his agency in the best possible light.[23]

To make matters worse, officials increasingly criticized the Pawnee Scouts. Of course, the departure of 200 men to help the army left the Pawnee villages without adequate defenses, but the warriors saw it as the best chance to get revenge on their enemies. The Indian Office, oriented in the peace policy's humanitarianism, perceived the practice as detrimental to making the Pawnees into "white men."

Grant's new commissioner of Indian Affairs in charge of the peace policy was Ely Parker, an old military friend of the president. Parker was an Iroquois Indian by birth, yet seemed to have little practical understanding of tribal war on the plains and the years of Sioux harassment of the Pawnees. In 1870, he advocated the discontinuation of the Pawnee Scouts because they "increase the bitter feeling and strife existing between these tribes." The army, which had found the scouts very useful, refused this advice that was seemingly given without any alternate plan to solve the Pawnees' problems.[24]

The massacre of 1873, following years of Pawnee demoralization, led in 1874 to the removal of the tribe to the Indian Territory. The decision to go was by no means unanimous within the Pawnee community, however. The Pawnees who favored it had support both from those whites who desired additional Pawnee lands and from those who felt that removal would promote the civilization process.

The years of Pawnee greatness and the tribe's subsequent agonizing decline at the hands of its enemies and well-intentioned whites were at an end. The Teton Sioux, Cheyennes, and Arapahos lost a challenging enemy. In the Pawnees' place, American settlers filled up the land and became much more of a threat to the hunting grounds than the Pawnees had ever been. As for the Pawnee Scouts, they were at least able to wage war for a few more years against their old enemies on the northern plains. The unit's military success enabled the Pawnees to practice their favorite pastime, even as their power as a tribe decreased.[25]

During the early 1870s, besides pressuring the Pawnees, the Sioux also helped force the Poncas from their home near the mouth of the Niobrara River in northeastern Nebraska. The Ponca sale of some land to the United States in 1858 had sealed their fate with the surrounding Sioux; the Poncas' situation worsened during the 1860s. Little American help came during the Civil War and the Minnesota War. The Poncas lived near white settlements that were more concerned about their own safety from the Sioux than that of the Poncas. In 1863, for example, the governor of Dakota Territory, John Hutchinson, put the matter very bluntly in refusing Ponca Agent J. B. Hoffman's request to transfer a cannon from nearby Fort Vermillion to the agency. No matter what the dangers present for the Poncas, he declared, "you may rest assured that I will never consent to disarm a white settlement, to afford protection to an Indian Village."

The situation continued to worsen during the late 1860s, especially after the government mistakenly transferred the rest of the Poncas' land to the Sioux in the 1868 Fort Laramie Treaty. The Sioux, resentful of the Poncas living on what was now Sioux land, and what the Sioux had long considered theirs anyway, continued their destructive raids.[26]

In the early 1870s, however, government protection for the Poncas improved. The United States supplied them with a few arms, although sometimes grudgingly. A small detachment of fifteen soldiers from nearby Fort Randall stayed at the agency, which sometimes lessened the damage of raids. This benefitted the government as well as the Poncas because the Indian Office had to pay for all horses the Sioux stole. But attacks still continued, especially by the Lower Brulés, who lived nearby on the lower White River near the Missouri. By 1874 the Poncas decided to move right into the agency and set up their village there. The Brulés and Oglalas still came and ran off horses and, for sport, shot the Poncas' cattle. The Sioux did not consider running off the cattle for food; next to a mouth-watering meal like the fat meat of the buffalo hump, beef was unfit for consumption.[27]

For several years, the United States considered simply removing the Poncas. Land-hungry white Americans would eventually benefit from the removal, of course, but Commissioner Ezra A. Hayt gave the reason based on the policy of ending tribal war: "The unfortunate location of the Ponca on account of their exposure to unfriendly contact with the Sioux, which has been a matter of frequent comment in the annual reports of this office, has led to the removal of that tribe to the Indian Territory, in accordance with provisions contained in the last two Indian appropriation bills." The United States finally moved the Poncas in 1877.

The Poncas preferred to move downriver with their Omaha relatives, but the Omahas were not interested. Neither was the government, which sent the Poncas all the way south to the Indian Territory. Some white citizens living near the Poncas' northern land joined the protest by those Poncas who did not want to go to the Indian Territory. These settlers near the Ponca Reservation also suffered from Sioux raids and appreciated the fact that the Poncas provided a modicum of protection. In 1879, the settlers even petitioned the president to have the Poncas brought back to the Niobrara because they would "feel safer if the Ponca were allowed to return because they [the Poncas] would stand between them and the Sioux." The petition and the protest of some Ponca leaders failed, however, and the last major target of the Sioux in the southeast theater was gone.[28]

The removal of the Poncas and Pawnees from the northern plains demonstrated the importance the federal government placed upon its policy of ending tribal war. The administrative difficulties derived from the conflict were intertwined with the problem of fighting against Sioux hostiles in the second half of the 1860s. In the beginning of the 1870s, the government had not been very successful in eliminating either problem. Grant's peace policy did not produce results, and intertribal raiding continued without letup. The removal of the Pawnees and Poncas essentially was an admission of the failure of the army and Indian Office to alter deep-seated tribal rivalries.

CHAPTER EIGHT

Superior in Daring and Enterprise

THE CLIMAX OF WARFARE, 1865-1877

The American contact with tribal raiding after the Civil War led to more attempts to control the warfare, a policy that increased particularly after the Sioux attack on the Pawnee hunting party on the Republican River in 1873. The government redoubled its efforts to keep the Indians confined to their reservations in order to "civilize" the warriors, restrain intertribal raiding, and stop war parties from taking out their aggressions on settlers. At first, American officials were mainly concerned with stopping Sioux hostility and confining those tribes to reservations. This meant that much of the effort to control intertribal warfare went into protecting the Sioux' enemies. A lot of raiding by tribes friendly to the United States went on without comment, particularly by the army, which often used these tribesmen as allies.

Much of the government's early efforts to control intertribal war centered on ending the decades-long conflict between the Sioux and the Three Confederated Tribes. From their earth-lodge village near Fort Berthold in present-day western North Dakota, 2,000 Arikaras, Mandans, and Hidatsas with perhaps 500 warriors faced 15,000 or 16,000 Teton and Yanktonai Sioux with 4,000 warriors. In spite of disparate numbers, however, this rivalry did not have the intensity of others. The Three Confederated Tribes, small in number, did little to challenge the Sioux for hunting grounds because the Sioux had already moved into the land farther west. Also, in this combat arena trade and raiding alternated to such an extent that war was never as threatening to the Three Tribes as it was to the Pawnees.[1]

Most of the Sioux raiders, when they were not roaming over the land west of the river tribes, travelled all the way from two Sioux agencies 200 to 300 miles down the Missouri. The Hunkpapas, Blackfoot Sioux, and some Yanktonais lived around Grand River (later Standing Rock) Agency in South Dakota. The Two Kettles, Sans Arcs, Miniconjous, and more Yanktonais lived south of them on the Cheyenne River Agency.

The rivalry between the Sioux and the Three Tribes thus took place in an area covered with forts and agencies. This meant that a number of army officers and Indian agents wrote detailed descriptions of the raiding. One of the more objective and realistic was Colonel Philippe Regis de Trobriand, commander of Fort Stevenson, twenty miles downriver from the Three Tribes, in the late 1860s.

A Frenchman who emigrated to the United States, de Trobriand was descended from a long line of military men. After a successful stint in the Union Army during the Civil War, he rejoined the army and made a career in the West. He was an imposing military figure, with deep-set, penetrating eyes, a prominent nose, and a full beard that was divided into two manicured points in the European style of the time. De Trobriand, however, was more than a military man. Originally trained as a lawyer, he later took up painting and writing.

The colonel had a fairly realistic view of intertribal conflict although he showed little appreciation for the military talents of the native plains cavalrymen. He recognized the limited character of Indian fighting, but went too far in denigrating the warriors' courage when he wrote of "their complete ignorance of what we call heroism." He added that the Indians "have no conception of the feeling that makes us scorn danger. . . ." De Trobriand was correct, though, when he explained the need for the typical war party to greatly outnumber its opponent before it would accept an all-out fight in the open. Indians, he pointed out, would not attack an army post directly. He emphasized their habits of fighting as individuals, not in formation, and of always taking care to save wounded and dead comrades. Though prejudiced, de Trobriand came as close as anyone trained in the European or American military tradition to understanding tribal war.[2]

Because he understood the limited nature of intertribal warfare, de Trobriand pointed out that the rivalry between the Three Tribes and the Sioux was not all one-sided. He noted that the Arikaras oftentimes went out against the Sioux with considerable bravado. On one occasion, they "floated" to war in some of their women's bull boats. Even the remnants of the Mandan tribe raided. In fact, in 1874 another army officer went so far as to accuse the Mandans of being the cause for the tribal conflicts being carried on without letup. Neither were the Three Tribes captives in their own village. They often went out to hunt buffalo, and the Hidatsas and Mandans continued to spend part of the winter hunting on the lower Yellowstone River.[3]

Since the Lewis and Clark expedition, the United States government had been concerned to some extent with the welfare of the Mandans, Hidatsas, and Arikaras. Now the Indian Office wanted to make greater attempts to protect them from the many Sioux who faced them. This was a major challenge because the army was reluctant to distribute guns, and officials were generally skeptical about becoming too involved in intertribal squabbles. Until the end of the Indian wars, the disagreements between the Indian Office and the army continued to thwart the possibility of a unified Indian policy.

The difficulty of following a definite policy was particularly evident in the complicated situation surrounding the river tribes. Many Sioux who attacked the Three Tribes were generally friendly to the United States. The Yanktonais and the Two Kettles were the best examples. Even the notorious Hunkpapa and Miniconjou tribes included factions that did not fight the Americans. When these "friendlies" fought the Three Tribes, however, it placed the government in a tenuous position. To keep as many Sioux as possible on the reservation and peaceful toward Americans was imperative; it would be disastrous to alienate friendly Sioux. Yet the Indian department also wanted to protect the Three Tribes.

Because of this delicate state of affairs, the army often tried to stay out of the conflict even though its job was to sell firearms to the Interior Department for the Three Tribes' use in hunting and defense. In 1867 the commander of Fort Rice, south of Bismarck, North Dakota, notified de Trobriand that a body of Sioux was heading for the Fort Berthold Agency. The colonel then warned the agent, but he also told the Hidatsas that his soldiers could not fight alongside the Indians because it would be wrong to help the tribes destroy each other. Later that evening, de Trobriand wrote in his diary his unofficial thoughts: "As both [the Sioux and the Three Tribes] are friends of the United States, we have no business interfering in any of their quarrels, and we have nothing to lose if the redskins devour each other." This attitude, typical of many army officers, horrified most Indian Office employees.[4]

In 1869 and 1870, with Sioux raids intense, the Fort Berthold agent called for aid and the army sent 300 Springfield muzzle-loading rifles and 30,000 rounds of ammunition for the Three Tribes. However, General Alfred Terry, commanding the Department of Dakota and fearing irresponsibility on the part of the rival Indian department, made precise stipulations on the use of the weapons. He would hold the agent responsible, warned the stringent general, for making sure that the guns were used only against the "hostile Sioux or against what are known as friendly Sioux only in case of attack from them. If on any occasion they are found to be used otherwise than as herein directed they will be taken back by the Government."[5]

In 1870, Lieutenant Colonel S. B. Hayman, the new commander of Fort Stevenson, downriver from Fort Berthold, demonstrated considerably more sympathy for the Indians than de Trobriand had. When the agent at Fort Berthold heard that a war party of Sioux was on its way north and called for help, Hayman not only sent a cannon to the agency, but also informed his own superior that he would consider any passing Sioux parties to be hostile because they were the ones who had broken the treaties with the Three Tribes and not the reverse.

The resulting engagement was not major — only one Arikara was killed — but General O. D. Greene, adjutant general of the Department of Dakota and the department commander's primary assistant, quickly quelled Hayman's ardor. He warned of the possibility of starting a war with the friendly Sioux and ordered Hayman not to treat the Sioux from downriver as hostile unless they actually attacked the Three Tribes in their village. Even then, the army's assistance should "only be necessary when an attack is made while the Indians are out hunting and leave but few warriors and many women and children not sufficiently defended — arms and ammunition having been provided them for that purpose. It is not our desire to commence hostilities nor to bring about an Indian War unnecessarily."[6]

The army was cautious because intertribal conflict in this case became closely tied to the overall peace on the northern plains. The army's position was precarious. Not wanting to antagonize friendly Sioux, neither did it want to appear reticent about helping the Three Tribes because during the occasional truces the Sioux attempted to get the village tribes to join in the war against the whites. In the end, however, given the long years of intertribal rivalries, this and other attempts at alliance were not very successful.

These rival traditions, plus a certain loyalty to the United States, led some men of the Three Tribes to follow the Pawnee example and serve the army as scouts in order to effect their revenge on the Sioux. George Armstrong Custer's most loyal and permanent scouts were Arikaras, or "Rees" as frontiersmen called them. A number of them died alongside Custer at the Battle of the Little Bighorn. His favorite scout, Bloody Knife, was fighting beside Major Marcus Reno at the south end of the huge hostile camp when a bullet struck him in the face, splattering brains and blood all over the major.

In the early 1870s, as the hostile Sioux became more active, the army catered more to the wants of friendly tribes that supplied scouts. In 1872 the War Department loaned the Fort Berthold Agency a gatling gun for its protection. The army also began to send out troops to help the Three Tribes. One good example occurred in June 1874, when Colonel Custer was preparing to launch his notorious expedition that eventually opened the Black Hills to gold miners. Abruptly, General Phil Sheridan, commander of the Division of the Missouri and a former Civil War cavalry leader, ordered the expedition delayed. A feisty, outspoken little bantam of a man, Sheridan had no love for the Indians; so for him to take steps to delay the expedition in order to help the Three Tribes illustrated the importance of the new policy coming down from high in the ranks. With numerous Sioux on the warpath against whites, intertribal conflict had become a major consideration in government actions.

Sheridan's instructions, as quoted by General Terry, were to "tell Custer to lay close for the party of Sioux on its way to attack the Rees. The Rees and Mandans should be protected same as white settlers." Terry endorsed and sent on the orders, adding to Sheridan's words by writing that "a chance to put an end to these forays of the Sioux may be more important even than your expedition and at any rate the expedition will not suffer by a few days delay in starting." As was usually the case, however, the war party was able to elude the eyes of the army and make its attack at 6:30 a.m. on June 13, 1874. The Sioux lured the Arikaras out of the village with decoys and killed five of them.[7]

This raid, however, proved to be the last large offensive against the Three Tribes. The next year Custer, commanding Fort Abraham Lincoln at Bismarck, North Dakota, helped conclude a fairly permanent peace between the Sioux and the Three Tribes. Later, the hostile Hunkpapas sent some small raids against the Three Tribes, but in general the rivalry declined considerably.

Two new additions to government policy helped cause this decrease in war. An 1875 government order required all Sioux to come into their reservations or be considered hostile. In this way the army could deal with the hostiles more effectively, but this also meant fewer intertribal raiding parties by friendly Sioux, at least those who obeyed the order. In 1876, as a result of a compromise between the War and Interior departments, the United States began to severely limit the distribution of firearms. Now traders could sell powder and ball to the Indians, but not modern breechloading rifles or fixed ammunition in cartridges.[8]

While the conflict surrounding the Three Tribes waned during the 1870s, the warfare in the western theater intensified. Here the Shoshonis and the Crows were the targets for the spearhead of the Sioux, Cheyenne, and Arapaho advance. The small Northern Arapaho tribe was in the van of the attacks against the Shoshonis of the mountains, often called Eastern Shoshonis to distinguish them from the many Shoshoni tribes farther west in the Great Basin and Columbia Plateau. Despite the Shoshoni-Arapaho Treaty of 1870, there was a rapid demise in the peace between the two tribes; Arapaho raids into the central Wyoming homelands of the Shoshonis reached new highs. The Northern Cheyennes and the Oglalas, often followed by the Miniconjous and Brulés, frequently joined the Arapahos.

The need to protect miners inundating the Sweetwater River country, as well as the need to protect the Shoshonis, led the army to station infantry at the Wind River Agency. For the first few years, the soldiers proved ineffective because they were on foot and the raiders were mounted, but by 1873 things had improved with the addition of a cavalry unit. Even so, the soldiers could not stop the raids, and in a way the troops were an added inducement to raiding parties. If the Shoshonis were away, the raiders could always attack soldiers.

The Shoshoni-army alliance did not always fail, however. In 1874 the Shoshonis, with the help of Company B, Second Cavalry, attacked an Arapaho camp near the Powder River, killed some of the Arapahos, and ran off more than 100 horses. The army had no qualms about helping the friendly tribes if their raids could disrupt the lives of hostiles.[9]

In 1876 Chief Washakie and 213 of his men went off to help the army in the Great Sioux War, the culmination of the years of Sioux hostility. Now an old man in his seventies, Washakie had a remarkable reputation as a warrior and held the high esteem even of his enemies. A handsome man with long flowing hair, his broad face denoted a vigorous character with its prominent nose, strong mouth, and expressive eyes. Washakie led his men to join General George Crook in one part of the three-pronged pincer movement that was supposed to surround the hostile Sioux west of the Powder River in southern Montana. At the Battle of the Rosebud, several days before the Custer massacre, the Shoshonis along with their Crow allies played a major role in helping to hold off the hostile Sioux and Cheyennes.

Although this was primarily an army battle, the Indians fought in their own peculiar style, and the Cheyennes, as was their custom, remembered the battle for what they thought was the most important war honor won that day. Probably more Cheyenne women than those in other tribes participated in war, and in the Battle of the Rosebud a woman named Buffalo Calf Road, sister of Chief Comes in Sight, performed the most outstanding feat of the battle. The Crows and Shoshonis had shot Comes in Sight's horse from under him and were closing in to finish him off. Suddenly, Buffalo Calf Road whipped her horse into the middle of them, her brother jumped up behind her, and she deftly zigzagged her galloping pony to safety, saving his life as well as her own.

Another incident also illustrated the techniques of tribal fighting used in the battle. "Jack" Red Cloud, son of the famous chief but not much of a warrior himself, was trying to make his mark. Unluckily, the Crows humiliated him in a fashion that was typical of intertribal confrontations when one side had the chance to insult the other's courage. After his horse was shot, Jack jumped clear and ran frantically for cover. But instead of killing him, three Crows merrily rode after him, lashing him with their whips and merely laughing at a warrior who ran away so quickly without facing his enemies or, at the very least, cooly taking time to remove the bridle from his dead horse. For a plains warrior, such humiliation was far worse than death. Ironically, this gamelike, yet deadly, fighting took place alongside the United States Army, a modern military force intent on the total conquest of the Indians and their land.[10]

Though the Shoshonis, Crows, and other tribes fought with the soldiers, they continued to use their own, rather inclusive, tactics. They allied themselves with the army in order to continue their old feuds and to keep the benefits of having American protection in their own tribal lands. The Shoshonis, considering how their enemies increasingly pressed them, needed American aid. In addition, their peace with the Crows helped the Shoshonis' tenuous position. The Crows also wanted American help, and, of all the tribes intimidated by the Sioux, none received more attention than they did. They had long been the Americans' friends and had proved themselves worthy by being, man for man, a match for any other tribe.

By the end of the 1860s, the Sioux alliance had permanently driven the Crows from the Powder River country. Although the Fort Laramie Treaty of 1868 recognized the Sioux' right to this land, the Crows never ceased to oppose Sioux harassment. No other tribe resisted the Sioux encroachment like the Crows. After the 1868 treaty, Chief Red Cloud, now at peace, even asked the army for weapons so his band of friendly Oglalas could better resist Crow raids. Even the mighty Hunkpapas complained of having to obtain their annuities far up the

Missouri because of the danger from Crow war parties.[11]

But the large Sioux population, in contrast to the limited Crow numbers, made it possible for the Sioux to use the same tactics against them as against the Pawnees — sending very large war parties to invade enemy territory. Each spring or summer during the 1870s, as if by tradition, the Crows and Sioux met in the vicinity of the upper Yellowstone and the Bighorn river country and had a large battle. The Sioux encroached on the Crows' abundant hunting grounds, and the Crows defended them. Despite the apparent seriousness of the situation, the fights were rather mild. Few casualties resulted from these battles, just enough bloodshed to continue the cycle of revenge.

The battles of 1873 and 1875 provide two good examples. In the spring of 1873, a very large party of Oglalas and Northern Cheyennes moved from their camp on the Rosebud River and went far to the west, past the Bighorn. At the point where Arrow (now Pryor) Creek flowed into the Yellowstone near Billings, Montana, they found 400 lodges of Crows with a few of their Bannock and Nez Percé friends camped nearby.

At the appearance of the massive enemy force, the Crow women quickly dug rifle pits and fortified their camp. The rival tribes spent the day, however, in exhibitions of daring charges that were more impressive in horsemanship and individual bravery than in military impact. In between the flashy assaults, the warriors called back and forth, learning the latest gossip about the people they both knew, such as the well-known mountain men Jim Bridger and James Beckwourth. Young warriors also indulged in plenty of jeering and exchanged the worst possible insults. At one point an Oglala sitting out in the open to show his courage — and miraculously escaping injury — called to his opponents, "Come closer. Come get some Lakota women! They are much better than Crows." At this, everyone on both sides laughed very loudly. Eventually, the invaders left. The only casualties occurred when the Crows stealthily followed the leisurely retreat and ambushed and killed two Oglalas. Not all large battles were so relaxed and sociable, but this type of confrontation was quite common and usually resulted in few casualties.[12]

The 1875 battle was only slightly more intense. A camp of 300 Crow lodges, sixty Nez Percé tipis, and a few Grosventres was moving down the Yellowstone, some distance from Crow territory, when it encountered 1,200 to 1,500 Sioux warriors. A long three-day battle resulted. Since the river separated the two forces, the battle was not very serious until the Sioux crossed the river and drove the Crows north to the Musselshell. The Sioux won the day, but the battle was inconclusive in terms of the standards of modern warfare.[13]

During the 1870s the Indian Office became increasingly concerned as Sioux war parties began to threaten the Crow Agency itself. In 1873 and 1875, the invaders killed some agency employees, and as a result the Indian Office requested military protection from Fort Ellis. But the fort, near Bozeman, Montana, was too far for any rapid response in an emergency and too undermanned to send a permanent military detachment. Besides, the post was too involved in combatting Sioux depredations against whites in southwestern Montana, particularly along the Gallatin River Valley west of Bozeman.

Governor B. F. Potts of Montana Territory, a great supporter of the Crows, continually requested more guns and ammunition from the Interior Department. "I do not believe a day passes that the Sioux Indians are not in some force on the Crow reservation, . . ." wrote Potts. But he favored the Crows and was so impressed with the number of Sioux raids that he was not very objective about the realities of intertribal warfare, as he illustrated in an 1874 letter: "I do not believe the Mountain Crows have ever left their own reservation to fight other Indians nor do I believe they propose to." Like some other officials, Potts believed the Indians when they told him of the overwhelming power and hostility of their enemies as compared to their own weakness and innocence. In this way tribes tried to obtain more help from the federal government. The framework of tribal conflict had not changed. All the tribes joined in when they could, whether they were weak or strong. Certainly, the Crows were one of the best examples of this.[14]

Not everyone agreed with Potts about the Crows' helplessness. Major N. B. Sweitzer, the outspoken commander of Fort Ellis, presented the army point of view. He thought the Crow agents were overly concerned with the need for protection. The Crows themselves, Sweitzer claimed, were perfectly capable of defending their own people and the agency. He contended that a mere ten or twelve Indians at the agency would be capable of defending it during the summer raiding season.

Sweitzer expanded his theory further in 1874, when he criticized Crow Agent F. D. Pease about his efforts to make peace between the Crows and the Sioux. Sweitzer's argument included the traditional army emphasis on the military solution of suppressing the hostile Indians and controlling the others, which was contrary to the Interior Department's humanitarian approach that gave the Indians considerable freedom of decision. That sort of peace, he maintained, "may be philanthropy to the Indians, but it is death to the whites."

Like many other Americans in southern Montana, Major Sweitzer perceived the Crows as protectors of the whites against the hostile Sioux. The expanding settlements of the Gallatin Valley were particularly grateful to the Crows. Of course, merchants also appreciated the protection. In 1874, the freighting and trading firm of Story and Hoffman wrote to the Crow agent to encourage government support for the Crows. According to the company, the Crows had always been friendly and were "considered by the people of Montana as their main Safeguard between the whites and the Sioux. . . ." Therefore, the letter continued, it was "considered a matter of necessity that these Indians be provided with ammunition sufficient to guard themselves from the raids of the Sioux with whom they are constantly at war."

As early as 1870, an unofficial military policy provided that the United States supply the Crows with arms in return for the tribe being a buffer for frontiersmen. By 1874, the agreement was an accepted fact. Settlers and soldiers viewed the Crow tribe as an extra "regiment of cavalry." Each side benefited; Americans felt safer, while the army did not hinder the Crows in their warfare.[15]

None of this was acceptable to the Indian Office, however, nor was it official government policy. In 1874, Secretary of the Interior Columbus Delano, representing the program of peace and civilized life for the Indians, reprimanded Governor Potts for excessive zeal in supporting and arming the Crows. Such an approach, he said, would only make the Sioux more hostile to the whites.

An example of the type of detrimental influence feared by Delano occurred in December 1876 among the Crow scouts working for Colonel Nelson Miles, an egotistical but supremely successful Indian fighter. Miles was receiving a delegation of Miniconjou chiefs under a flag of truce. Suddenly and without warning, twelve Crow scouts rushed the Miniconjous and, before the soldiers could stop them, the Crows killed five of their old rivals. The furious Miles attributed the incident to the Crow desires for revenge on a bitter enemy. The Crow action seemed to corroborate Commissioner Ely Parker's earlier fears concerning the negative aspects of the Pawnee Scouts.[16]

Most army officers, however, valued the use of Indian allies. And the Crows often volunteered. During the 1876 Sioux War, the three-pronged invasion of the Powder River country utilized many Indian auxiliaries. In this large operation, which ended in Custer's demise, Lieutenant James Bradley, later to die in the short Nez Percé War of

1877, commanded the Crow scouts. The Crow tribe, like the Shoshonis and some others, seemed to sense at an early date who would be the ultimate victor in the red-white contest on the northern plains. Accordingly, the young warriors joined the winning side, but their specific reason was to gain revenge and individual war honors against a long-standing enemy.

The Crow scouts with Custer, in applying their own views of war, thought little of his attack on such a large hostile camp. Several Crows accompanied Custer's column on its fateful ride along the bluffs overlooking the Little Bighorn River. A seventeen-year-old, mixed-blood Crow nicknamed Curley was one of them. A tall, handsome youth with prominent cheekbones and wavy hair, Curley gained recognition as being the first one to pass the word of Custer's fate to other American troops in the area. In escaping before the battle, Curley was simply following the natural inclination of a plains warrior. Attacking such a huge camp was suicidal; it was better to await a better day to fight.

Three other discouraged Crows also left, even though they stayed a little longer at Custer's side: Goes Ahead, Hairy Moccasin, and White Man Runs Him. Goes Ahead was married to Pretty Shield, a woman with strong medicine who in 1931 told her life story to cattleman Frank Linderman. Goes Ahead had told her how the three Crow scouts barely escaped before Custer and his troops were annihilated. Afterward, they joined the remnants of Major Reno's men defending themselves on the bluffs south of the huge village. A short while later, they also left this fight and headed for home. On the way, Goes Ahead was able to kill a lone Sioux and catch his horse for them to ride, since all three had lost their mounts in the battle. So the venture with Custer benefitted Goes Ahead because he was able to win a war honor, something in which he was deficient.

Pretty Shield spoke of the importance of war honors for a man in being able to win a wife. She had married Goes Ahead, a good man, even though he had never counted coup and had only one honor to his credit — rescuing a friend in battle. But his case must have been similar to many warriors. Certainly, they could not all have had numerous feats to their credit when so many battles were of limited conflict.[17]

Ironically, even though the Crows left the battlefield before all was lost for Custer, the Sioux alliance fought the Battle of the Little Bighorn much like intertribal contests. It is likely that in overrunning Custer's detachment the Indians charged in groups from different directions, much as they did in their own battles while in competition with each other. The massacre occurred because the warriors had a huge numer-

The Crow warrior Curley, who was one of the first to pass the word of the disaster at the Battle of the Little Bighorn. *Courtesy Smithsonian Institution National Anthropological Archives, Bureau of American Ethnology Collection.*

ical advantage and had to defend their camp. They were therefore willing to suffer casualties in order to win such a stunning victory.

A good example of the Indian approach to the battle appears in the memoir of Wooden Leg, a Northern Cheyenne who was a young man when the soldiers attacked the village on the Little Bighorn. Even after he knew that the soldiers under Reno were attacking the southern end of the camp, he paused to prepare himself for battle. His father had retired from war when Wooden Leg was of age to fight, according to Cheyenne tradition, so the elder man went to catch his son's horse while Wooden Leg quickly painted himself, arranged his hair, and donned his best war clothes. All this complied with his medicine; to do otherwise was to risk death because one would have no spiritual power.

One's tribal identity was also important. In this very battle, the Sioux mistakenly killed a Cheyenne named Lame White Man. They mistook him for one of the Arikara scouts with Custer because he had neglected to dress properly like a Cheyenne ready for war. Lame White Man had rushed off to fight wearing only his breechcloth, later picking up a dead soldier's blue coat. Considering the Indians' painstaking preparation for war and their habit of not guarding their camps, it was no wonder that Custer's units got so close before the heavy fighting began.

When Wooden Leg finally joined the fight at the point where Major Reno had attacked the village, the Hunkpapas, whose circle of lodges was at that end of the encampment, were already forcing the soldiers to retreat. Wooden Leg and his friend Little Bird ran down one badly frightened soldier who was frantically lashing his horse toward the river. They came up on either side of him and both counted coup by striking him with the elkhorn handles of their whips. The soldier immediately turned and fired his carbine, the bullet striking Little Bird in the thigh. But Wooden Leg managed to knock the "bluecoat" off his horse and grab the valuable carbine at the same time. They did not bother to go back and kill the soldier. Wooden Leg had already attained two war honors and simply killing a man as such, did not show courage. At any rate, he said, "It seemed not brave to shoot. Besides I did not want to waste my bullets."

Although this type of combat was significant in intertribal conflict, in the long run it had little effect in fighting the modern army of the United States. The day had arrived when this type of individualistic warfare could not exist within a technically advanced society. In the case of Custer's defeat, the Indians simply had a vast superiority in

numbers and highly charged emotions to add to their individual courage.[10]

The army's Crow allies, seeing this ultimate American power, determined to make the best of their alliance with the whites in order
to carry on their raiding. They became better armed with the help of
the government, and they often fought with the Americans' blessings,
at least of those in the army. This set of circumstances allowed the
Crows to successfully carry out their individualistic brand of war for
many years, whether helping the army or fighting on their own.

The Crow approach was evident in the 1877 Nez Percé War. When
Chief Joseph led his people on the long journey across the mountains
and plains to avoid the army, the Crows volunteered to help the
soldiers even though the Nez Percés had been friends. The Crows
soon revealed their true intentions when the army unit they accompanied discovered a Nez Percé camp. According to one of the regular
army scouts, "at the sight of 2,500 head of hostile horses the Crows
went wild, charged one corner of the rear of the herd, and cut out
300 horses, which they stampeded over the hill and rushed back to
their reservation." The embittered army scout continued, "Horses
were all they were after, so they did not stop to help the whites in
the impending battle."[19]

In the 1860s and 1870s, of course, the Crows had major conflicts
of their own. The Mountain Crows were so busy fighting the Sioux
that their conflict with the Blackfeet sometimes became less important.
Meanwhile, the River Crows and their new friends, the Grosventres
of the Prairie and the Upper Assiniboins, persisted in the old rivalry
with the three Blackfoot tribes.

While the old competition continued during these decades, there
was also considerable change in the battleground of northern Montana
and southern Alberta. Sioux migration along the Missouri and the
arrival of other tribes brought about the new developments. The upper
Missouri still teemed with buffalo, Here resided the last of the great
herds. Edwin Denig's earlier prophecy of a last battle over the buffalo
seemed to be coming true. This made the 1870s the climax of decades
of intertribal conflict.

The Yanktonais, with some Santees, had already been moving into
the area through most of the 1860s. Then and in the 1870s, other
outsiders also arrived, creating a crowded territory of hunters and
raiders. From Canada, the Plains Crees, Plains Ojibwas, and Red
River mixed bloods increased their hunting trips to the south. The
Mountain Crows went north from their land both to hunt and fight.

Hostile northern Sioux bands, particularly the Hunkpapas, also inundated the area.

As buffalo became scarcer to the south, even the Northern Cheyennes and Northern Arapahos moved north and tried to make a new home for themselves near the Grosventres of the Prairie, distant relatives of the Arapahos. The Cheyennes and Arapahos even had a white man who championed their cause, George Clendinin of Musselshell, Montana (eighty miles northeast of Billings). He petitioned the Indian department, unsuccessfully, to have the two tribes moved north. All the time, Clendinin had another interest in the matter besides the welfare of the Cheyennes and Arapahos. As an important businessman in Musselshell, he had been able to obtain a trading license with which he hoped to monopolize the Cheyenne and Arapaho trade.[20]

The influx of the tribes into the Northwest created difficulties for the Indian Office. For a time, all the permanent tribes in northern Montana were on one large reservation stretching from the Blackfoot lands to the eastern border of Montana. Only one agency, Milk River, administered all the tribes east of the Blackfeet.

The agents had a tense situation on their hands because a number of enemy tribes either drew annuities at the Milk River Agency or lived in the area: Yanktonais, Santees, Assiniboins, Grosventres, and River Crows. For a time Agent A. J. Simmons had to draw on all his diplomatic skill to keep each party happy. He distributed presents and provisions to the newcomers at the expense of the annuities of the Grosventres and Assiniboins of his agency. He was able to persuade some of the old chiefs to accept peace, but it was not possible to end the rivalries for long. To solve the problem, in 1871 the Indian Office established Fort Peck Agency, 100 miles downriver on the Missouri, for the use of the Yanktonais and their new friends the Lower Assiniboins.

By the 1870s, a triangular-shaped conflict had developed in northern Montana. The western corner consisted of the Blackfeet, who raided east against the Indians of the two other agencies, Fort Belknap (formerly Milk River) and Fort Peck. These two agencies provided the other two corners of an elongated triangle stretching east and west. All three groups raided each other, but the tribes in the middle — Grosventres, Upper Assiniboins, and the associated River Crows — held the most exposed position.

Montana Superintendent Alfred Sully, the former general, recommended that the Grosventres and Assiniboins have their own agency "for their mutual protection against their more powerful neighbors." General Sheridan was concerned about the River Crows. Technically, they belonged to the Crow Agency far to the south beyond the Yellowstone, but they preferred to stay between the Missouri and the Milk River with their new Grosventre allies. Sheridan thought they needed support because they were "legitimate prey for the Sioux on one side, the Blackfeet and the roaming bands of Yankton [Yanktonai] Sioux on the other until there is little security left for them."[21]

Considering the intricacies of tribal conflict, the three tribes were not in the extreme danger their defenders feared. They persisted in raiding their enemies in all directions. In 1869, Peter Koch of Musselshell, Montana, witnessed one typically inconclusive battle. Koch described how he watched as some River Crows in a camp near the Musselshell River noticed twenty-five Sioux, probably Yanktonais, appear across the river. The Crows quickly crossed the water and charged the enemy, then the Sioux turned and charged the Crows. This fighting lasted all afternoon. First one set of warriors would make a flashy attack, swooping down on the opponents, glorious in their paint and feathers and filling the air with arrows and bullets. When the enemy got sufficiently reorganized, the warriors whirled their mounts and attempted their own attack. The Indians wasted a lot of ammunition, but the only casualty was one unfortunate Sioux horse.

Of course, there were exceptions to this bloodless fighting. Koch wrote of another contest in which the Sioux caught thirty-two Crows trying to run off Sioux horses. The Sioux surrounded the thieves, but the Crows fought off the attackers for several days behind quickly constructed breastworks. Finally, the Sioux made a determined charge and killed all but two men. In a custom not uncommon in tribal war, they allowed the two Crows to go free in admiration for their bravery.[22]

In the 1870s, among all the tribes involved on the upper Missouri battleground, the Yanktonais emerged as the most aggressive and wide-ranging. Koch described them as being "superior in daring and enterprise to any of their brethren." Not only did this occur on the far upper Missouri; various Yanktonai bands stretched across the breadth of the northern plains. In 1871 Colonel David S. Stanley, commanding Fort Sully at the mouth of the Cheyenne River in central South Dakota, reported that the Yanktonais, often accompanied by the Santees, made "constant war on the Blackfeet, the Crows, the Crees, and the Assiniboines, and their war parties are always out."

But the tribe was most worrisome in the Northwest. Four hundred miles northwest of Colonel Stanley at Fort Sully, Milk River Agent Simmons found the Yanktonai Sioux to be the greatest threat to the people of Montana, both red and white. In 1871, Simmons pointed out how, for years, the Yanktonais had been coming into the area to hunt. Recently, he continued, they had been trying to live there permanently and had been followed by the eastern Sioux, or Santees, who had lost their war in Minnesota. All of them, he wrote, were well-armed and, as warriors, were "superior to the neighboring Indians."[23]

American officials believed these Indians were trying to push the other tribes away from the rich Milk River hunting grounds. Major W. H. Lewis, a special inspector for the army in 1871, reported on the situation. He used the attitudes of the white people around Fort Benton, Montana, as one source for his study. It was their opinion that the Grosventres and Assiniboins would not fight the Sioux except in self-defense. His informants told him that even the famed Blackfeet would flee to Canada before they would face the mighty Sioux. All this was overstated, but it does give an example of the difficulties the many indigent Sioux created for the upper Missouri tribes.[24]

In 1875, things became worse. Indian Office inspector E. C. Watkins reported that Sitting Bull and his hostile Hunkpapas moved at will along the Milk River, not only inflicting depredations on whites but also making "war on the Arickarees, Mandans, Grosventres, Assinaboins, Blackfeet, Pagans, Crows, and other friendly tribes on the circumferences." Like the Yanktonais, the Hunkpapas covered a wide area in their warfare, from the Three Tribes villages all the way to the Blackfoot country.[25]

The Sioux wars against the army, which reached a climax in 1876 and 1877, did not much change intertribal conflict on the upper Missouri. All the tribes fought their usual enemies whether they were hostile or friendly to whites. Even so, the Sioux made a last-ditch effort to convince old rivals to join them against the whites, thus prompting the government to give more protection to the friendly tribes.

Regardless of American fears of a mammoth Indian war, there was little chance of that happening. Tribal rivalries were usually too intense to allow a man to switch over to the enemy's side. Why could he not simply continue to raid that enemy as he always had? Even after Custer's defeat, when the hostiles were at the peak of their triumphs, no large movement to join them took place.

The army could then breathe more easily, and Commissioner of Indian Affairs John Q. Smith could boast that the friendly tribes "have braved all threats and resisted all inducements offered by these adventurers, and, in spite of repeated losses by depredations, have steadfastly adhered to their friendship to the Government. . . ." In his analysis, the commissioner gave their loyalty to the government as the Indians' motive; he made no mention of the intense tribal loyalty and the love of fighting. In this way the government often ignored or misunderstood the significance of intertribal warfare as a motivating factor in Indian behavior, a common perception since whites had first entered the northern plains.[26]

In 1876 and 1877 most of the hostile Sioux, Cheyennes, and Arapahos, run down by military units and short of food, surrendered and retired to reservation life. The army disarmed them and took away many of their horses. Except for Sitting Bull, his band, and a scattering of other followers who escaped into Canada, the war years were over for the hostile elements of the Sioux alliance. But not so for the friendly tribes. War still went on, especially on the upper Missouri. Since 1873, however, the United States had gradually put into effect the machinery to terminate intertribal raiding, so the Indians' time for enjoying war was coming to an end.

The army's enforcement of the policy against tribal raiding, spurred by the Sioux massacre of the Pawnee hunting party in 1873 and other events, began to have a real effect in the mid-1870s. Gradually, the government established more control on reservations, allowing Indians to leave only with a pass. The army increased its patrols to reinforce the rules and limited the outlay of firearms. By 1875 and 1876, as officials carried out these polices more assiduously, the stringent measures began to have some impact. In 1875, for instance, Agent H. W. Bingham of Cheyenne River noted that "the habit of organizing and directing war parties, so long in existence among the Indians, is beginning to lose the great interest and excitement formerly felt in such expeditions."[27]

Bingham did not mention it, but another cause for the decline in raiding was the agents' use of Indian leaders to discourage war parties together with the role played by the Indian police, a method used effectively at Fort Peck Agency. The Indian department was beginning to recognize the benefits of using Indians to help institute discipline on the reservations. The old, respected chiefs already had some influence, and tribal police could be effective because they continued some of the traditional duties of the warrior societies. In addition, a man might be able to gain status from being a policeman, status that he previously obtained through warfare.

Events showed, however, that these early signs of decreasing warfare were regarded too optimistically. Tribal rivalries were not to be stopped that easily. Proving one's bravery in warfare was too impor-

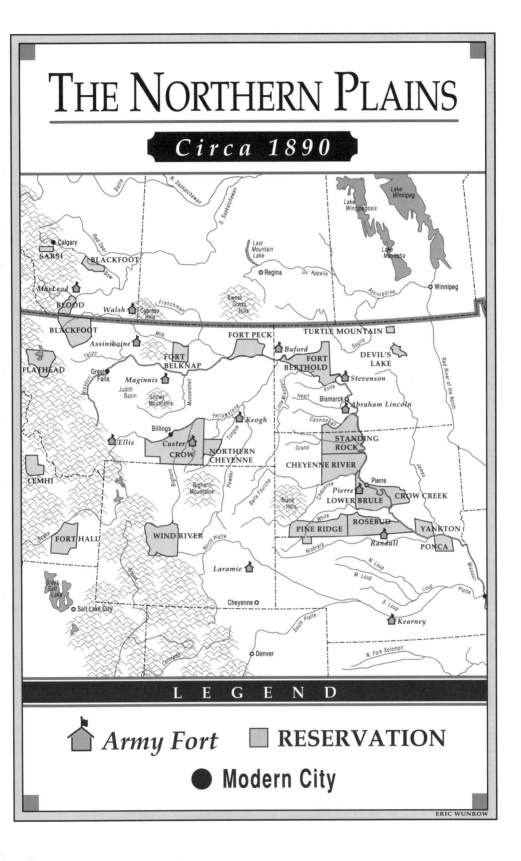

THE NORTHERN PLAINS

Circa 1890

LEGEND

Army Fort   ▢ RESERVATION

● Modern City

ERIC WUNROW

tant a factor in plains Indian society. Throughout the region the white hunters were rapidly exterminating the buffalo. But along the Yellowstone, upper Missouri, and Milk rivers, grazed herds large enough to support a number of tribes. This support for the traditional nomadic life permitted warfare to continue. In a sense, fighting became better because the federal government isolated the hostile Sioux on their reservations, thus giving warriors in the smaller tribes a more even chance to enjoy the pleasures of cutting horses, stealing women, and competing for war honors.

CHAPTER NINE

A Source of Grave Apprehension and Anxiety

THE END OF SIOUX SUZERAINTY, 1877-1881

The Sioux alliance, comprised of Sioux, Northern Cheyennes, and Northern Arapahos, reached the height of its power in the 1870s. Until 1877, it was able to stand with pride against the army in a number of battles, large and small. The Sioux alliance had been even more successful in maintaining its unstoppable movement southwest, west, and northwest. For the first time on the northern plains, a tribal combination seriously threatened the livelihood of the other tribes. The Teton Sioux and their friends forced the Poncas and the Pawnees from their homes in the Southeast; surrounded and harassed the Three Tribes in the Northeast; pushed back the Crows in the Southwest; and drove the Shoshonis into the Wind River Valley. Finally, the Tetons and Yanktonais moved all the way into the northwest theater and challenged the Grosventres, Assiniboins, and Blackfeet.

With the defeat of Colonel George Armstrong Custer's Seventh Cavalry in 1876, the Sioux reached their pinnacle of power, but it was short-lived. The strong army reaction, led by colonels Nelson Miles and Ranald MacKenzie, forced most of the hostiles onto reservations in 1877. The American power was too much to resist, coming as it did when the northern buffalo herds began their dramatic decline. Hide hunters had already eliminated most of the southern and central plains herds; now they worked on the northern plains buffalo. Unable to sustain their nomadic life while fighting the whites, the hostiles of the Sioux alliance reluctantly filed into the agencies, riding tired and foot-sore horses, dragging worn-out tipis on patched and broken down travois, and wearing tattered clothing. The army confiscated the Indians' guns and soldiers kept careful watch to stop the warriors from leaving the reservations.

A few hostile Indians resisted. Sitting Bull, chief of the Hunkpapas and the best known and most powerful of all Sioux leaders, fled to Canada, the "Grandmother's Land" to the Indians. Some Sioux from other tribes joined him in slipping across the international border, where the American army could not follow. In their raids across the 49th parallel, these diehard hostiles maintained their wars against the whites and also helped to keep intertribal rivalries burning hotly along the upper Missouri from 1877 until Sitting Bull's surrender in 1881.

In the other theaters of war, however, the conflicts between tribes slowly ground to a halt. Controlling the hostile Tetons was an important factor in this development because they had been the focal point of recent intertribal raiding. Reservation life, by supporting the Indians and forcing "civilization" upon them, gradually undermined the raiding life. But the army, as an increasingly pervasive force, also kept close watch to stop warriors from leaving the reservations.

Scattered intertribal incidents occurred, but they were few in number. In the southeastern part of the plains, with the departure of the Pawnees and Poncas, all was quiet. In 1879, a group of Poncas under their stubborn chief, Standing Bear, returned to the northern plains, determined to stay in their old homeland. The Sioux forgave their old enemies and even gave them land in the southeast corner of the large Sioux reservation. Because of this friendship between old enemies, a common phenomenon after the end of tribal wars, the Poncas were able to stay in the North.

In the West, at the mountainous border of the plains, warfare sputtered to a halt, but the retiring Sioux and Cheyennes could not resist a few parting shots before they gave up their way of life. In May 1877, shortly before Crazy Horse's band surrendered at Fort Robinson in northwestern Nebraska, ten of his men went off on a raid against the Shoshonis. But after this war party, only the Oglalas who fled north to join Sitting Bull could continue warfare.

Northern Cheyenne Chief Dull Knife, a handsome man with chiseled features and a majestic air, led a band that refused to give up tribal raiding, but his people suffered greatly during the winter of 1876 after an attack by troops under the impulsive, abrasive MacKenzie, who next to Nelson Miles was the army's most successful Indian fighter. On November 25, 1876, MacKenzie's 1,000 soldiers and Pawnee mercenaries appeared out of a misty dawn to make a savage attack on Dull Knife's village near the Powder River. Most of the Cheyennes escaped, but the soldiers and Pawnees burned the 200 lodges and the food supply and captured 700 ponies, leaving the Indians destitute for the winter.

The Hunkpapa Sioux chief Sitting Bull, one of the last irreconcilables. Photograph by David F. Barry. *Courtesy Western History Department, Denver Public Library.*

Despite this catastrophe, the famed Cheyenne warriors continued raiding. In the spring, a war party reputed to be about 400 strong left the camp to attack the Shoshonis. Their agent, James Patten, maintained that the battle was one of the "fiercest ever waged on these plains" and "lasted until after sundown, when the hostiles withdrew." The results, however, were typical — a small number of casualties: five killed — one man, two women, and two children.

In the Shoshoni country, little happened after this last Cheyenne raid and the hostiles' surrender, even though in 1879 a Crow war party drove off some horses and killed a herder. The Crows did not always care whom they raided, even if they were old friends, but the attack probably came because the Northern Arapahos now inhabited the Wind River Reservation. The Indian Office had placed the Arapahos there in spite of their old rivalry with the Shoshonis, a situation that often led to quarrels.[1]

Meanwhile, far to the northeast, the Three Tribes, after decades of fighting off the attacks of numerous foes, finally settled down to a more secure existence. These village people, as well as the Sioux downriver from them, began to concentrate on periodic visits to other tribes, an Indian pastime second only to warfare. Indians traveled long distances to visit friends or even past enemies. The customary exchange of presents, as well as dancing and feasting, could go on for days or even weeks. In 1879, for instance, the Three Tribes exchanged visits and presents with the Crows, Assiniboins, Canadian mixed bloods, Cheyennes, Santees, and other Sioux tribes.[2]

Intertribal visiting and celebrating had long been an important part of the truces that occasionally slowed the pace of war. The Arikara, Mandan, and Hidatsa villages had always been especially important for these meetings because they were trade centers. According to Agent William Courtenay, the Three Tribes still had a great desire "to visit other tribes, especially their old enemies the Sioux. . . ." Certainly, visiting was more common now that the violent side of intertribal relations had come to take second place to more peaceful gatherings. Old enemies still carried out formal adoption ceremonies, and war maintained its important role, if only as a topic of conversation. Warriors, as they had done in the past, told each other the stories of their exploits. Now, however, it became a subject of nostalgia, the activity of an idyllic past that increasingly moved farther out of reach.

Unfortunately, officials at the Indian Office were not well disposed toward this peaceful and harmless mode of intertribal contact. In their attempt to turn Indians into white people, the agents saw little good in this side of Indian culture because it was not related to the American ideals of hard work or Christian beliefs. To nineteenth-century Americans, nothing could be more benighted or less civilized than sitting around telling stories and being engaged in no apparent worthwhile activity.

Agent J. A. Stephan of Standing Rock became worried in 1879 because the Yanktonais, Hunkpapas, and Blackfoot Sioux were becoming too friendly with the Three Tribes. Two hundred and seven Indians from Fort Berthold Agency had visited his agency in August. The disgusted agent reported five days of continuous feasting and merrymaking. The Indians neglected their crops, although it is doubtful if many of them were actually farming. If this were not enough, complained Stephan, he expected his Indians would ask for passes to Fort Berthold to make a return visit that would consume even more time.

Earlier in the year, when this particular round of visiting had begun, Fort Berthold Agent E. H. Alden had requested passes for a separate visit by forty Arikaras to return an earlier social call from the Standing Rock Sioux. Commissioner of Indian Affairs Ezra A. Hayt's answer, reflecting the growing impatience with visiting, was short and to the point: "You are informed that, in the judgment of this office, the Indians would in no way be benefited by such proposed visit and therefore the permission cannot be granted."[3]

As if to break up the long rounds of visiting, a few instances of raiding still occurred. The Lower Brulés, their rivalry with the Poncas finished, sent two war parties against the Three Tribes in the summer of 1879. Apparently, the raid was unsuccessful because nothing more was heard of it until the Lower Brulés returned and denied they had been on the warpath. As late as 1881, some men from the Yankton tribe, peaceful for a long time, took some horses from the Arikaras.[4]

These few raids were rather harmless. In some cases, it seemed like more bloodshed might result from agents' rivalries than from fighting between Indians. One chain of events leading to an agent feud began early in July 1880, when a war party of Brulés left Rosebud Agency on the White River in South Dakota and headed for Fort Berthold Agency. On October 22, they killed an Arikara and ran off twenty horses. The Fort Berthold agent believed the raiders had come from the Cheyenne River Agency. Agent Leonard Love of Cheyenne River indignantly denied this, stating that his Indians had been disarmed and dismounted in 1876 and had no way to secure ammunition. Apparently not understanding the mobility of war parties, he insisted that Fort Berthold, 400 miles away, was too far for a raid. Love then proved that he could account for all the males over sixteen at his agency during the specified period of time because they had been present for the ration issue.

This fairly typical quarrel went on into 1882, when Fort Berthold Agent Jacob Kauffman still insisted the Cheyenne River Indians were responsible. Then officials discovered what had actually happened: A Rosebud warrior named Horn had led the party that took the horses, then on the way home had given ten of the animals to friends at Cheyenne River and those Indians received the blame.

With rapid communication between agencies and forts, together with the army's increased activity, war parties found it more difficult to function. But some agents made the government policy inefficient by being less than objective about the Indians on their reservations. Many agents were determined to establish either "model" agencies or, if they were dishonest, to make themselves illicit cash profits. In each case they needed to show off their work and their Indians in the best possible light to the Indian Office. At times the agents' defenses of their little "empires" were almost laughable.[5]

As always, the agents at Fort Berthold were able to make good progress with their complaints because of the small size of the Three Tribes. But despite their detractors or apologists, these tribes were always ready to take the offensive. They had done so for generations. In September 1880, for instance, a band of Plains Ojibwas killed a herder named Walking Wolf and drove off the herd he was watching sixty miles northwest of Fort Berthold. As soon as word reached the village, near the fort, a war party of fifty Hidatsas and Mandans mounted their horses and followed the trail, heading northwest into Canada. Near Fort Peck Agency the pursuers killed a Yanktonai woman, either by mistake or for revenge. Eventually the war party found the culprits, now joined by some Assiniboins, and a fight ensued near the Moose Mountains of southeastern Saskatchewan. The Mandans and Hidatsas lost five warriors killed and six more wounded, but they killed eight or ten of their opponents.

Like the raid by Horn a month later, this confrontation turned into a fiasco, but it also became international in scope. In October, James Taylor, United States consul at Winnipeg, informed Assistant Secretary of State John Hay of the affair. Taylor saw future difficulties, "so universal is horse-stealing among the Canadian Indians."

Lieutenant Governor David Laird of the Northwest Territories gave the Canadian perspective of the problem. He had heard from a chief among the Plains Ojibwas and Assiniboins of Canada that the Mandans and Hidatsas "switched" their enemies while chasing them, then killed several of them. Presumably, Laird was referring to the practice of counting coup.

Although independent of Great Britain since 1867, Canada was still under Dominion status; so the mother country conducted Canadian foreign policy. By December, the British minister to the United States, Sir Edward Thornton, had also entered the rather amusing fray. He officially brought the matter to the attention of Secretary of State William Evarts. Anxious that Queen Victoria's subjects had sufficient protection, Thornton expressed his hope that the culprits could be caught. In his diplomatic note, he enclosed Governor Laird's concern that the invasion of Canada by the Mandans and Hidatsas meant that "the dangerous impression will be apt to gain ground among our Indians that Her Majesty the Queen is powerless to protect her people from such wholesale slaughter." Fortunately, Anglo-American relations were usually based on more significant matters. However, the Three Tribes were left alone. Their warfare was quickly dying out, even though these few remaining conflicts attracted a degree of attention not usual in northern plains war.[6]

These conflicts involving the Three Tribes were superficial, but on the upper Missouri tribal warfare became localized from 1877 to 1881 and continued to be as violent and intense as ever, if not more so. The conflicts continued to be complicated by the rivalries derived from the migrations of the 1860s and 1870s, but Sitting Bull's presence across the international boundary supplied an important new catalyst. From 1877 to 1881, the tribes of the Northwest — Blackfoot, Sioux, Assiniboin, Grosventre, and Crow — managed to enjoy a few last years of almost totally free raiding. The government, worried and even embarrassed about Sitting Bull's continued hostility, permitted and at times even encouraged the friendly tribes to fight in order to force the irreconcilable Hunkpapa hostiles and their allies to come in and surrender.

The territory for war extended from the Milk River south across the upper Missouri all the way to the Yellowstone. The region had grown into a major meeting ground for hunting parties and hostile bands from the middle of the 1800s on. For this reason Edwin Denig, the fur trader writing in the 1850s, had predicted that it would be the site of the last Indian war, to be fought over the buffalo. It was an expansive land, with dry stretches varying from yellow buffalo grass to gray-green sage and dry brown brush. Small ranges of large hills, such as the Bear Paw Mountains and the Snowy Mountains, interrupted the arid expanse. The wide beds of the Missouri, Yellowstone, Milk, and their tributaries in lonely fashion cut through the vast plains, occasionally broken by the violent pitch and drop of steep buttes, mesas, ravines, and eroded badlands.

Much of this land appeared sterile to the eye, but the buffalo found its stubby dry grass appealing and nourishing. By the late 1870s and early 1880s, the last of the great herds of the plains were living here. They gave the Plains Indians a few more years of independent life and provided the last large profits for the white hunters who used booming long-range rifles.

Between 1877, when most of the hostiles surrendered, and 1881, when Sitting Bull finally went onto the reservation, the region became crowded with various tribes taking advantage of the bison herds. The peoples who had inhabited the area for several decades or longer predominated in terms of land and government support: the Piegans at Blackfoot Agency; the Grosventres and Upper Assiniboins, sometimes joined by the River Crows, at Fort Belknap Agency; and the Lower Assiniboins and Yanktonais at Fort Peck Agency. Other tribes who had often used the hunting grounds in the past now needed them more than ever. From Canada, the Blackfeet and Bloods came down to join the Piegans; the Plains Crees and Plains Ojibwas moved south to hunt; and the Flatheads, Pend d'Oreilles, and Kutenais continued to hunt on the land that had once been theirs.

The Red River mixed bloods from Canada also arrived in greater numbers to challenge the Indians for the last of the buffalo herds. The mixed bloods were hard-working people who engaged in hunting and trade just like their ancestors, the Cree trappers and French voyagers, had done. For years they had travelled to the plains to hunt the buffalo both for meat and for hides to sell, but since the middle 1800s the migrating and diminishing herds had forced them to go farther west. The mixed bloods, often called Métis, moved in well-organized bands, travelling on horses and two-wheeled carts made entirely of wood. They made a colorful and merry cavalcade. Their bright and variegated clothing was a unique mixture of the dress worn by their two sets of forebears. A fun-loving people, their camps rocked with laughter and good times. But the Red River mixed bloods were also well-disciplined, and it was very difficult for plains warriors to defeat them. The men were formidable, well-armed fighters, constantly on the lookout, waiting ready to circle the two-wheeled carts into an effective fortification at the first sign of danger.

Much of the conflict on the upper Missouri continued as it had for more than fifty years. Flatheads, Pend d'Oreilles, and Kutenais came to hunt and capture horses. But now, varying their activities somewhat, they made more truces with the Blackfeet and instead raided the Crows and the Sioux.

The Blackfeet, although having lost some of their former power in the smallpox epidemic of 1869, remained avid raiders. After 1877, almost all of the Blackfeet on the Montana reservation were Piegans. In that year most of the Bloods and Blackfeet had agreed to pledge allegiance to Canada and live on a reservation in that country. Of course, many of them continued to hunt in the United States. Blackfeet on both sides of the "medicine line," as they called the 49th parallel, slipped back and forth to collect rations from both governments. In 1879, the American government counted the people living on the Blackfoot reservation at 7,500, although this probably included many of those living in Canada. Certainly, the count was much too high because it was the same number given to the entire Blackfoot confederation in the 1850s. Nevertheless, the Piegans were more numerous than any other tribe on the upper Missouri except the Yanktonais.

The Piegans continued their old competitions with the Crows, Crees, and Assiniboins. In 1881, General John "Black Jack" Davidson, commander of the District of the Yellowstone, telegraphed headquarters from Fort Custer that the Piegans were "stealing horses from the Crow every night" and the Crows were asking for protection. A tough and disciplined veteran from the pre-Civil War frontier, Davidson was an effective commander despite occasional bouts of "strange behavior" attributed to the effects of an earlier sunstroke. His report was borne out by the Crow agent, who stated that fourteen Piegan lodges were camped near the Crow Agency. The Piegans, however, not only stole horses, but also during truces sold whiskey to the Crows and generally disrupted what the agents called the "civilizing" process at the agency.[7]

The Blackfeet also fought the Plains Crees (whom they called Liars), whether in southern Alberta and Saskatchewan where the Crees lived or on the upper Missouri where they often hunted. In the winter of 1879-1880, the Crees arrived on the Musselshell River accompanied by their mixed-blood relatives from the Red River. About the same time, a group of Blackfeet and Bloods also arrived from Canada. Before a confrontation could take place, Joe Kipp, a trader in the area, stepped in and arranged a peace agreement. From this truce a new friendship developed between the Crees and the Blackfeet and improved through the years, but the Bloods were less willing and the chiefs had a hard time holding back their young men. The Piegans would have none of this peace, and their conflict with the Crees endured.[8]

The Crees' old Assiniboin allies, while still fighting the Blackfoot confederation, developed friendships with other tribes. The Lower Assiniboins lived with the Yanktonais at Fort Peck Agency and the Upper Assiniboins shared Fort Belknap Agency with the Grosventres.

During the late 1870s, one Upper Assiniboin warrior named White Dog gained considerable notoriety for his assaults on Piegan horse herds. James Willard Schultz, a so-called squaw man among the Piegans, told the story of the man's feats. For years, wrote Schultz in his memoirs, White Dog stalked Piegan camps, taking horses and stealing women, until his name became a subject of dread in Piegan tipis. Finally, in 1879, the Piegans formed a special war party to find and wreak revenge on the invincible raider.

Six men under the leadership of Many Tail Feathers set out east for Milk River, the country of the Fort Belknap Assiniboins. This expedition was typical of Blackfoot horse raids — a few men traveled on foot, carrying the bare essentials: extra moccasins, lariats for capturing horses, weapons, and, of course, the magic clothes and paraphernalia that made up their medicine. The men followed the tactics of cautious war parties, making no sign of having passed through the countryside. They traveled by night and hid and rested during the day.

As the leader, Many Tail Feathers took care of the all-important spiritual side of war. At each hidden camp he "made medicine" by saying prayers and seeking visions. A war party's success depended upon the power of the leader's medicine together with his ability to seek extra help from the forces of nature. Over the course of this venture, Many Tail Feathers not only had one positive vision but also one that he considered bad. This was not a good omen, but the men decided to persevere, such was the importance of their mission.

The war party found White Dog's camp and during the night quietly stole some horses, the one form of booty that Indians almost never overlooked, even on revenge expeditions. Then, near dawn, the men were lucky enough to spot White Dog on his way out of the camp. They ambushed and killed him, but in the scuffle he killed one Piegan and wounded another named Bear Head. The Piegans fled, and the incensed Assiniboins followed. Eventually, the Piegans were overtaken and had to stop to make a stand. Normally, such a situation would have meant certain death, but the defenders possessed new repeating rifles. Not needing to load their weapons as often as required for the old muskets, the Piegans poured a withering fire into the ranks of their pursuers until it was dark enough to escape. Unfortunately, in this skirmish they left another of their number dead.

Days later, when the Piegans reached home, their people welcomed them as heroes. It was a Pyrrhic victory, however, despite the killing of White Dog. Two of the six men were dead, and their widows mourned them in the traditional way. Using sharp knives, they slashed their arms and legs, cut off their hair, and tore their clothes. Although Many Tail Feathers was pleased about the killing of White Dog, he said that the loss of the men came from his one bad vision, which meant the Above Ones were not protecting his war party.[9]

While the once mighty Blackfeet continued the rivalries of almost a century, their new contest with the Yanktonais became just as important. Drawing from his life of hunting and raiding with the Piegans, Schultz believed that the Yanktonais and other Sioux became the Piegans' major enemies at the end of the 1870s and the beginning of the 1880s. At the same time, however, some elders in these two tribes, as with other northern plains bands, shifted their attitudes toward peace. In the spring of 1881, for example, the Blackfeet captured thirty-six Yanktonai ponies. Then, when an expedition prepared a pursuit, the Yanktonai leaders restrained it and reported the incident to the commanding officer of Fort Keogh, at the mouth of the Tongue River near Crow territory.

While a few Yanktonais tried to keep peace, many were still busy making war. The portion of the tribe at Fort Peck, together with their Assiniboin allies, numbered over 7,000 people, thus outmanning the other upper Missouri tribes. Because the Yanktonais had remained at peace with the whites since they had aided the Santees against the Sully and Sibley expeditions of 1864 and 1865, the government did not exert the control over them that it did over the hostile Sioux.

With these advantages, the Yanktonai tribe, a relative newcomer to the area, became a power in the northwest plains and made war on all the surrounding tribes. The Crows became a major adversary. In the late 1870s, after years of separation, the River Crows began to return more often to their old homeland and reside near the Mountain Crow division. The Yanktonais still greatly outnumbered the Crows, but the Crows kept up their part of the new rivalry.

The Yanktonais also ran into their old enemies from the East, the Red River mixed bloods. The antagonists often met in the Judith Basin of central Montana, a favorite hunting ground for both. One clash occurred in November 1880, when the Yanktonais managed to get away with forty horses from the watchful Métis.

By 1881, the number of Yanktonai war parties on the loose astounded observers. In May, the commander of the Poplar River Army Camp near Fort Peck Agency reported that "war parties of Yanktonais numbering in all from 150 to 200, have been here last night and this morning, and are still traveling. Some have gone north, others towards the Yellowstone, ostensibly to fight the Crees and Crows."[10]

In addition to these expeditions, the Yanktonais also carried on a major conflict with the Grosventres of the Prairie at Fort Belknap Agency. It was perhaps the most intense contest of the time, or at least it was one of the rivalries the agents most publicized. From 1877 to 1879, war parties seemed to be almost constantly in the field. In addition to the usual motives, the Indians battled over the rich buffalo herds. The tribes native to the area had long contended that the Yanktonais, though recent arrivals, were trying to control the dwindling herds. Another problem for the Fort Belknap Indians, besides the competition for the buffalo, was that the Indian Office discontinued the agency between 1876 and 1878 due to a shortage of congressional funds. The Grosventres and Assiniboins were supposed to pick up their annuities at Fort Peck, but they refused to do so because of the Yanktonai presence.

After the Fort Belknap Agency was reestablished in 1878, the new agent, W. L. Lincoln, was quick to complain of Yanktonai attacks. He noted that the tribe seemed interested only in fighting the Grosventres because the Upper Assiniboins were relatives of the Yanktonais' own allies. But by this time, the Grosventres and Upper Assiniboins were almost like one people, and both considered the Yanktonais bitter enemies.

Fort Peck Agent William Bird retaliated against Lincoln's accusations, and soon a war of words was on between the two agents, neither of whom was particularly well informed about the Indians' activities. Bird claimed that the hostile Hunkpapas did much of the raiding. Besides that, he said, enemies had stolen 189 Yanktonai and Lower Assiniboin horses. He pointed to the infamous White Dog as the main culprit. Lincoln shrilly retorted that he had caused White Dog to return all stolen stock and that as far as the Grosventres were concerned, they had not been at war for four years! Any stealing, he added, was the Crows' work.

Lincoln's vociferous charges must have had some impact, and perhaps there were more Yanktonai war parties. At any rate, in both 1878 and 1879, Commissioner Hayt entered the intradepartmental conflict to reprimand Bird and demand that the agent stop the raids and return any stolen horses.

This two-year battle of memos between morally incensed agents gave the policy of control the appearance of a ludicrous farce. It also retarded attempts to end Indian warfare. Yet, in addition to the unrealistic views of the agents, it was in fact difficult to determine just who was raiding whom and to what extent. Few agents, even if they were objective, could gain that thorough a knowledge. By 1880, Agent Bird had lost his job partly because he was ineffective in controlling Yanktonai warfare. But raiding did not seem to decrease. Bird's replacement, N. S. Porter, like many previous agents, ran up against the cultural importance of horse stealing. Porter had success retrieving horses stolen from whites, but, he wrote, those "horses stolen from other Indians they [Yanktonais] do not like to give up, as they claim it is one of their customs to steal from one another, and the more horses an Indian steals the greater Indian he is considered among his tribe."[11]

Across the Canadian border, the hostile Sioux provided support for the Yanktonai power. From 1877 to 1881, Sitting Bull was the magnet that attracted dissatisfied Indians. Using the international border as an effective barrier to cross and recross in raiding both whites and Indians, he was the catalyst for an almost constant state of excitement and anxiety among the tribes of the region.

From the beginning, the Canadian government was apprehensive about Sitting Bull's presence. According to American Commissioner Hayt, the Hunkpapas were "a source of grave apprehension and anxiety on the part of both the Indian and white population of that part of Canada. . . ." The Canadians, showing some concern for the Indians within their borders, insisted that the Sioux stay at peace with them. Lieutenant Colonel James MacLeod, commissioner of the Northwest Mounted Police, believed that the Indians living in Canada, although enemies of the Sioux in the past, now wished to be at peace with them. For their part, the hostiles from America realized the need to be peaceful in order to remain and use the Grandmother's Land as a refuge where the American army could not enter.[12]

In the winter of 1877-1878, the hostiles camped and hunted at Cypress Hills in southeastern Alberta. Canadian tribes were close by — Blackfeet, Bloods, and some Assiniboins and Crees. All were looking for the already dwindling buffalo herds. A few skirmishes took place, the warlike Blood warriors being especially anxious to fight the Sioux. But Sitting Bull and Crowfoot, the chief of the Moccasin band of the Blackfoot tribe, met and established a peace. Both of them saw the need to avoid an outbreak of fighting in a time of growing food shortages.

During his years in Canada, the stocky Sitting Bull, thick braids enclosing his moon-shaped face, met the old chief of the Blackfeet on several occasions. Crowfoot had been a great warrior during his youth in the 1840s but had begun to realize the need to live at peace with the whites and others in order to ensure Blackfoot survival. In the councils with Sitting Bull, he appeared very different from the powerful Sioux leader seated cross-legged on the ground next to him. A large hooked nose protruded from Crowfoot's weathered and seamed face, a face that had seen many winters and that was lined with worry for his people. His hair was not braided, but fell loose to his shoulders, with his medicine, an owl's head, twisted into the hair at the top of his head. Through the years the two leaders, in preserving the peace, developed a close acquaintance and mutual respect. Before he left Canada, Sitting Bull honored the Blackfoot chief by naming his own eight-year-old son Crowfoot.[13]

The peace benefitted not only the security-minded Crowfoot but also the warlike Sitting Bull. By having peace and a secure home in Canada, the Hunkpapas were free to fight the whites and other tribes south of the border. Sitting Bull's camp was therefore a tempting destination for northern plains warriors. With Sitting Bull they were able to have their last round of glory. Some men from defeated hostile tribes, their hopes renewed, came north to join Sitting Bull. Straggling Nez Percé refugees, escaping their defeat at the Bear Paw Mountains in 1877, entered the camp. A few warriors from friendly tribes also attached themselves to Sitting Bull's charismatic leadership: Blackfeet, Grosventres, Bannocks, Flatheads, even some Colorado Utes and Great Basin Paiutes.

Though only a small number left any one tribe to go to Canada, Sitting Bull's camp swelled to 4,000 people. At first, life was good, with plenty of raiding and enough game for food. But by 1879 and 1880, the buffalo had become very scarce in Canada, leaving the large camp without sufficient food. The massive settlement dwindled as one group after another went back to the reservations, until, in 1881, Sitting Bull himself returned to the United States with fewer than 200 followers.

In the meantime, the Hunkpapas and their friends fought all the tribes, from the Piegans, Grosventres, and Assiniboins north of the Missouri all the way south to the Crows on the upper Yellowstone. In between times, they hunted along the Milk River or in the Judith Basin or raided white settlements in the Gallatin Valley and along the Musselshell River.

In the fall of 1877, the Hunkpapas were hunting between the Marias River and the Sweet Grass Hills near the international boundary and, according to the commander of Fort Benton, Major Guido Ilges, scaring the Piegans off their hunting grounds. In 1879, the hostiles camped

200 miles to the east at the base of the Little Rocky Mountains south of Fort Belknap Agency and raided in all directions. The next year they were again in the Milk River country. Agent Lincoln of Fort Belknap once more let fly with exaggerated fears for his Grosventres and Assiniboins, now accusing the Hunkpapas instead of the Yanktonais. The Grosventres and Assiniboins, he reported, "have a mortal fear of the Sioux so that although buffalo are the one thing they most desire . . . they are afraid to go to them for fear of coming in contact with the Sioux."[14]

Depredations made by hostiles based in Canada were intolerable to the United States. After the war against the Sioux appeared to have been won in 1877, this new belligerence was an insult that could not go unanswered. The government thus took various kinds of action, and the army and Indian Office calmed their traditional rivalry enough to present a united front to the new threat.

In 1878, the army provided rations for the Grosventres, Assiniboins, and mixed bloods because it feared they might join the hostiles. In 1879, the Eighteenth Infantry Regiment under Colonel Thomas Ruger built Fort Assiniboine close to the Milk River (near Havre, Montana) in order to protect the area against Sitting Bull. In the same year, General Miles, commander of the District of the Yellowstone, led an expedition north of the Missouri to confront the Sioux coming south to hunt buffalo. He reassured the Grosventres and Assiniboins of army protection and those tribes moved down toward the Missouri to be close to the troops. Twenty Assiniboins then joined the army as scouts.

Federal officials also made other attempts to help the friendly Indians against the hostiles. Troops chased horse raiders on occasion. The Indian Office even countenanced drastic departures from its traditional humanitarian approach. Some agents, sounding less like representatives of the Interior Department and more like army officers, actually encouraged their wards to take retaliatory action against hostile raids. In 1880, for example, after the Crow agent gave permission to a war party to pursue Sioux horse thieves, the Crows caught the Sioux and killed five of them. The United States and Canada also began a cooperative effort to return stolen horses across the border.

Some army action, however, went beyond the desires of the high command. Army policy was reverting a bit to the cautious approach more common before the crises of the 1870s. William Tecumseh Sherman, now commanding the entire army, outlined the accepted policy to Miles when he reminded him that his job was to defend the Missouri River traffic and beyond that simply to "protect, defensively, our own

peaceable Indians, not to adopt their quarrels and to fight their battles."[15]

Despite the complaints of friendly tribes and the agents' calls for
help, the Indians of the upper Missouri needed little aid against their
enemies. Of course, their position in opposition to the hostile Sioux
made it possible for them to obtain more things from the government,
especially guns, but actually, the days of Sioux suzerainty were past
anyway. The Sioux in the area outnumbered the other tribes, but not
to the extent they had in the 1860s and 1870s. All tribes were on a
more equal status. Fewer Sioux were raiding and the shortage of
buffalo meant that all the tribes had to spend more time hunting other
game. This was especially true for the hostile Sioux, who did not
receive agency rations like their enemies. Because of the new "equality," the Piegans, Crows, Grosventres, and Assiniboins were more
easily able to carry on offensive action against the Sioux in Canada.
Canadian officials were concerned about these raiding parties crossing
the border because the United States Army often showed little interest
in controlling them.

For its part, the army saw the Piegans, Crows, Grosventres, and
Assiniboins as an adjunct to protecting American settlements. And
the Indian Office, with its new approach to tribal war, did its part to
help in the effort against the hostiles. Piegan Agent John Young, for
example, volunteered his tribe as a convenient barrier against the
Sioux. The Piegans were the equal of the Sioux in "courage and intel-
ligence" and "now become a sort of guard against any sudden irrup-
tion." Young even suggested a more definite arrangement in which
the Piegans would "by scouts make widely known the movement [of
the Sioux], so that the military and settlers outside the reservation
could be prepared."[16]

The Grosventres and Assiniboins, though together numbering only
about 2,000 people, were not timorous about raiding the Sioux. In
1879, a 200-man war party managed to run off fifty-nine horses from
Sitting Bull's camp. Agent Lincoln, like Agent Young, saw his tribes
in a possible role as a military adjunct to the government. Accordingly,
he abandoned his former position that they were in peril from the
Yanktonais and Hunkpapas and sang their praises as protectors. He
now advocated them as "a sort of Bulwark and our only protection
(in the absence of the military) against the hostile Sioux north of the
Border."[17]

The Crows seemed to be responsible for a very large portion of the
raiding against the hostiles in Canada. Many years later, Black Elk,
the famous holy man of the Oglalas, reminisced about those days,

when he was a fifteen-year-old boy and his band left the reservation after the death of Crazy Horse and traveled north to join Sitting Bull. He mentioned two incidents in Canada in which large Crow war parties attacked his people. Both times, said Black Elk, he had a premonition that something was going to happen. This, he believed, was the beginning of his spiritual power.

The first incident occurred while he watched, as two Sioux, chasing buffalo behind a distant hill, were trapped and killed by fifty Crow warriors. Later that summer, a large war party of Crows attacked Black Elk's band while it was in transit on a hunting trip. Two old people and their daughter got their travois stuck in a creek as the mounted Crow war party pounded down on them. A warrior named Brave Wolf "jumped off his horse, which was a very fast bison-runner, and made the beautiful girl get on. Then, he stood there by the two old people and fought until the Crows killed all three of them. The girl got away on the fast horse." Still another Oglala named Hard to Hit, a cousin of Black Elk, "charged back alone at a Crow who was shooting at a Lakota in a bush, and he was killed."[18]

The River Crows were especially tenacious in their raids against the hostiles of Canada. One warrior, Two Leggings, left a memoir of those years in interviews he gave to William Wildshut, a field researcher for the Museum of the American Indian.

Two Leggings had a large hawk nose and prominent cheekbones that made his face look like it was carved in granite. He was not the usual subject for ethnological studies, most of which focused on famous chiefs. He was a more representative warrior, however, because he had had to work hard to attain his medicine and successes in war, none of which came easily. In the 1860s and 1870s, Two Leggings conscientiously followed a path designed to make himself a great warrior. His story was one of a very ambitious man trying to gain the good medicine that the Crows felt was the major prerequisite for success on the warpath. Two Leggings used the self-torture of the sun dance. He made numerous fasts to gain visions, and during one of these fasts a friend cut horse-track shaped pieces of skin out of his arm in order to give him luck in capturing horses. Despite his efforts, Two Leggings was frustrated over and over again when his numerous visions did not bring good results in war.

Finally, he was able to obtain a powerful medicine from another warrior. This man was Looks at a Bull's Penis, whom Two Leggings called his "medicine father." The man's name came from an incident when, as a child, he had pointed at a buffalo penis that his mother had cut off in butchering the animal. An observant old man then gave boy his name, either from the ribald Crow sense of humor or because he saw some religious significance in the incident. (Wildshut, writing with predictable Victorian sensitivity, discreetly changed the name to Sees the Living Bull.)

As he became more successful at war, Two Leggings joined in the strong competition between Crow warriors. The rivalry for war honors was intense and sometimes led to hard feelings that could hold over for years. On one occasion, Two Leggings killed a Sioux and was reaching for the dead man's weapon. Abruptly, another Crow from Two Leggings' own warrior society, the Lumpwoods, pushed him aside and got the gun for himself, thus robbing Two Leggings of the honor of taking an enemy's weapon. Usually society members worked together, however, and against rival societies, which they often taunted over their lack of war exploits. One particular incident of harsh ridicule from members of the rival Fox society made Two Leggings so angry that he took out a war party just to prove himself to his rivals. He returned successful, brandishing a Sioux scalp. This gave him the advantageous position needed to ridicule the Foxes in turn. Then he even went farther and stole the wife of a Fox warrior, a peculiar form of rivalry used between these two societies.

By the late 1870s, Two Leggings was fighting as often as possible against both the Piegans and Sioux. One challenging expedition came in the months following Custer's defeat. Two Leggings' friend Medicine Crow, his usual companion on war forays, joined the party. The son of Looks at a Bull's Penis, Medicine Crow was a starkly handsome man with aquiline features surmounted by the brushed up forelock, a common hairstyle among Crow men. After preparations including prayer, sweat baths, and advice from Looks at a Bull's Penis, the eleven young men set off, travelling north through a winter blizzard.

When they reached the Missouri River, they sighted a Sioux village on the opposite side. Both banks were frozen, and large ice blocks bobbed dangerously along the swift current in the middle of the river. The war party had a harrowing experience guiding its horses and small rafts carrying equipment and clothes through the icy waters. Numb with cold, the warriors finally struggled up the frozen north bank. After briefly attempting to warm themselves, they quietly approached the enemy camp. Horses were abundant and during the night the Crows set about quietly slipping them out of the camp, trying to get the good ones that were tied in front of the owners' lodges. Two Leggings was conservative enough to stop before there was much chance of being discovered. He and his companions quietly

The Crow warrior Medicine Crow, a companion of Two Leggings on innum-
erable raids against the Piegans and Sioux in the last years of intertribal
fighting. *Courtesy Smithsonian Institution National Anthropological Archives,
Bureau of American Ethnology Collection.*

made off with 100 horses, galloped the herd continuously for several days to escape pursuit, and safely returned home. The village belonged to Sitting Bull, although the Crows only learned this later.[19]

Two Leggings and other Crows also raided Indians and mixed bloods in Canada. Canadian authorities became increasingly upset about this. According to Major J.M. Walsh of the Mounted Police, the Crows stole twice as many horses from Canadian territory as Sitting Bull's warriors did on the American side. Colonel Miles tried to placate the Canadians by suggesting that the friendly Indians be kept from crossing the international line and that the River Crows be persuaded to spend more time at the Crow Agency farther south. But the army was not going to try this type of control even if it was possible. The army's main concern was still Sitting Bull, not intertribal rivalries.[20]

The truth of the matter was that the army by no means minded the Crow help. In fact, the soldiers welcomed it. In May 1880, thirty Crows led by Bear Wolf attacked a party of hostile Sioux and Nez Percés, killing two of each tribe. Colonel Davidson, commanding Fort Custer, requested a fitting complement from General Terry, commander of the Department of Dakota, since the Crows were working so hard to guard the "line" of the Yellowstone. It seemed as if Davidson considered the Crows a special troop of cavalry. Terry sent a note, expressing his pleasure at the Crows' conduct and assuring them they could continue to expect the army's support and protection. The Crows were probably secretly amused at the idea that they needed any protection, but they could take comfort in the fact that their activity had helped them to stay on the good side of the whites. And, after all, the United States government was the source of many of the good things in life.[21]

The army felt that this kind of motivation for the friendly tribes, if it did not go too far in encouraging intertribal conflict, was beneficial. The government was afraid there might be some kind of a mass exodus to join the hostiles. Throughout the far western frontier, Americans had always had this fear — that a grand alliance of tribes would bring down thousands of warriors upon unprotected frontier settlements. Few people, even in the military, recognized what a minute chance there was of this ever happening. Most intertribal rivalries were too strong to permit an alliance of this type, notwithstanding the fact that the Indian style of warfare would have necessitated many more thousands of warriors than were available to defeat the whites. Besides, most warriors preferred fighting other Indians. Considering their individualistic tactics, it made for a more challenging battle.

Therefore, despite persistent rumors, few Indians joined the hostiles permanently. Sitting Bull, who made many efforts to establish an alliance against the whites, was doomed to failure because of strong tribal ties holding long traditions of intertribal rivalries on the northern plains. These facts, together with rapidly decreasing Canadian buffalo herds, ruined Sitting Bull's plans. The Hunkpapa chief never gave up trying to induce recruits into his camp. But whether he talked to Crows in America, Blackfeet and half breeds in Canada, or threatened the Pend d'Oreilles to get them to join him, all the leaders refused him.

Most warriors who got involved at all in the red-white conflict preferred to work for the army. It was much more profitable than joining the hostiles in terms of guns, supplies, and even fighting opportunities. The army paid the scouts and even provided their wives with pensions if they died in battle.

General George Crook had effectively used these Indian allies in his campaigns against the Apaches of present-day Arizona. On the northern plains Colonel Nelson Miles was most innovative in the use of Indian auxiliaries, following the initial success of the North brothers with their Pawnee battalion and Crook's scouts in the 1876 campaign against the Sioux. During 1877, Miles was responsible for forcing most of the remaining hostiles onto the reservations or, at least, into Canada. He first engaged, as scouts, some of the Sioux and Cheyennes who had surrendered to him at Fort Keogh. They joined the Crow scouts already signed up, even though they were old enemies.

Miles' scouts were responsible for much of his success. Not only did he use them to find and attack the hostile camps, which was the one effective way to defeat the nomadic Indians, but he also sent them into the hostile camps as spies. Many of the former hostiles, accepting the victory of the white man, felt little culpability in using their military skills against former relatives, friends, and allies now joined with Sitting Bull. What was helpful to the army in being able to hire these scouts was the fact that among some Indian nations, especially the Sioux, serious political rivalries existed between bands and families. Some individuals were willing to avenge these old feuds through helping the Americans.

With only the Sitting Bull hostiles left, Miles also had many Indians living on the upper Missouri who were anxious to hire out as scouts. At one time or another he used Assiniboins, Grosventres, Bannocks, Cheyennes, Sioux, and Crows. In 1879, when the hungry Hunkpapas moved south of the Milk River in search of food and Miles led an expedition against them, Indians from a variety of tribes helped him. One hundred and forty-three of the Cheyenne and Crow scouts found the Hunkpapas, attacked them, then weathered a fierce counterattack

Cheyenne scouts who served under General Nelson Miles. (Seated, left to right) Jacob Tall Bull, Thaddeus Redwater, and Big Head Man. (Standing, left to right) Willis T. Rowland, Lone Elk, and Samuel Little-Son. Photo by de Lancey Gill. *Courtesy Smithsonian Institution National Anthropological Archives, Bureau of American Ethnology Collection.*

until the troops came up and chased off the hostiles with two rapid-firing Hotchkiss guns.[22]

In their willingness to help the army stop Sitting Bull, the Indian auxiliaries were unknowingly destroying their own ability to wage the free-wheeling raids of plains warriors. During Sitting Bull's exile, tribal war was localized in the Northwest and even there was crowded by the growing white population. Once Sitting Bull surrendered, there was no justification for the government, whether in the guise of officer or agent, to allow tribal raiding to continue. The Hunkpapas' ominous presence in Canada and on the upper Missouri had been the only rationale that led the government to allow the last few years of unfet-tered warfare.

It was grand while it lasted, this last fling, or, as Edwin Denig had prophesied thirty years earlier, the final war over the buffalo. Within two years after the surrender of Sitting Bull, all of the good-sized buffalo herds had been annihilated by Indians and white hide hunters. After that, the Indians in the Northwest had to live on the annuities distributed at the agencies. Warfare, the culture's basic social ingre-dient, continued, but it could not last too long, because the economic base of the people's freedom was gone. With the disappearance of those magnificent herds of thousands of shaggy buffalo, the warrior culture of the plains, equally impressive in its unique way, would inevitably be forced to pass away.

CHAPTER TEN

Those Days of Which I Now Only Dream

THE END OF INTERTRIBAL WARFARE, 1881-1889

It was October of 1883. The flat, autumn-yellowed plains stretched out in every direction to meet the rocky buttes that surrounded the upper waters of the Grand and Moreau rivers. Here, where the boundary of North and South Dakota reached out to touch Montana, Sitting Bull and his people found a herd of 1,000 buffalo that white hunters had driven east of the regular migration routes.

The hunt followed the predictable pattern ingrained in generations of plains people. Well-disciplined by the warrior societies, the hunters moved in quietly near the herd, spread out, then at a the given signal charged all at once. The ponies swept across the grassy sod and swiftly closed in on one target, and then another and another. As an animal was brought closely alongside, each hunter sent an arrow or bullet crashing into its thick hide toward the vulnerable heart and lungs. Women, children, and old people followed in the wake of the hunters. The women, helped by the old people, deftly butchered the animals and packed the meat on horses. The children enthusiastically ate the delicacies of fresh brains from cracked skulls, soft and full intestines, and warm blood.

The hunt was a great success. In two days, the Indians annihilated the herd, providing themselves with meat and hides for many months.

Thus ended the Indians' last major buffalo hunt on the plains. No large herds existed after 1883. That same year white hunters wiped out another herd that had wandered into North Dakota and shipped the skins east from the railhead south of Fort Berthold. Inhabitants of Montana sighted a very large buffalo herd in 1883 crossing the Yellowstone River, headed north. Nobody knew what happened to that herd, but 1883 was the last year that the railroads shipped large numbers of hides out of the northern plains for sale in the East. Sitting Bull's band had been fortunate; many Indians on the reservations of the Northwest were going hungry due to declining buffalo herds and short rations from the United States government.[1]

Incredible but true — a resource once so vast that observers had reported how herds blackened the terrain in all directions to the surrounding horizons — this cornerstone of Plains Indian society was eliminated in less than a quarter century by the concerted effort of hunters dealing in hides. With the buffalo gone, tribal life could not continue as it had in the past.

The last of the old ways to continue, however, were the intertribal struggles, a custom less affected by the demise of the buffalo and equalling the buffalo in its significance to plains culture. Survival and status, the buffalo and warfare were the twin pillars of Plains Indian society. Raiding persisted and sometimes even flourished during most of the 1880s in the face of growing resistance. Yet, more than any other factor, it was the last gasp of a dying culture.

Tribal warfare's decline had begun two years before the end of the buffalo, when Sitting Bull finally surrendered. On July 19, 1881, he led his 186 remaining followers into Fort Buford at the junction of the Missouri and Yellowstone rivers. Dressed in a ragged calico shirt and patched leggings, the once-indefatigable chief had found survival in Canada untenable. His surrender was the culmination of a proud but hopeless struggle against the increasing white domination on the northern plains. In terms of intertribal conflict, Sitting Bull's presence across the Canadian border had made raiding on the upper Missouri acceptable to the government. Now all that began to change.

With the last hostile Sioux contained on reservations, the federal government had no more need for friendly warriors to fight hostile Indians. Therefore, both the Indian Office and the army reverted to a strong program to stop tribal raids. The friendly tribes, however, not as closely watched on their reservations as the hostiles, had other attitudes about raiding. The plains warriors, following years of ambiguous and contradictory government policies on tribal war, were unlikely to stop raiding because white officials suddenly reversed their thinking.

Given this situation, many warriors continued intertribal conflict as before. The field of battle, still localized as during the years of Sitting Bull's exile, centered on the territory surrounding the Milk, upper Missouri, and Yellowstone rivers. The Crows and the Piegans were the most irreconcilable tribes, but the Bloods and, surprisingly, the Plains Crees from Canada were not far behind them. The Assiniboins, Grosventres, Yanktonais, and the Red River mixed bloods contributed in a slightly lesser degree to the conflict, which now consisted primarily of capturing horses.

The Upper Assiniboins and Grosventres of Fort Belknap, living in the center of the arena, suffered from numerous raids. In 1882, the Crees and mixed bloods, the Piegans, and occasionally the Bloods and Blackfeet from Canada all made war on them. In addition, the Plains Crees stole Piegan horses and the Yanktonais and Crows exchanged attacks.

Evidence suggests that the Piegan-Crow rivalry was particularly violent. The two tribes had apparently signed a truce in the winter of 1881, but shortly thereafter the Crows had treacherously murdered a Piegan couple who were visiting them. The victims' relatives were not going to be deterred from revenge, and war broke out again, now with the Flatheads often travelling with the Piegans. Crow Agent Henry J. Armstrong complained mightily of Piegan raids and the resulting loss of horses and the disruption of the "civilizing" process.[2]

The Piegans seemed to be most responsible for continuing the rivalry. In November 1882, Commissioner of Indian Affairs Hiram Price warned Blackfoot Agent John Young that various reports on the subject "appear to locate the principle blame on the Indians of your Agency." Therefore, Price ordered his agent to "promptly and heartily cooperate with the Military in this behalf and give to them such timely notice of contemplated raids, that may come to your knowledge, by rumor or otherwise as will enable the Military to be properly prepared to meet the emergency and punish the perpetrators."

In his directive, Price also expressed what became the government's greatest concern about tribal war: that it would "possibly embroil the whites of the adjacent regions in trouble" with the Indians. In fact, this was already happening. Major Lewis Merrill, commanding the escort for the Northern Pacific Railroad, which was laying rails across the southern portion of Montana, noted some examples. He said the raids were a great threat, because "neither Crows nor Piegans distinguish very carefully among the horses they steal and white men frequently suffer as well as other Indians."

The United States government, seeing tribal warfare begin to reach a crisis, put great energy into a plan to eliminate it. Officials who had previously condoned and even encouraged raiding now suddenly were aghast at the continuation of intertribal conflict and wanted it ended immediately. But it was not going to be easy to end such an ingrained habit; Crow Agent Armstrong said as much when he noted the many Piegan raids on the Crows. He noted that Agent Young was doing the best he could to stop the Piegans, but much more was needed. Armstrong suggested two methods. One was to force the Piegans off the warpath by threatening to stop their rations, which, he qualified, would be a dangerous thing to try with the Blackfeet. The second solution he suggested was to greatly increase army patrols.[3]

In 1883, the Crow-Piegan contest and other rivalries, far from declining, seemed to increase in volume. Hastily now, the various government officials tried to coordinate a unified effort after years of vacillation and diverse approaches to the problem. In April, the commanding officer of Fort Ellis, Major Gordon, asked his superior, General Terry, if he should send troops that were requested by the Crow agent. Terry replied, "It is very important to put a stop to the thieving of the Piegans and other Indians from the Crows. Send troops as requested. Act promptly and effectively, go yourself if you think it best." In June, General Sherman took a hand, with his usual direct, no-nonsense approach. He ordered that all stock stolen from the Crows be confiscated from the offending Indians and when problems occurred, "if necessary, fire on them [the Indians]."

The army found its new job of controlling the small horse raiding parties difficult to carry out and the Indians' style of raiding incomprehensible. Lieutenant F. D. Holton, who helped the Crows locate stolen horses, found the warriors very uncooperative. They constantly exaggerated the number of animals taken and refused to work closely with the troops. Holton apparently had no idea how Indian warriors operated in war or he would have understood why they preferred to use their own methods of revenge.

Colonel Thomas Hatch, commander of Fort Custer, openly reported the difficulty of protecting the Crows from raiders. He pointed out that it was impossible for a modest number of troops to patrol the whole Yellowstone River, the Crow Reservation's northern boundary. The Crows' enemies came quietly in small parties of two to four men. They crept into Crow camps, stole the best horses, and were 100 miles away before the owners discovered the loss. Why, Hatch wanted to know, could the Crows not guard their herds? Unknown to Hatch, Indians seldom guarded their horses except the very best ones, which were tethered within the camp. Even when some horses had been kept in a corral at the agency, Hatch continued, enemies had stolen them. It would help, the colonel continued, if the Indian Office would make the offending tribe pay for the horses.[4]

While the Crows received all this attention, they were no more innocent than other tribes in the area. Both the Crows and Grosventres of the Prairie took horses from the Blackfeet during 1883. But the tribe that gained the greatest notoriety in that year was the Plains Cree. They often raided into the United States, sometimes accompanied by their mixed-blood relatives. They attacked a number of tribes, but their expeditions against the Grosventres, their old enemies; the Assiniboins, once their allies; and the Piegans, long their opponents in war, became newsworthy items in another round of diplomatic altercations between Great Britain and the United States.

International difficulties stemming from tribal conflict dated back to the 1840s, when so many Canadian mixed bloods invaded America to hunt and as a result clashed with the Yanktons and Yanktonais. Nothing of serious diplomatic nature occurred, however, until Sitting Bull's band stirred up rivalries in Canada, and the Mandans and Hidatsas made their short raid north following Plains Ojibwa horse thieves. Now, as the 1880s progressed, a number of crises across the international boundary followed one after another, beginning when the Plains Crees and mixed bloods, coming into the United States to hunt the last buffalo herds, became involved in tribal war.

The first international problem began in March 1883. A group of Piegans, following Crees who had stolen their horses, found the Crees near fur trader Joe Kipp's ranch on the Marias River. The Crees' attention was directed toward butchering one of Kipp's steers when, taking the Crees by surprise, the Piegans charged their enemies and killed several of them before the others fled to Canada. This incident led to rumors that Cree warriors were massing along the Canadian border ready to take revenge. Agent Young asked Commissioner Price to relax the rules on the amount of ammunition sold to Indians. Price refused, saying that the army would provide any protection needed, but nothing came of the rumors. The fear of massive gatherings of hostile Indians was still common in the 1880s, even though, by this time, large war parties bent on revenge were a thing of the past.

By June, the indignation changed to the Canadian side. The British legation in Washington, D.C., forwarded a complaint from Fort Walsh across the border (in Canada) that Canadian Indians, like the Crees, were "afraid of the South Piegans who are out in numerous small war parties trying to steal what few horses our Indians have left." When General Sherman got word of the situation, he stated that the problem could be solved if the army was allowed to confiscate all stolen animals, which was the policy used by Canadian officials. Sherman hoped that the Interior Department would agree to this. The two government agencies were working more in concert on tribal warfare, but the Indian Office was still skeptical of allowing too much army interference in Indian affairs. Sherman and other army officers felt that the agents did not closely regulate the warlike tendencies of the Indians. Since interdepartmental rivalry did not allow for a solution to the Piegan-Cree situation, Agent Young and the Canadian authorities temporarily averted further tension by meeting on their own and facilitating the return of some stolen stock.[5]

Soon after the Piegans had responded to the Cree challenge, the Grosventres and Assiniboins chased Cree raiders into Canada and recovered thirty-seven stolen horses. The incident resulted in another rumor from Canada which stated that the Plains Crees were preparing a massive attack on the Grosventres and Assiniboins who, the Crees said, "have been killing their soldiers." As usual, the story turned out to be larger than reality. Lieutenant Colonel Guido Ilges, Fort Assiniboine commander, asked the Fort Walsh Mounted Police to cooperate in thwarting the expected offensive. However, Major Albert Shurtliff, commanding Fort Walsh, assured Ilges that such an attack was unlikely, and indeed it was, since tribal fighting during the 1880s was on a much more limited basis.[6]

All in all, 1883 was a trying year for the Indian Office. There were large numbers of tribal raids as well as other small irritations. Within various reservations dissatisfied warriors, at a loss without the action of war, sometimes turned to minor theft, something previously uncommon to plains societies. Also, the visiting continued. Fort Berthold Indians and Standing Rock Sioux visited each other. A group of Crows tried to visit Standing Rock Agency, but soldiers turned them back. In October, forty Oglalas arrived at Fort Custer under the leadership of Young Man Afraid of His Horses. A famous chief in the wars against the whites, he now had papers from the Pine Ridge agent permitting this visit to the old Crow rivals. Colonel Hatch decried visits like this because they helped to cause a reversion to war. What happened, he said, was that the dancing and celebrations always led to war stories and bragging about fighting prowess; this, he said, in turn, could always lead to violence.

But these problems were minor compared to the continuation of almost full-scale raiding on the upper Missouri. The intensity of the warfare seemed to take government authorities by surprise, and they began to organize a more stringent system of controls, particularly over the distribution of arms. Agents carefully watched for potential war parties leaving the reservations. The army, steadily becoming an all-pervasive force, increased its patrols of the routes commonly used by war parties.

By the end of 1883, the regulation was taking form but was still

The Horse Thieves by Charles M. Russell. This painting depicts the Piegan warrior White Quiver's raid in the 1880s. *Courtesy Amon Carter Museum, Fort Worth, Texas.*

beset by the old rivalry between the army and the Indian Office. Although the army was working diligently to trap the elusive war parties, Commissioner Price insisted on deemphasizing the role of the military men compared to that of the Indian Office. He wrote in his annual report that the War Department had supplied the Indians with "scalping knives by the thousands" when it had handled Indian affairs, but that the Interior Department was teaching the Indians worthwhile pursuits. In displaying the worst possible pomposity and self-righteousness of his day, Price continued, "Thus we are substantially changing their 'swords into plowshares and their spears into pruning hooks,' and educating them to 'learn war no more.'"[7]

The two years following Sitting Bull's surrender, 1882 and 1883, brought no relief to government officials surprised by the tenacity of warriors in carrying out their favorite pastime. Meanwhile, the United States moved into the middle of the decade of the mid-1880s as a modern, advanced nation. Grover Cleveland was elected president of a sophisticated, representative democracy, and the country moved closer to becoming the world's greatest industrial power. In the Far West, the frontiers of mining, cattle, and farming gradually came to a close and developed into modern businesses. The time was near when the Dakotas, Montana, and Wyoming would become states.

Yet, paradoxically, on the upper Missouri an ancient cultural tradition of aboriginal peoples continued. The competition for horses, coups, and glory seemed to increase in intensity in 1884 and 1885 despite white settlement and the impact of more army patrols. Small war parties continued to avoid the authorities and lead ever larger army units on wild goose chases. It seemed to Americans an appalling misuse of a great industrial nation's manpower.

The Piegans were particularly active, and their efforts seemed to reach a new apogee. Late in the winter of 1884, Crow Agent Armstrong listed the statistics for the last two years: 500 ponies stolen in 1882, 200 to 300 in 1883. Now, February of 1884 had not yet passed and already more than 100 horses were missing. The Piegans even stole thirty-five horses from the famous chief Plenty Coups. The Crows, with the help of some white men who were victims of the same thieves, followed the Piegans and killed three of them. The commissioner ordered the Blackfoot agent to threaten the tribe with military intervention, but this had no effect. The Piegans captured forty-one horses in March, although the sheriff of Chouteau County in northwestern Montana confiscated and returned thirty-five of them. Thus, even civil authorities were becoming involved in the raiding. In September 1884, fourteen Piegans cut out 100 Crow horses, and the army pursuit found only a cold trail pointing north.

The warring continued with the same intensity in 1885. By September, Piegan war parties consisting of three to ten men, often joined by Bloods, invaded Crow country every three or four days. Usually the army patrols, when alerted, were too late to pursue effectively. The Piegans, to avoid having their stolen horses confiscated when they returned to the agency, often took them across the border and sold them to other Blackfeet in Canada.

While the Piegans were probably the greatest aggressors in these years, the role of the Crows is harder to measure. As usual, government officials tended to favor them because they had always been friendly and had helped in fighting the Sioux alliance. Westerners had always appreciated Crow aid in protecting settlers from hostile

Sioux while admiring the tribe's courage in defending its land against all invaders. Praise for the Crows, however, often extended well beyond reality. Commissioner of Indian Affairs John D. C. Atkins naively maintained that the Crows "are peaceable, inoffensive people, unused to the practices of war and being unarmed are wholly unable to protect themselves against their more war-like neighbors in the North."

This example of bureaucratic favoritism belied the statistics, which proved a much different situation. The Crows were by no means peaceful toward their Indian enemies. General Terry's reports for September and October of 1885 showed that his patrols picked up as many Crow raiders as Piegans. The government's friendship for the Crows certainly did nothing to hinder the tribe's warlike efforts.[8]

The Crow-Piegan rivalry was not the only one. Piegans continued to fight the Assiniboins and Grosventres at Fort Belknap and raided as far as the new Northern Cheyenne Reservation along the Tongue River, next to the Crow Reservation. The Crees still fought the Piegans, although many Crees now turned their efforts to helping the mixed bloods in the 1885 rebellion led by Louis Riel against the Canadian government. The continuing conflict in the Northwest even encouraged some tribes outside the northwestern arena to once more take up their weapons. The Bannocks of Wyoming and the Shoshonis and Arapahos of Wind River Reservation exchanged minor raids, and the Plains Ojibwas made several small attacks on the Three Tribes at Fort Berthold.[9]

Despite the widespread intertribal conflict of 1884 and 1885, the period was also a watershed. Tribal warfare was on the decline and doomed to imminent extinction. The army, Indian agents, and Canadian officials were becoming much more effective in coordinating their efforts, especially now that telegraph lines stretched into more remote areas of the Northwest. Usually, the army and agents caught horse thieves and returned the stolen animals. The concern about stolen animals, reflecting the frontier antipathy toward horse stealing, was diametrically opposite to the Indian view, which saw stealing horses as an act of war. It was not like stealing from one's own people, which seldom happened in plains Indian communities. Yet, carrying their own attitudes to a logical conclusion, American and Canadian officials went farther and eventually prosecuted raiders for crimes such as theft and murder.

By the middle 1880s, controlling the warfare was more effective because with few buffalo remaining the Indians depended on the agencies for food. When men went raiding they missed the ration issues, and the agent could more easily discover the expedition. It was difficult for men to quietly disappear on raids, and, when they did go, Montana was becoming so populated with farmers and cattlemen that it was laborious for a war party to negotiate undetected the countryside that was now cluttered by farms, ranches, and towns.

But the system of control, though much more effective, was not foolproof and could be beaten by cunning warriors, as seen in the case of a raid by a warrior named White Quiver. He was certainly one of the most talented Piegan raiders. In 1885, at the age of thirty-five, he set off alone against the Crows on a revenge raid that became so phenomenal it was almost inconceivable that one man could have accomplished it.

Finding a Crow village on the Yellowstone, White Quiver waited until nightfall, fired into a lodge, and killed three people. This was his retaliation for the deaths of several relatives. After this attack, however, he did not take flight, but stayed hidden all the next day. On the following night, White Quiver crept quietly into the camp and cut loose four prize horses tied to the fronts of their masters' lodges. On leaving the camp, he ran off more horses from the herd nearby and, with a total of fifty, rapidly made his way home.

The Crow agent telegraphed ahead, however, and when White Quiver arrived at the Blackfoot Reservation, American authorities confiscated the herd. Not to be dissuaded, this ingenious man waited his chance, stole the horses back, and headed for Canada to sell the animals to the Bloods.

Again, technology caught up with him. The Americans telegraphed Fort MacLeod and the Mounted Police took the horses. Undismayed, White Quiver retrieved part of the herd from the police corral the next night. He headed home, where he distributed the horses to Piegan friends who agreed to keep quiet about the matter. Of course, this feat was unusual. With army patrols and the telegraph constantly at work trying to stop men like White Quiver, warriors had an increasingly difficult time getting away with raids. The fact that they did succeed so often is a tribute to their talents.[10]

Part of the miraculous nature of White Quiver's raid was that it came at a time when Americans were forcing the decline of intertribal competition. White Quiver seemed to be an anomaly when compared to government sources that testified to the waning of tribal war. In 1884, Indian department reports noted a gradual diminishing of the conflict and a decrease in forays. Secretary of the Interior Henry M. Teller even went so far as to herald the end of the wars with an optimistic but wholly inaccurate statement: "It affords me great satisfaction in my third and last report to be able to say that the past year has been one of peace among the Indians, and that no outbreaks have occurred. All the tribes are at peace with each other and with their white neighbors."

This was quite an exaggeration, but white people who were knowledgeable about the subject did believe that 1885 was indeed a real turning point. Agents noted fewer warlike expeditions and the development of friendships punctuated by visiting between such old and bitter enemies as the Crows and the Oglalas and Northern Cheyennes.

More important, such close observers as George Bird Grinnell and James Willard Schultz, both of whom had close ties with the Blackfeet, recorded 1885 as the year when intertribal warfare came to an end. Grinnell said that the geographic spread of white settlement made facile passage of war parties over the plains impossible, while Schultz maintained that the government put an end to contests between the tribes. Both factors were important in bringing tribal war to an end, along with the general decline of the buffalo hunting culture.[11]

By 1885, white Americans in the northwestern plains felt strongly that tribal war ought to end soon because of its detrimental effects on white society. According to Blackfoot Agent R. A. Allen, "On many occasions when the Indians fail to capture horses belonging to other Indians they steal from the whites, and thus the country is kept in a constant state of excitement."

A "state of excitement" was an accurate description, and it took only hearsay to create the excitement. James Terrell of Banner, Wyoming, started a rumor in February 1885 by saying he had received information from Indians of the Sioux, Cheyenne, Crow, Arapaho, and Shoshoni tribes that they had "formed a league, and will go as soon as grass grows to fight the Piegans, Bloods, Blackfeet, and other tribes north of the Yellowstone." The result, said Terrell, would be "a conflict with the whites, as the game is gone and they will have to subsist off the country." Terrell raised the alarm with United States Senator J. B. Beck, and this resulted in a thorough investigation by army officers and Indian agents. The conspiracy was found to be an absurd notion turned into bureaucratic nonsense that simply cost the government money and raised some resentment in Wyoming. The residents of nearby Johnson County, soon to be made famous with its cattlemen's war, complained of people avoiding the area as a place to settle because of the rumor of an Indian war.

Travelling war parties, however, sometimes had detrimental effects on ranchers. At the end of 1886, J. R. Dilworth, a rancher in Gallatin

County, Montana, was still writing to the secretary of the interior trying to get federal compensation for stock stolen in May of 1885. Piegans had taken the animals on the way to fight the Crows and the agent, said Dilworth, made little effort to stop the raids.[12]

Late in 1885 the powerful Montana Board of Stock Commissioners petitioned the federal government to put an end to the Crow-Piegan war. Led by the well-known rancher Granville Stuart, an early pioneer, the board recommended that the Indians be disarmed and dismounted and their land divided into family allotments, forcing the Indians to live more like the whites. The remaining land could be sold to benefit surrounding ranchers. This attitude led to the passage of the notorious Dawes Act of 1887, which tried to break up tribalism and tribal land. Its purpose, to sell all tribal land except plots given to individual Indian families, was a serious threat to Indian culture.

In the petition, Stuart continued to explain the cattlemen's complaint. He accused the Indian agents of simply allowing their wards to carry on their warring habits freely. Depredations against settlers resulted — horses taken and cattle slaughtered for food in the absence of buffalo. In his memoirs, Stuart provided an example of one negligent Crow agent who, Stuart claimed, gave the Crows permission to raid the Piegans. "This same agent," Stuart wrote, "knew that his wards would have to cross two hundred miles of country, partially settled and occupied by white people, and that while on this raid they would necessarily have to live off of the white men's cattle, and that when stealing and plundering, Indians do not discriminate between white or Indian enemies. They take anything at hand."

There was some truth to the ranchers' complaints, but they were overstated. General Thomas Ruger, now the Department of Dakota commander and a realistic commentator on the Indians, gave less credence to the idea of transient war parties' wholesale depredations. He attributed many incidents to unprincipled whites taking advantage of a situation in which Indians would be blamed for the rustlers' thievery.[13]

But the grievances filed by frontier citizens, whatever their accuracy, were influential. In the late 1880s, the government became increasingly less tolerant of intertribal struggles and agents and soldiers redoubled their efforts to stop it. That meant more army patrols, restricting Indians to reservations, seizing tribal land, and even criminal prosecution.

Despite opinions to the contrary, tribal warfare was not completely ended by 1885. Controls tightened as never before, but during 1886 and 1887, a number of warriors hung on to perpetrate raiding, struggling to continue a way of life that was expiring. Much of the action still centered around the Piegans and Crows, but the Bloods from Canada once again became active participants.

As in years past, a few less-than-honest white settlers benefitted from tribal raiding. Some white Canadians in the Porcupine Hills, near Fort MacLeod in southern Alberta, helped Blood war parties with their spoils of war: In exchange for a share of the stolen horses, the whites shielded Indian raiders from American and Canadian authorities.[14]

In another arena, Agent Henry E. Williamson believed the Crows to be peaceful and much put upon by their enemies, but reality proved otherwise. In September 1886, these "inoffensive" Crows stole 200 ponies from the Piegans. According to government authorities the proliferation of visiting was influential in preserving tribal competition among the Crows and others.

If anyone could inflame the mood for war, it was the great chief Sitting Bull. At one point, he and a few followers visited the Crows. F. C. Armstrong, an Indian Office inspector, noted that the influence was bad, since "Sitting Bull and other visiting Indians have done much harm here by bad advice and boasting talk."

The Crows, besides their conflict with the Blackfeet, in 1886 revived the quarrel with the Yanktonais of Fort Peck Reservation. The Yanktonais were less involved in raiding in the 1880s than previously, but a certain group of men remained inveterate warriors. In September 1886, the Crows, retaliating for an earlier Yanktonai raid, killed two Lower Assiniboin women at Fort Peck Agency. The government reacted strongly. There had been little killing in recent tribal war and, furthermore, these victims were women. The United States government found twenty Crows responsible for the killing and prosecuted them under a new act of Congress placing Indians under civil law. The court found the men guilty and ordered them confined at Fort Custer for a time.

This government action helped reinforce the peace efforts being made by Fort Peck Agent H. Heth. The raiding, said Heth, had caused the Indians to live close to the agency for protection, thus interrupting the effort to spread them out on separate farms. A similar situation existed on the Crow Reservation, where the government was already attempting to divide part of the reservation into individual allotments.[15]

Another of the now infrequent bloody incidents occurred between the Bloods and the Grosventres of the Prairie. In September 1886, after having lost sixty horses to rapacious Blood raiders, the Grosventres took the initiative. Although soldiers turned back one group of Grosventres when they came near Fort Assiniboine, a second party of twenty-three men managed to slip away from the reservation. They found eight Bloods at the Sweet Grass Hills near the international boundary. The Bloods, caught unaware and trapped, dug trenches on a hill to defend themselves, but they had little chance. In an act of bravado, the Grosventres assaulted the position, killed four of the enemy, and returned home triumphantly with the scalps.

This battle spurred rumors that Bloods and Blackfeet were massing at the international boundary for a revenge attack. American forts went on alert, and troops from Fort Maginnis and Fort Custer in central and southern Montana marched toward the Sweet Grass Hills. Fort Belknap Agent Edwin Fields asked permission for his Indians to buy ammunition to use in their defense. The Indians did not receive the ammunition, however, because of complaints coming from the Great Northern Railroad, which feared for the safety of its workers.

No Blood attack came. The day of large revenge parties was past. Nonetheless, four Assiniboins added to the tension by stealing four Blood horses. But the Assiniboin agent confiscated the ponies on the war party's return. In June, government officials arranged for a peace. Canadian Blood Agent Major William Pocklington, together with an inspector of the Northwest Mounted Police, brought the well-known Chief Red Crow and other Blood leaders to Fort Belknap. The Indians exchanged presents and held a dance, and both parties returned stolen horses and made promises of better conduct. This truce, unlike most intertribal agreements, was fairly effective in limiting raiding, although it was briefly broken the next year.[16]

The Plains Cree was the one tribe that was not part of this tumult. The Crees had been the scourge of the upper Missouri in the early 1880s, but after their experience in the losing cause of the Riel rebellion they generally gave up intertribal warfare. When the Crees again came to the United States in the late 1880s, they came as friendly visitors to the Assiniboins and Grosventres, and eventually some of them lived for a while with the Piegans on the Blackfoot Reservation.[17]

The years 1886 and 1887 made up the last truly active period of intertribal conflict. At the end of 1886, warfare had not increased and had been localized to fighting primarily among the Piegans, Crows, Yanktonais, and Canadian Bloods. War parties took more stock from whites, but that was the exception, and it probably occurred only because many more ranches dotted the countryside. Ranches were hard to avoid, and cattle were available.

By 1887, the situation had changed even more. The contestants were the same, but, wrote General Ruger, "There has been a decrease in the present year, as compared with former years, in Indian depredations and in raids between reservation Indians, and also of predatory incursions by Indians of the Canadian Northwest Territory." The general's explanations for this phenomenon were the facts that the Indians were becoming more civilized; that the treaty between the Bloods and the Grosventres and Assiniboins was successful; and that troop patrols were more active.[18]

Without doubt, massive army patrolling was becoming more effective along with cooperation between agents and officers using the telegraph to report raids. Ruger, for example, recorded pursuits of war parties by six or seven troop detachments just in a two-week period in October 1886. In addition, the use of these troops did not include the months of general scouting in certain areas where war parties passed regularly and sometimes hid stolen ponies. The army made regular searches of the Snowy and Belt mountains of central Montana. Periodic patrols also traced the established routes that both Blackfoot and Crow war parties had taken for over fifty years to and from Crow country: across the Judith Basin, past the Crazy Mountains and along the Sweet Grass River, and on to the crossing of the Yellowstone River at Pompeys Pillar near Billings, Montana.

On the reservations, the Indian police supported the army's job. As tribal competition declined, policing became an increasingly attractive job for retired warriors. During 1887, Blackfoot Agent M. D. Baldwin proudly informed the commissioner how, while the Bloods continued to raid, the Piegan raiding was decreasing, in part because of active Indian police. On one occasion, the police confiscated some horses stolen by Piegans in retaliation for a Crow raid and a court sent the Piegan perpetrators to the penitentiary at Deer Lodge, Montana.

This judicial prosecution was one of several examples of using the new law that placed Indians under civil court jurisdiction. This solution was not used extensively, but it was another threat to discourage the warriors. Now a kind of double jeopardy covered Indian raiders: Parallel to the civil law that made criminal prosecution possible, the army continued its own military control of the Indians, a situation that would have been illegal if applied to any white American citizen.

A circular policy letter from Commissioner of Indian Affairs Atkins, dated February 2, 1887, greatly benefitted the army. Atkins prohibited visits between tribes except for unusual special reasons. Controls on Indians leaving the reservation dated back to the 1870s, but now the Indian Office stiffened this policy. The idea was that, besides helping the civilizing process, the elimination of visiting would stop some potential raiding parties. Now officials simply turned away visiting bands, which is what happened to a group of Oglalas and Brulés trying to visit the Crows in 1887. The agents believed this would help alleviate the men's desires for war and also preclude any opportunity for Indians to take the warpath while pretending to go visiting.[19]

Restricting Indians to reservations with the idea of placing them as farmers on small plots of land and the frontiersmen's greed for more land all led the government to limit the size of reservations. J. K. Toole, Montana Territory's delegate to Congress, presented a bill to break up Montana's large northern reservation that included the land of the Blackfoot, Fort Belknap, and Fort Peck Indians.

Finally, in 1888 the government broke up the large reserve into three distinct and small reservations. The secretary of the interior, rather conveniently it seems, gave the reasons as emanating from intertribal conflict. The big reservation, he said, lay too close to Canada; therefore, it was "quite difficult to keep our Indians upon their reservations or to keep foreign Indians from coming upon them. The visiting, roaming, or raiding of Indians to and from their reservations presents a serious obstacle to the civilizing efforts which are made possible among them under the provisions of the agreement recently ratified."[20]

With these examples of white determination to end tribal war, opposed to some warriors' resolute intention to continue fighting, it became evident how much deep feeling and principle each side had invested in the concept of tribal war. The incidents of the Crows killing the Assiniboin women and the Blood-Grosventre debacle were examples of how the issue could become so controversial. But the best example of how tribal raiding became an emotional point of contention was the Sword Bearer incident at the Crow Agency in September 1887.

Sword Bearer was a young Crow of recognized spiritual power. In 1887, he led a horse raid against the Piegans, but on the war party's return in September the warriors heard that the agent was going to have them arrested for their illegal activity. The men, having gotten quite drunk from celebrating, painted themselves for war and galloped angrily to the agency. One warrior leaped from his horse in front of Agent Henry Williamson's interpreter and pointed his rifle directly at him. Then at the last moment, as he pulled the trigger, he moved the rifle so it fired over the interpreter's head. Meanwhile, other men painted for war rode wildly through the agency, threatened Williamson and the employees, and shot at buildings.

Williamson, a retired general, had been the Crow agent since 1885. The Crows knew him as a domineering and power-hungry man as well as a drunk. Much of the war party's reaction to his order was obviously directed toward him personally. The Crows undoubtedly remembered his drunkenness, his violent temper, and his misuse of funds received from leasing Crow land.

Williamson's reaction was to wire the commissioner and call for troops. When they arrived from Fort Custer, this further incensed the Crows, and other warriors joined the original war party to resist the soldiers, one being a well-known chief, Crazy Head. A brief fight resulted. The Indians killed one soldier and wounded another, but Sword Bearer and seven other Crows also died in the fighting.

The government saw this challenge by the usually friendly Crows as very serious. It sent nine Crows, including Crazy Head, to prison far away at Fort Snelling, Minnesota. Most of the men were released after a year, during which time some of them attended the Carlisle Indian School to be educated in white ways. Chief Plenty Coups, now one of the most important Crow leaders, was instrumental in the release of the prisoners, giving the government his own guarantee for the men's good behavior. It was not until 1889, however, that Plenty Coups achieved the release of an older man, Deaf Bull. The old warrior had seemed at one point to be going insane in prison and even attacked and stabbed several of the other Crows with a penknife. But by 1889, he was calm enough to go free.

The punishment of the Crows was much harsher than any past penalties dealt out for intertribal war. The Crows had challenged American authority and federal officials were determined to put a final end to intertribal conflict. A number of people, however, remembered the Crows as staunch supporters of the United States and wanted to be as lenient as possible. President Grover Cleveland was among them. Soon after he heard of the incident, the president wrote Secretary of the Interior Lucius Q. C. Lamar, agreeing that the Crows should be jailed but also saying, "I feel like treating them with as much moderation as is consistent with safety."[21]

The Sword Bearer incident and the fairly solid treaty between the Bloods, Grosventres, and Assiniboins were indicative of how difficult it was for young men to carry on their warlike adventures. Obviously, the United States was no longer going to tolerate the conflict to any extent. After years of vacillation, the military and the Indian Office had reached an accord of purpose. The end of raiding was at hand.

In 1888, General Ruger reported the greatest decrease in tribal war in northern plains history. Before that year, he wrote, raiding had been frequent, but now there were only rare war parties. Ruger maintained that although raiding "by small hostile parties of the Yanktonais Sioux of the Fort Peck Agency, and Piegans of the Blackfeet Agency, against the Crows, and the reverse, has not entirely ceased, there have been fewer of such raids, particularly by the Piegans."[22]

Nonetheless, the Bloods and Yanktonais seemed to get a second wind and take up some of the efforts previously made by the Piegans and Crows. A scattering of Blood and Yanktonais forays seemed a final flurry of effort by individuals trying to gain one more war honor, attempting to salvage what had been the most important aspect of their lives.

Although most signatories respected the 1887 treaty, several Bloods lost little time in breaking it. In the spring of 1888, on two occasions three weeks apart, Blood war parties captured Assiniboin ponies. Fort Belknap Agent Fields claimed that few horses were returned and accused Canadian officials of protecting their Indians' thieving habits.

Fields believed the warriors under his charge were living peacefully, but it was not long after the first Blood raid that three Assiniboins stole twenty Blood horses. When the Assiniboins returned to the agency, however, they turned the animals over to the agent and stated that the purpose for the raid was "to show the Blood Indians that they too could go to war (to steal horses) if that was the game of the Blood Indians." Tribal war was not far from over when warriors gave up their booty so easily.

The Northwest Mounted Police proved themselves more honorable than Agent Fields' accusation. They tried to maintain an international trust by inviting Americans to come north to examine the Blood herds. A combined Indian-military delegation took advantage of the offer and did find a number of stolen animals. As late as September, however, the Bloods were at it again, this time stealing twenty-one Assiniboin horses. But it was the Bloods' last raid against the Assiniboins, and a century-old rivalry sputtered to an end.[23]

While this action was taking place in the Milk River country along the international boundary, the small group of inveterate Yanktonais warriors of Fort Peck Agency set out to carry on the fifty-year rivalry with the Crows. Early in the morning of June 15, 1888, three of them crept up on a Crow camp and stole forty-three horses. They got only as far as the Yellowstone. The Crows picked up the trail, pursued rapidly, and discovered the thieves on the river bank at the Pompeys Pillar crossing. The Yanktonais scattered into the brush, but not before the Crows shot one dead. The other two, according to the Crows, drowned while attempting to swim the rapid current.

In August 1888, nine Yanktonais left for the south on a raid. Well-armed with Winchester rifles and plenty of ammunition, they headed for the Crow Reservation. Throughout the rest of August and into early September, army patrols, now going on full alert with every potential raid, scoured the possible crossing points of the Yellowstone without spotting the nine warriors. On September 4, three of them returned to the reservation empty-handed. Then, on October 1, after being out for five or six weeks, the other six men reappeared with thirty stolen horses. The reservation police spotted them and gave chase. When the warriors saw the danger, they abandoned twenty of the horses. The police captured one man, but the rest of them galloped for the safety of the Canadian border with the remaining ten horses.[24]

In this way, 1888 ended with only six raids reported, a far cry from perhaps scores of raids in 1886 and 1887 and hundreds in the years before that. Only two raids were reported in 1889 as the raiding life came to an end.

On the night of May 2, 1889, a Blood war party, at first mistaken for both a Piegan and a Yanktonais group, stole between thirty-five and forty-five horses from a Crow camp. The now efficient system of army control immediately went into operation. Twenty Fort Custer soldiers immediately quickly saddled their horses and took to the trail. The Fort Custer commander telegraphed the commander of Fort Assiniboine far to the north near the border, who also sent out a cavalry unit. The commander of Fort Maginnis, halfway between forts Custer and Assiniboine, did the same. thing. The troops managed to recover ten of the horses. The army also notified the Canadian authorities, who arrested three of the Bloods when they got home. Yet, in spite of this increasing lack of success, the Indians attempted still another raid. In June, five Yanktonai warriors slipped out of Fort Peck Reservation, headed for the Crow Reservation, but they returned empty-handed three weeks later.[25]

This was the last recorded "formal" war party on the northern plains. Undoubtedly, other small secret raids were carried out, and there is evidence of some kind of warlike activities continuing. Certainly, the Ghost Dance uprising of 1890 had some influence in rousing Indian emotions throughout the northern plains. As late as 1892, the Court of Indian Offenses for the Blackfoot Agency tried the famous Piegan White Quiver for allegedly stealing four Crow horses. However, the court released him for lack of evidence. Also in 1892, the army received a rumor that the Canadian Bloods were once again on the warpath and headed toward Fort Belknap Reservation, but a patrol found no war party and no other evidence. Essentially, with the final futile efforts of 1888 and 1889, intertribal conflict ground to a halt.[26]

In part, traditional visiting, trading, and celebrating between old friends and enemies replaced intertribal competition. In the same way that they had provided a major focus of warfare, the Crows now became a favorite focal point for social visits. Indian Office officials continually bemoaned the consequential interference with the civilizing process. After feasting and dancing ended, reminiscing about old rivalries and recounting heroic deeds were the next items on the social agenda of any gathering. The results were sometimes tense situations between men of all ages, from the young warriors to the craggy old fighters of a generation past.

Sometimes talking about war was not enough; men had to at least make the motions of going out to fight. In the last days of tribal war, a Sioux medicine man named Frosted, from Standing Rock Agency, led a secret war party of 150 men off the reservation to repel a supposed Crow invasion. In two days they were all back. Apparently, Frosted had simply created a deceptive ploy to increase his personal power.[27]

This vicarious appreciation of warfare could not long support the strong cultural pull toward individual combat. Words were not enough without actions to support them. The collapse of tribal raiding paralleled the entire defeat of a culture. Change came slowly and with many backward glances at the old "buffalo days." The warriors soon realized that their way of life was over, but farming, running cattle, and raising horses were no replacement for the exhilarating competition of counting coup and cutting horses.

Some men, with nothing to replace their old activities, turned to dissolute lives of uselessness and drunkenness. The formidable White Quiver spent several years in and out of jail on charges of drunkenness until, finally, the agency gave his life more purpose by making him an Indian police sergeant.

Already in 1888, Chief Plenty Coups saw the detrimental effects of the lack of fighting: "There were few war parties, and almost no raids against our enemies, so that we were beginning to grow careless of our minds and bodies." His fellow Crow, Two Leggings, did not have the political power of Plenty Coups to fall back on. He had lived for warring and faced the end of that way of life with difficulty. The Crows changed with the end of raiding, said Two Leggings: "Their hearts were on the ground. . . ." For himself, he welcomed death and the afterlife it promised: "Soon I shall live again those days of which I now only dream. . . ." The end of the buffalo and of raiding signalled the end of everything. "Nothing happened after that [his last fight]. There were no more war parties, no capturing of horses from the Piegans and the Sioux, no buffalo to hunt. There is nothing more to tell."

John Stands in the Timber, historian of the Cheyenne tribe, the tribe whose warriors made such a name for themselves as individual fighters, noted the men's difficulty adjusting to life without raiding. They were learning to settle down, but it took a long time since because there were no more war honors. Now, "there was no way for them to show the women how brave they were unless they got into trouble with white people, or at least got away with stealing some beef." The Cheyenne warrior Wooden Leg put it more simply. As an old man in 1930, he appreciated the security of the reservation against enemy attacks, but, he said, "I like to think about the old times when every man had to be brave." For younger men, still full of enthusiasm, raiding and fighting were inappropriate behavior now that white culture dominated the Indians. These men did not have much of a life left to them.[28]

For the northern plains warriors, life seemed to end when the raiding was over. It was difficult to find something in the white man's culture to replace the excitement and deadly competition of intertribal warfare. A few men could be policemen, others army scouts. But when the frontier period passed there were even fewer possibilities. Reservation life made it difficult to be exposed to other types of "competition" in white society, such as athletics. Two generations after tribal warfare ended, World War II provided a historic opportunity for some Indian men to continue the fighting tradition, but such opportunities came all too infrequently.

And this modern war was only temporary, not like the conflicts of old. The plains warriors of the 1880s had the greatest adjustment to make when their culture changed because the old contest for glory was difficult to reproduce in the new society they had to try to join. The activity upon which they had spent most of their time and energy, both physically and mentally, was lost to them in the 1880s. Nothing would ever again be the same. It is with a sense of finality approaching sorrow that one reads the lyrics of a Brulé veterans' song from World War II, a song all too similar to the death songs or medicine songs of old:

"They charge with it.
The President's flag, they charge with it.
He is the bravest Sioux boy so he charges with it."[29]

BIBLIOGRAPHICAL ESSAY

The study of intertribal conflict, as with any historical study of the American Indian, requires a variety of sources that must be compared and cross-referenced in order to reach objective conclusions. Historical records vary widely from travel diaries to expert treatises to government documents. In addition, because of the social importance of tribal war, an anthropological, or ethnological, perspective is necessary alongside the historical sources. Closely related to ethnologists' work is the oral history of the period — stories told in the early 1900s by old Indians who lived in the "buffalo days." Ideally, the best approach to the study of tribal war, and for that matter all Indian history, is a historical analysis combined with an understanding of the cultural characteristics of the plains people. Adjuncts to the scholarly approach are the Indians' feelings of closeness to the land and the importance of tribalism, beliefs that even today continue to motivate plains tribes.

Through time, three major issues have been important for people who have written about tribal warfare. The first issue is the military methods used by nomadic warriors. Early white men on the plains did not understand the limited, individual nature of Indian raiding. Also, nineteenth century Americans were shocked at the brutality of tribal conflict — killing women and children and horribly mutilating corpses. Ethnologists were able to explain the brutality in cultural terms, but many writers, perhaps uncomfortable with things like mutilation, tended to ignore the practice or emphasize its use by some American soldiers. Moving away from the subject of the actual violence, modern writers often concentrated on the significant impact of the horse and the gun on the tactics of Indian warfare.

The second issue is the motivation for intertribal conflict. Countless raids to prove one's courage by stealing horses and counting coups were very puzzling to Europeans and Americans. In modern times some ethnologists have explained the curious reasons for fighting in terms of particular types of cultural status. Other writers have often interpreted the motives as economic drives for territory, thus providing a more understandable concept to the twentieth-century mind.

The third issue is white involvement in tribal warfare, either through

195

the influence of the newcomers or from the detrimental effects of raiding upon travelers and settlers. From the beginning, Europeans and Americans, especially fur traders, became involved with the warfare. As a result, ending the conflict became a policy propounded by private companies, individual settlers, and the United States and Canadian governments. While this involvement was an important issue to those writing in the 1700s and 1800s and a crucial part of government Indian policy, historians have given it little attention except in the example of Indian allies and the case of tribal war's relationship to Indian-white wars.

The earliest historical sources dealing with these three issues are the fur traders of the middle 1700s. In the early years of the fur trade, contact with the Indians was often brief; the traders concentrated on acquiring pelts and promptly returning east. Nevertheless, some of the information on tribal war and trade is rather complete considering the fur men's lack of understanding of the area and the variety of tribes. *The Journals of Pierre Gaultier de Varenness de la Verendrye and His Sons* and the *Journal of a Journey Performed by Anthony Hendry* show that these men were fairly thorough observers of tribal warfare even though they did not visit the tribes for long periods of time.

In the 1780s and 1790s, the Hudson's Bay Company and the North West Company established permanent trading posts in western Canada along the tributaries of the Saskatchewan River. Now the traders had more contact with the Indians. The result was a number of journals which included comments on passing war parties and the writer's opinions of tribal conflict. Often the traders provided interesting commentaries on battles or pertinent insights into tribal warfare, but few white men took the time to learn about Indian culture.

Jean Baptiste Trudeau and David Thompson were exceptions to the rule. Trudeau's *Journal*, in which he depicted his life and trade with the Arikaras, demonstrates an understanding of tribal war's ambiguity. He also recognized the true nature of the relations between the Arikaras and surrounding tribes. *David Thompson's Narrative of his Explorations in Western America, 1784-1812* proves the writer to be a phenomenon among traders of the late 1700s and early 1800s. Thompson was not only well-educated, but also had a true intellectual curiosity about the people with whom he traded, as well as an enlightened attitude about their importance in the frontier's future. His writings about the Piegans and his discussions with the old Cree-turned-Blackfoot warrior, Saukamappe, comprise the most informative of the early narratives of the plains and mountains. Saukamappe's story has been the most significant, and often the only, source for ethnologists studying the 1700s. Overall, however, Thompson's own objective observations have been of the most importance. Not only did he give an accurate description of tribal war itself, but also he went much farther than other traders in describing the often futile European attempts to control or stop the raiding between tribes.

With the exception of Trudeau and Thompson, the eighteenth-century diarists supplied rather minimal information. Their journals are important, however, in providing information on the location and migration of early tribes, as well as the early impact of horses and guns.

After the tentative eighteenth-century beginnings, the nineteenth-century brought with it a burgeoning fur trade and a greatly increased white interest in the northern plains. After the United States acquired Louisiana Territory, Americans traveled up the Missouri River to compete with traders coming south from British territory. The Lewis and Clark expedition opened the way for more explorers, traders, military expeditions, and even casual travelers during the first two decades of the century. The Missouri became a thoroughfare; more people and permanent fur posts meant increased observation of the Indian cultures. For the first time men studied a few of the tribes of the northern plains in a more systematic and purposeful way.

The Lewis and Clark expedition set a precedent for the thorough exploration of the 1800s. President Thomas Jefferson instructed the two leaders not only to outline trade routes and underscore America's right to her new empire, but also to investigate the new land's flora, fauna, and human societies. In addition, they were supposed to control Indian warfare. As a result, the *Original Journals of the Lewis and Clark Expedition, 1804-1806,* supply the earliest source on that United States government policy. Because of their precise instructions, Lewis and Clark tended to be more detailed than many early observers. But like the fur traders, they were not always objective and tended to favor one or more tribes in wars with stronger foes. Nevertheless, on the whole, Lewis and Clark's efforts to understand Indian culture and their attempts to bring peace to the Missouri area resulted in descriptions that are among the era's best sources.

While the American explorers stayed with the Mandans, downriver Pierre Antoine Tabeau, an experienced trader, lived and traded with the Arikaras. In his detailed *Narrative*, Tabeau recorded valuable information, particularly about the ambiguities of trade and war and the ambivalent relationship between the Arikaras and the Sioux tribes.

While the Americans moved up the Missouri in the early 1800s, the aggressive North West Company sent its representatives south to the

Big River, or Missouri, and west into the mountains. A number of the company's traders wrote copious journals commenting on the Indians with whom they did business. Alexander Henry, one of the most prolific diarists, described in depth the warfare of several tribes, especially the Blackfeet, as well as the traders' attempts to control the war. Antoine Larocque and Charles MacKenzie, traded along the upper Missouri as well as in Crow territory. MacKenzie wrote "Mississiouri Indians," in which he added important information about the people in these areas. Larocque, a well-educated man, in "The Missouri Journal, 1804-1805" and "Journal of Larocque from the Assiniboine to the Yellostone, 1805," showed insight into the working of tribal culture and war.

Among the American fur traders, Wilson Price Hunt and Robert Stuart provided information on tribes far from the well-traveled routes. Washington Irving used Hunt's journal for help in writing *Astoria*. Despite its romantic air, the book provides accurate information on the Cheyennes and Crows. Stuart's journal of his expedition east from Astoria, edited by Kenneth A. Spaulding as *On the Oregon Trail*, presents conscientious and precise observations of the Crows and Arapahos and their warfare.

The fur men's purpose, of course, was to make money in a business which at that time depended on the cooperation of the Indians to supply the furs. The traders certainly had biased attitudes. Indians who continually brought in furs to sell and did not steal goods and horses from the whites appeared to the traders to be more justified in their intertribal squabbles than Indians who disrupted trade. At the same time, most traders, while easily working with the Indians and admiring parts of their culture, considered them all to be savages, as exemplified by their constant raiding and stealing. Because of this attitude, the white men provided sort of an unintentional objectivity to their writings. They described all Indians as on the same level; therefore, the recorders treated tribal warfare in a generally consistent and straightforward manner.

In 1811, two travelers, John Bradbury and Henry Marie Brackenridge, stepped into this wilderness scene of fur traders and warring tribes. Bradbury's *Travels in the Interior of North America* and Brackenridge's *Journal of a Voyage up the River Missouri* provided other, non-entrepreneurial perspectives of the northern plains conflicts. While lacking the trader's expertise born of long observation, Bradbury and Brackenridge noted important events and viewed the Indians with some accuracy.

The War of 1812 and a recalcitrant Congress delayed the American exploration of the northern plains until almost the 1820s. Then, the Long Expedition of 1819-1820 began a new era of government interest in the area. Edwin James, one of the scientists accompanying Major Stephen Long, kept an extensive journal later published as *An Account of an Expedition from Pittsburgh to the Rocky Mountains.* In it, James logged important information about the Pawnees and Omahas. The *Account* is a valuable historical source because of the author's precise scientific conclusions.

A new era for the observation of western Indians began in the 1820s when the United States sent permanent officials into the northern plains. In 1824, the Indian Office established the St. Louis Superintendency of Indian Affairs, a large division of the department encompassing the Missouri country. Soon afterward, the department created the Council Bluffs Agency and the Upper Missouri Agency operating under the superintendency. In 1825, the Atkinson-O'Fallon Expedition ascended the Missouri River as far as the Yellowstone. Atkinson and O'Fallon made several treaties with the plains tribes, some of which attempted to stop intertribal conflict. This began the long-term federal policy of trying to end tribal war, but in the early period, agents and soldiers had little close contact with the nomadic tribes; as a result, government documents of this era are not as valuable as the reports dating from the midcentury and later.

During the 1830s and 1840s, despite the continuing lack of thorough and complete government documents, in general, the sources for intertribal warfare improve dramatically. A number of factors brought great numbers of Americans and Europeans to and across the northern plains: steamboat travel on the Missouri and Yellowstone; increased use of the Platte River trail for emigrants to Oregon and California; the zenith of the beaver trade; missionary efforts; and greater government interest in the area. This massive migration meant more people to write about the "peculiar" military habits of the northern plains warriors.

As in the late 1700s and early 1800s, the fur trappers and traders were the white people who most often observed tribal warfare. A number of literate mountain men wrote accurate accounts of their work and adventures. Some, like John Work of the Hudson's Bay Company (*Journal of John Work* and *The Snake Country Expedition of 1830-1831*) and Russell Osborne of the Rocky Mountain Fur Company (*Journal of a Trapper*), left thorough records of actual events. Francois Chardon, at the American Fur Company's Fort Clark, kept a detailed daily diary. *Chardon's Journal at Fort Clark, 1834-1839* notes passing war parties and the results of raids and battles. Warren Ferris of the

American Fur Company, in his *Life in the Rocky Mountains*, and Zenas Leonard, who worked for the Gant-Blackwell Company and for Captain Benjamin Bonneville (*Adventures of Zenas Leonard, Fur Trapper*), gave accurate observations of tribal fighting.

Higher ranking fur traders, directing fur posts and learning much from the Indians and from their own Indian wives, added educated observations. Edwin Denig was the best example of these men. His book, *Five Indian Tribes of the Upper Missouri*, though not published until 1961, is the single-best source for the mid-nineteenth century. Denig passed on his knowledge to travelers who enjoyed his hospitality. The Jesuit priest, Pierre-Jean De Smet, a valuable source for the 1840s and 1850s, apparently gained much of his Indian knowledge from Denig. Other knowledeable fur traders were Alexander Culbertson, who gave information to others without writing it down himself, and Charles Larpenteur, who wrote *Forty Years a Fur Trader on the Upper Missouri*.

These fur men, learning so much about the aboriginal inhabitants of the northern plains, admired the Indians' military abilities. But like their predecessors in the business, they also tended to take sides according to which tribes were customers and which were friendly. The Flatheads and the Snakes, long-time British and American clients, often acted as allies. The Blackfeet, however, traded with the British and were for years hostile to Americans. As a result, writers often described the mountain Indians as brave warriors defending their outnumbered people against the overwhelming Blackfeet. Americans recorded the Blackfeet as warlike and savage people. Of course, all of this influenced the business at hand — buying fur pelts. Through many sources runs the perennial theme of the problem of trying to control the warfare in order to improve trade.

Besides the fur traders, beginning in the 1830s, a stream of private travelers ventured into the northern plains. Their purposes varied from science to art to pleasure. Their lack of monetary ties to the Indians often made them more objective in describing the tribes, although they were not immune from selecting favorite tribes. Of all the travelers, Maximilian, Prince of Wied, was perhaps the most accurate. Science was a serious hobby for Maximilian, and he pursued the truth with some determination and precision. His *Travels in the Interior of North America* portrays Indian warfare in important details not found in other sources.

The artist George Catlin traveled up the Missouri River the year before Maximilian and later recorded his observations in the book *North American Indians*. Catlin was an idealist and romantic, and this colored his views. But the attention to detail in his drawings carried over, somewhat, to his writings. Catlin wrote in depth about the culture of the village tribes. In addition, his portraits of Mandan, Blackfoot, Cree and other Indian leaders added to his precise written descriptions because the paintings depicted men who had gained their positions by daring acts in intertribal raiding.

Other artists added their expertise in illustrating Indian life and warfare even though their comments were not always as detailed as those of Catlin. Alfred Jacob Miller painted and recorded information about the mountain Indians and their wars with the Blackfeet; his works were collated in *The West of Alfred Jacob Miller, 1837*. Paul Kane, a Canadian artist, gave a complete picture of some of the Canadian tribes in the 1840s; his work was published in *Wanderings of an Artist Among the Indians of North America*. Rudolph Kurz traveled and painted along the Missouri in the late 1840s and early 1850s. He commented upon tribal warfare and other topics in his work, *Journal of Rudolph Friedrich Kurz*, published in 1937.

Jesuit missionaries made up another group of important observers. Led by Father De Smet, the priests set up a mission among the Flatheads in the early 1840s. Father Gregory Mengarini and Father Nicholas Point helped De Smet. They became the first whites to have a significant nonfinancial influence on the Flatheads and some members of plains tribes like the Blackfeet and Sioux. "Mengarini's Narrative of the Rockies" (1938) and Point's *Wilderness Kingdom* (1967) illustrate the fathers' religious intentions and their rather realistic views of Indian culture. The Jesuits had no qualms about tribal fighting as long as it was done on the defensive and in a righteous cause; they often perceived their converts as "fighting the good fight" for Christianity. Predictably, in their close accounts of the tribes they were serving, the missionaries spent considerable time on the subject of warfare.

De Smet, especially, made an extended study of the people he was trying to convert; it was later published in 1905 as his *Life, Letters, and Travels*. His interests went beyond proselytizing. He learned as much as he could about the Indians and used his knowledge to improve the Indians' situation as he saw it. This meant a need to stop the fighting, and De Smet was helpful in orchestrating the Treaty of Fort Laramie in 1851.

By the time of this treaty, the plains Indian culture had reached its apogee. Hundreds of warriors led the way in the constant search for prestige on the warpath, and by this time, a variety of white people had observed and written about the war culture for two decades. Each of them had his own particular bias, whether it was the traders' pecuniary one, or the artists' romantic and sensitive view, or the missionaries' religious approach. All of them entered the plains possessing, to one extent or another, the nineteenth-century attitude of superiority over primitive people. In spite of these shortcomings, the 1830s and 1840s were the first time observers described tribal competition for a large area and in terms of numerous tribes. The result was a valuable collection of historical material.

In the mid-nineteenth century, the government took a much greater interest in tribal warfare on the northern plains. The United States had acquired a great deal of land from Mexico, and the west coast beckoned with potential. California provided a wealth of gold, and the Oregon country offered excellent farmland. Wagon and stage routes opened, and exploration for railroad routes proceeded. The Interior Department, formed in 1849, took over Indian affairs from the War Department. Under the Interior Department, the Office of Indian Affairs quickly grew in size as agencies and reservations increased. In the decade and a half before the Civil War, government documents, supplemented by more civilian journals, provided increasing amounts of information on tribal conflict.

The most valuable government documents of the era are those relating to the Fort Laramie Treaty and the Judith Treaty. Both agreements tried to end intertribal warfare, and the commissioners documented the conflict both before and during the negotiations. At the same time, explorers such as Lieutenant Gouverneur Warren and the men searching for a northern railway route to the Pacific Ocean dealt with specific tribal rivalries. After the treaties, the reports of Indian agents became important sources because the agents were trying to make the Indians adhere to the new rules against war. In particular, agents of "border" prairie tribes to the east and southeast of the plains found themselves in the midst of an increasingly intense Sioux invasion. The Omaha and Pawnee agency reports give examples of how far tribal war could be carried and the extent to which the American representatives reacted to the often-violent conflict.

American Fur Company traders, who still ran posts along the Missouri River after the beaver trade collapsed, persisted in keeping accurate records of intertribal raiding. Henry Boller worked for one of the companies in opposition to the giant American Fur Company in the late 1850s and early 1860s. In his book, *Among the Indians: Eight Years in the Far West, 1858-1866*, Boller recorded in some detail, the tribal competition swirling around the Three Tribes. Farther west, at Fort Sarpy and Fort Benton, several employees of the American Fur Company, in particular James H. Chambers, made journal entries of how many war parties passed their forts over a period of more than a year during the mid-1850s.

Historical information on tribal conflict increased greatly after the Civil War because of the greater diversity of sources and the volume of government documents. Americans streamed into the West after 1865 and conquered the last frontier in a few short decades. As inter-tribal competition reached a climax and then waned in the late 1800s, it drew the attention of many people, particularly government employ-ees who described it in reports, journals, and reminiscences. A vast quantity of documentary material resulted from writers dissecting in print as never before, the characteristic military practices of the plains nomads.

The northern plains soon bristled with military posts and Indian agencies. Reports of agents and army officers flooded Washington, D.C. These records, increasing year after year along with the bureauc-racy that supported them, provide the best sources for the post-Civil War years. The correspondence is included in the records of the Inter-ior and War departments. Annual reports are in the bound "serial sets" of yearly government publications for each session of Congress. They are helpful for major events and policy statements. Government officials, however, frequently padded their reports in order to make themselves appear in the best light.

The day-to-day correspondence kept at the level of the fort or agency is much more in depth than annual reports. Much of it is stored at various branch Federal Archives and Records Centers at Denver, Colo-rado; Kansas City, Kansas; and Seattle, Washington. Most of the important correspondence, however, reached Washington, D.C., and is now stored in the National Archives. Some areas of this correspon-dence are on microfilm with copies in the branch archive centers and in many university libraries.

Of the army reports, perhaps the most useful are the Records of the Adjutant General's Office. On microfilm at the National Archives, this collection of records includes most of the army correspondence; all army units sent their reports to the adjutant general of the next highest command (the Office of Adjutant General being the record keeping agency of the miltary). The Records of the United States Army Continental Commands is of additional help. These records cover large and varied collections of army documents and correspon-dence, some of which cannot be found in the Adjutant General's records.

In the Interior Department files, the most significant documents are found in the correspondence of the Commissioner of Indian Affairs. The Letters Sent by the Commissioner include a few notations over the years, often important policy statements. But the information is scarce. The Letters Received by the Commissioner comprise the single-best government source on intertribal conflict and attempts to stop it. Microfilmed and organized according to Superintendencies and Agencies and located at the branch archive centers and, in small quantities, at university libraries, this set of records comprises more pertinent information than any source. The Letters Received not only contain the agents' writings, but also include copies of important correspondence by army personnel, as well as letters from other people directly or indirectly involved in Indian affairs: traders, freighters, peace commissioners, missionaries, and soldiers.

Government documents include the most extensive information on tribal war after the Civil War and provide wide varieties of viewpoints. But there are other sources of note which give different perceptions of the subject. First are a number of autobiographies by men involved directly or indirectly with the Indians and their warfare. Retired army officers like Captain John Bourke (*On the Border with Crook*, 1892) and Colonel Henry Carrington (*AB-SA-RA-KA, Land of Massacre*, 1879) wrote about their careers, often including information on intertribal fighting tactics. The best book of this kind is *Military Life in Dakota: The Journal of Philippe Regis de Trobriand*, published in 1951. In describing the action surrounding the Three Tribes, de Trobriand made precise and thought-provoking analyses of Indian culture, including warfare. Another informative autobiography is the one by the Montana pioneer, Granville Stuart. In *Forty Years on the Frontier* (1925), Stuart wrote from the point of view of a cattleman concerned about the detrimental effects on stockmen of the last days of Indian raiding, but he did so with some expertise and attention to facts.

The reminiscences by Indians, or white people very closely involved with Indian culture, also comprise important late nineteenth century sources. These stories often reached far back before the late 1800s. The work done in the 1870s by the young Lieutenant James Bradley is an example. As commander of scouts for Colonel John Gibbon in the Sioux campaigns, Bradley studied in some detail his Crow scouts' culture. He questioned his men about Indian lives and warfare and wrote down information that in some instances extended back to the 1780s.

Later, in the early twentieth century, a number of individuals did work similar to Bradley's, in this case transcribing the dictated experiences of old Indians. George E. Hyde did a very thorough job of recording George Bent's experiences, which became the *Life of George*

Bent (1967). George Bird Grinnell wrote about the cultures of the Cheyennes, Pawnees, and Blackfeet, drawing on interviews with people he was close to in those tribes. The resulting books, *Pawnee Hero Stores and Folk Tales* (1889), *Pawnee, Blackfoot, and Cheyenne* (1912), and *The Fighting Cheyennes* (1915), contain helpful information on tribal war. In the 1920s, the anthropologist William Wildscut wrote a manuscript dictated by the Crow warrior Two Leggings. Published in 1967 by Peter Nabakov, *Two Leggings, The Making of a Crow Warrior* (1967) provides a very personal and specific account of one man's drive toward success in warfare. In the early 1900s, John Stands in the Timber, historian for the Cheyennes, collected documents and stories alike to portray his tribe in the old buffalo days. In 1967, aided by Margot Liberty, he published *Cheyenne Memories*. Amateur scholars also contributed to the accumulation of oral history. Frank Linderman, a rancher who was friendly with the Crows, prepared the dictated biographies *Plenty-Coups, Chief of the Crows* (1930) and *Pretty Shield, Medicine Woman of the Crows* (1932). Together, they provide male and female perceptions of intertribal fighting. Thomas Marquis, a physician working on the Crow and Northern Cheyenne Reservations in the 1920s and 1930s, wrote a biography of a well-known Cheyenne warrior, Wooden Leg. This book, *Wooden Leg, A Warrior Who Fought Custer* (1931) provides excellent information on a young man's search for military status near the end of tribal confrontations.

White men who married Indian women and lived with a tribe — "squaw men" in the contemporary jargon — often amassed a vast knowledge of their adopted tribes. Such was the case of Thomas Leforge for the Crows and James Willard Schultz for the Blackfeet. Their stories are good sources because they obtained information both from their own experiences in raiding and from the stories of Indians with whom they were well-acquainted. Leforge wrote *Memoirs of a White Crow Indian* (1928) and Schultz was responsible for two books, *Blackfeet and Buffalo* (1962) and *My Life as An Indian* (1935).

These books, coming primarily from remembrances of old people, have both positive elements and historical problems. They include a wealth of authentic experiences. Even though the Indians sometimes mixed up names and time periods, their memories in some areas, like those of most nonliterate people, were remarkable. Yet it is important to deal objectively with these stories. An account of raiding done by one tribe might vary from another in the particulars of grading war honors, the size of war parties, the emphasis on various types of raiding, and so on. In addition, warriors far advanced in age sometimes maintained a certain animosity towards other tribes and even towards their old comrades who were also their rivals in competing for coups. One warrior's perception of warfare should be cross-checked with other sources, just like an Indian agent's words must be compared to the opinions of other people or an agent supporting an opposing tribe. As an example, Two Legging's concept of the importance of war might be compared to that of Plenty Coups, a very important chief of the same tribe. Two Leggings' view of the Crows' success in war and how war was ended could also be compared to army and agent records on the same subjects. In this cross referencing a more objective picture appears.

After the end of intertribal warfare in the late 1800s, in addition to army officers' autobiographies and warriors' reminiscences, other works recorded the phenomenon of tribal war. Myriads of young anthropologists, spurred on by the new approach of the influential scholar Franz Boas who advocated firsthand observation of Indian culture, entered the plains and other Indian lands in the early 1900s to do field work with various tribes. The result was a number of ethnological studies. Some of them included important cultural information on tribal warfare: Frances Densmore's *Teton Sioux Music* (1918) and *Mandan and Hidatsa Music* (1923); Robert Lowie's *The Crow Indians* (1935); James Teit's *Salishan Tribes of the Western Plateau* (1930); David Mandelbaum's *The Plains Cree* (1940); and Clark Wissler's *Material Culture of the Blackfoot Indians* (1910).

It was not long before tribal warfare became involved in the anthropologists' theoretical debates. A major area of contention was the idea that Indian societies were static and unchanging versus the theory that they were dynamic cultures and that outside influences continually changed them. The impact of the horse on the plains culture and its association with warfare became a point of contention early in the debate. Clark Wissler, in *Material Culture of the Blackfoot Indians* (1910), maintained that the horse had no significant effect on an already-established society. But A. L. Kroeber, in "Ethnology of the Gros Ventre (Atsina)," *Anthropological Papers of the American Museum of Natural History* (1908), contended that the horse was revolutionary in changing the culture. More recently, John C. Ewers took more of a middle position in *The Horse in Blackfoot Indian Culture* (1955), but emphasized the idea of the strong economic and tactical impact of the horse upon warfare. Horses provided a new form of wealth, caused more close combat, but probably made for fewer large massacres. Gilbert Roe, in *The Indian and the Horse* (1955), added to the discussion by pointing out that the horse did not revolutionize warfare, but did perpetuate it and forced a change in some techniques.

Over the years, two major schools evolved. One in agreement with Kroeber's ideas followed the concept of dynamic change and the importance of economic determinism in Indian culture and war. Scholars pursuing Wissler's position supported the theory of unchanging societies which included warfare that was essentially a "gamelike" social phenomenon not economically determined.

Among Kroeber's disciples, Bernard Mishkin, in *Rank and Warfare Among the Plains Indians* (1940), emphasized changing plains cultures and the overwhelming importance of economics in warfare. Oscar Lewis applied this economic approach to Blackfoot culture in his 1942 monograph, *The Effects of White Contact Upon Blackfoot Culture, With Special Reference to the Fur Trade*. Frank Raymond Secoy's *Changing Military Patterns on the Great Plains* (1953) stresses the importance of the horse and gun in changing warfare and causing the struggle to be one for survival. In 1962, Symmes Oliver's monograph, *Ecology and Cultural Continuity as a Contributing Factor in the Social Organization of the Plains Indians* supported Secoy's view. Oliver emphasized the evolutionary aspects of the plains tribes and their wars.

The most sophisticated explanation of tribal warfare from the "dynamic" school of ethnologists is W. W. Newcomb Jr.'s article, "A Re-Examination of the Causes of the Plains Warfare," *American Anthropologist* (1950). After reviewing the literature, Newcomb argued against the theory that warfare was essentially a "game." He favored the economic motive. Newcomb pointed to the all important impacts of the horse and gun, along with tribal migration and decreasing game, as causes for the wars to become economic struggles over the diminishing buffalo herds. Newcomb's thesis, however, became rather inconclusive and almost contradictory when he explained individual motives for war. The warrior, he maintained, might have lived for war because it was an expression of his society, but in reality, he fought because of long range economic and political forces.

The "static" school, against which Newcomb argued, is one that has interpreted warfare primarily as an unchanging competition between warriors for honor and status, fought against enemies over whom the warrior must prove his superior courage. Besides Wissler's studies, the classic work by Harry Holbert Turney-High, *Primitive War* (1949), is a basis to this theory as well as a pioneering effort to describe all aboriginal warfare. The book provides a sweeping view of tribal conflicts as compared to the warfare of civilized societies. It is a good starting point for the subject of intertribal conflict. Robert Lowie, in *Indians of the Plains* (1954) and other works, followed the idea that the real objectives of war were not to acquire land but to attain horses, revenge, and glory. Marian Smith, in her article, "The War Complex of the Plains Indians," *Proceedings of the Amerian Philosophical Society* (1938), made a close study of plains warfare and concluded that it was one of the most important socializing institutions of the culture. She wrote that the practice of war was not economic, but was primarily for the purpose of showing one's superiority over an opponent. George Bird Grinnell, in "Coup and Scalp Among the Plains Indians," *American Anthropologist* (1910), wrote about this extreme competition especially in terms of counting coup, most tribes' ultimate war honor.

Besides the efforts of the two distinct schools examining plains warfare, one anthropological study used quantitative analysis, extending the study of tribal conflict into a new research area. Donald G. Callaway, in his unpublished Ph.D. dissertation, *Raiding and Feuding Among Western North American Indians* (University of Michigan, 1978), examined far western tribal conflicts in the Great Basin, Southwest, California, and Northwest Coast cultures. He concluded that not only economic forces at work in many of the tribes, but also many other factors determined whether a culture was oriented toward raiding to a greater or lesser extent. Callaway's study and all the anthropological works have value in providing the historian with an understanding of the strictly cultural side of intertribal warfare, in particular distinguishing between the unique methods and motives of war in different nomadic tribes.

The drawback of the ethnological approach is the absence of the historical perspective: when and why events happened; what was the continuity of historical development; and most of all, what was the influence of various historical periods when whites recorded intertribal fighting as they perceived it and then tried to control it and bring it to a close. The school of anthropologists which emphasizes the dynamic changes in society has taken a major step in the use of historical sources. This is particularly true of Lewis and Secoy. However, the documentation is sparse according to historical standards and often depends on a few well-used sources. For instance, the major historical source for ethnologists showing changes in warfare, from foot nomads to mounted warriors with guns, is the old Cree, Saukamappe. Admittedly, David Thompson's interviews with him are a valuable source, but they still provide only one person's interpretation of several decades.

One scholar who has managed to combine both anthropological and historical materials to give a balanced view of Indian culture and war is the ethnohistorian, John C. Ewers. He effectively used this methodology in his study, *The Horse in Blackfoot Indian Culture* (1955) and particularly so in his tribal history, *The Blackfeet, Raiders on the Northwestern Plains* (1958). More recently in his article, "Intertribal Warfare as the Precursor of Indian-White Warfare on the Northern Great Plains," *Western Historical Quarterly* (1975), Ewers pointed out how Indian wars and alliances with the whites were both a continuation and an integral part of old intertribal enmities and alliances.

Other historical coverage of intertribal conflict has been sparse, too often replaced by the more popular books on the wars between the plains Indians and the United States Army. The 1960s and 1970s, eliciting popular books on the struggle of the Indians to defend their land, did bring about at least one book that sought a similarly popular appeal for tribal war. *Seven Arrows*, written in 1972 by Hyemeyohsts Storm, is an interesting story of plains Indian life, told from the philosophical approach of Indian spiritualism. The theory of tribal warfare, however, is absurd. The author claimed that the white man's influence changed an intertribal warfare that was somewhat idyllic into a conflict based on greed and materialism.

A number of good tribal histories besides Ewers' book do exist and include material on intertribal rivalries. George E. Hyde's histories of the Brules and Oglalas, *Spotted Tail's Folk* (1961) and *Red Cloud's Folk* (1937) are the foremost examples of the use of intertribal conflict in tribal histories. Hyde pointed to raiding as a primary part of Teton Sioux culture which extended into the wars with the white soldiers. Royal M. Hassrick, in *The Sioux: Life and Customs of a Warrior Society* (1964), also dealt with tribal warfare. His coverage was brief and more general, but included the important social and psychological aspects of warfare in the Sioux's cultural pattern. Ewers, in his history of the Blackfeet, went beyond the years of raiding to show the problems that developed for the warriors when the old raiding habits were lost during reservation life.

Other tribal histories also include information on intertribal conflict. Grinnell's *Fighting Cheyennes* and *Pawnee Hero Stories and Folk Tales* have significant sections devoted to tribal war. Virginia Cole Trenholm and Maurine Corley, in *The Shoshonis: Sentinels of the Rockies* (1964), wrote of that tribe's many wars, including the Shoshonis' importance as allies of the whites against the hostile Sioux and Cheyennes. *Flathead and Kootenay*, written in 1969 by Olga Weydemeyer Johnson, not only detailed wars with the enemy Blackfeet but also explained the ambiguity of tribal warfare. Michael S. Kennedy, editor of *The Assiniboines* (1961), included stories illustrating the importance of warfare in that northern plains tribe.

A recent tribal history of a different sort is *People of the Sacred Mountain*, written by Father Peter John Powell and published in 1981. Powell wrote a history of the Cheyennes using mainly the people themselves and their stories which have been passed down through the years. The book is primarily concerned with the individual battles of the Cheyennes against other tribes and the Americans. Photographs of individuals, most of them warriors, fill the two volumes. Pictures drawn by the Cheyennes complement the photographs. The pictures are nineteenth-century pictographs, drawn by warriors on the white man's ledger paper, to portray the artists' battle feats. It is significant that such a book, put together from the memories and traditions of a plains tribe, gives a primary cultural position to warfare.

Besides tribal histories, several biographies place tribal war in a place of importance. Mari Sandoz' *Crazy Horse* (1942) and Stanley Vestal's *Sitting Bull* (1957) show the significance of warfare in establishing the careers of these important Sioux leaders. Sandoz also described the ambiguity of Indian warfare and how Crazy Horse attempted to go beyond the limited type of combat in order to prepare a more effective military challenge to the whites. More recent is Hugh Dempsey's biography of the Blackfoot leader, *Crowfoot* (1972). Dempsey dealt primarily with Crowfoot in his later years after he retired from the warpath, but it is obvious that his great prestige came from previous courage and leadership displayed in battle.

In 1975, Stephen Ambrose wrote a different kind of biography, *Crazy Horse and Custer*, in which he described the parallel lives of these two leaders. Several good examples of tribal conflict are included in the book. Of most interest was a spontaneous competition between Crazy Horse and Sitting Bull to see who was most brave. They carried it out in front of white soldiers defending the Northern Pacific Railroad crews. Considering that both of these leaders attempted to organize Indian alliances to fight the Americans using white men's tactics, this incident is illuminating in showing the extent to which all Indian leaders and warriors were inextricably tied to their unique traditional methods of making war.

A few historical works have dealt more directly with intertribal conflict. In 1972, Thomas E. Mails wrote *Mystic Warriors of the Plains*. Essentially a technical description of plains Indian culture, the book includes much detail on equipment and techniques used in fighting. Mails' own illustrations add to the book's completeness and accuracy.

Arthur Roy Buntin's M.A. thesis, *Battleground* (Montana State University, 1952), covers tribal warfare in the area of eastern Montana and regions close by. Considering the sources he used, which are limited, Buntin gave an accurate description of the fighting. His conclusion that economics was responsible for the warfare is also limited in scope and tends to oversimplify a complex system of conflict. Buntin did go beyond other authors, however, in attempting to explain how tribal war came to an end, even though in this area he lacks sufficient sources. Buntin saw the United States government as active in ending the war, but he gave too much credit to the idea of the Indians turning to farming as a reason for warfare ending, a conclusion that is hardly justified by historical records.

An important part the white influence on, and indirect encouragement of, tribal warfare was the hiring of friendly warriors to fight the hostile tribes. Ewers, in his article "Intertribal Warfare as the Precursor of Indian-White Warfare on the Northern Great Plains," noted that it was natural for the Indians to ally with the whites when it helped them against their other enemies. Grinnell's 1928 book, *Two Great Scouts and Their Pawnee Battalion*, gives a thorough description of the Pawnees' use of the system of alliances to wreak vengeance on their old Sioux and Cheyenne opponents. Thomas W. Dunlay's book, *Wolves for the Blue Soldiers* (1982), is a definitive study of this portion of Indian studies. He gave background to earlier frontier use of Indian auxiliaries but concentrated on the far west. Despite his thorough coverage, Dunlay's explanation for the Indians' role in the alliances fell somewhat short of the whole picture. He emphasized the economic aspects of war without doing much with the important motive of warriors wanting to continue a way of life that gave them social status.

In recent years, several significant articles have been written about intertribal conflict. Although Ewers' "Intertribal Warfare As the Precursor of Indian-White Warfare on the Northern Great Plains" adds no particularly new information, it is important as a reminder that the time-honored intertribal competition operated long before the wars with the whites. Ewers emphasized the important power of tribalism and the resulting aggressiveness that brought about years of war and alliances as well as trading patterns.

Colin G. Calloway has written two articles that speak directly or indirectly of tribal war. "Swordbearer and the 'Crow Outbreak,' 1887," *Montana, The Magazine of Western History* (1986) shows how important raiding was to the Crows. The practice of war even led them to challenge the authority of their long-time American friends. "The Inter-Tribal Balance of Power on the Great Plains, 1760-1850," *American Studies* (1982) demonstrates the great importance that the white man's trade had as an integral part of the wars between the plains tribes. However, Calloway's description of tribal war is based only on survival and economic motivations and does not include other explanations. Another article, dealing with the relationship of trade to tribal conflict, is Gary Clayton Anderson's "Early Dakota Migration and Intertribal Warfare," *Western Historical Quarterly* (1980). This led to his book, *Kinsmen of Another Kind: Dakota-White Relations in the Upper Mississippi Valley, 1650-1862* (1984). These works cover an area peripheral to the northern plains, but the author presented the new conclusion that the attractiveness, to the Sioux, of European trade was as important to the nation's migration out of the woodland area as was any pressure from the Ojibwas. In his book, Anderson emphasized the importance of kinship in Sioux dealings with each other and outsiders. This is closely related to Ewers' emphasis on tribalism as a key adjunct to intertribal conflict.

Another article relating trade and tribal war is one by William Cronon and Richard White, "Indians in the Land," *American Heritage* (1986). Although not a documented scholarly article, it is nevertheless important in bringing out major ideas of two important environmental historians. In their article, written as a conversation between them, one of the significant points was how stealing in warfare closely related to the various ways in which tribes exchanged goods, including trade. This idea, combined with Ewers' stress on tribalism, Anderson's emphasis on kinship, and the many examples of the Indians' formal adoption in order to have a truce, illustrates the complexity of intertribal relations. American and Canadian officials saw Indian warfare only in terms of white culture; it was therefore impossible for them to thoroughly understand it. In trying to stop the warring, whites never realized the depth of cultural meaning they were invading.

Adding to the economic definition of this cultural complexity and coming before the *Amrican Heritage* article, in 1978, *The Journal of American History* published Richard White's article, "The Winning of the West: The Expansion of the Western Sioux in the Eighteenth and Nineteenth Centuries." Most important of the recent studies, this article takes the old argument of dynamic plains societies fighting an economic warfare and applies it to a historical interpretation of tribal war. White reviewed the literature briefly, though by no means completely, mainly choosing to emphasize those scholars who favored the economic interpretation of warfare. While including a general look at anthropological scholarship, White did not do much with the brief historical literature on tribal conflict. Instead, the value of the article lies in its examination of important ideas.

White contended that nineteenth-century warfare, in particular that associated with the Sioux advance, was not static but was a constantly changing conflict. He illustrated this with the Teton Sioux, reinforced by their Yanktonai brethren, moving inexorably through the northern plains. Through the power of numbers, the strong nation was able to push aside some tribes and seriously threaten the livelihood of others. White saw this as an economic conflict over hunting grounds and asserted that it was not a "game," but a deadly battle for survival with dire consequences for the weaker opponents of the Sioux. In particular, White effectively described when the Sioux conquered specific hunting grounds held by other tribes.

In general, this thesis is correct, but it must be qualified. A number of scholars have shown how tribes in the plains were constantly replacing others in the ongoing search for game. Secoy, in *Changing Military Patterns on the Great Plains*; Hyde, in *Indians of the High Plains from Prehistoric Times to the Coming of the Europeans* (1959); and others have demonstrated how the Pawnees, Shoshonis, Crows, Blackfeet, Comanches, and other people replaced resident tribes in their movements through the plains. Beginning in the eighteenth century, migrations of Europeans, Americans, and other Indians, and the introduction of guns, horses, and disease continued this migrating process. Both historians and contemporaries argued that the Sioux (and the Blackfeet at an earlier time) threatened the existence of smaller tribes. Ewers, for instance, pointed out the possibility that the Blackfeet might have eventually destroyed the Crows.

This description of intertribal conflict and the direction it took in the 1800s, however, is an oversimplification of a complex cultural and historical phenomenon. Certainly, tribal warfare was concerned with the economics of trade and hunting grounds; its impact could also be devastating to some tribes, especially the sedentary ones, as the conflict changed with technology and increased migration. What White and others left out were the tremendously influential effects of noneconomic motives and the fact that, while warfare changed and the Sioux became more dominant and threatening, much of the fighting remained the same in terms of the methods used and the results attained.

By the time the Sioux achieved their military supremacy after the Civil War, the custom of raiding had long been the major cultural force in each of the tribes of the northern plains. The major impetus for war was still the individual motives that Newcomb said were only subliminal causes. Cutting horses, counting coups, and performing other feats of daring comprised the only way a man could gain importance in tribal society. Warfare was intermixed with other customs to such an extent that all tribal institutions strongly supported it. Even women, who had so much to lose in terms of husbands, brothers, fathers, and sons, as well as their own lives, directly and indirectly encouraged war. As White pointed out, the Sioux sent their war parties to attack other tribes and take their hunting lands. But in most cases the Sioux hunted at will anyway, particularly on Pawnee land. Then they went on to harrass that nation for the usual variety of purposes: obtaining revenge, taking horses, and gaining other war honors.

The belief that the Sioux "armies" had great destructive power has a long historical background, much of it based on the mistaken thinking that the plains Indians were an effective modern military force that challenged the United States Army. White, supported by the ideas of Ewers, saw the potential Sioux destruction of small tribes. This theory of tribal war has often been based on the theories of some early traders as well as statements made by a few old warriors reminiscing about the early glory days and reliving apparent tribal greatness. Much of this information was inaccurate and often based on the bravado and boasting that was typical of plains combatants.

In reality, while the war parties of the Sioux (and the Blackfeet before them) were numerous, the methods of fighting defied any consistent success or the destruction of another tribe, although over the years there was a definite drain in the forces of most small tribes, the sedentary ones in particular. The system of warfare placed utmost emphasis upon not losing men who provided food for their societies. In battle, individual feats were of key importance, overriding the success of the group as a whole. These characteristics kept warfare at a level of individual competition with such limited casualties that the losses were manageable in the closely-knit tribal society.

In terms of tribal destruction, it is difficult to say what would have happened to some small tribes if the United States had not motified the Sioux threat in the late 1870s. As White and other historians have pointed out, the continual Sioux raids definitely threatened the livelihood of sedentary tribes like the Pawnees. Eventually the Pawnees moved to Indian territory, in part because of this threat. Yet, at the same time, their warriors continued to raid the Sioux and Cheyennes, and in addition, many of the Pawnees did not want to leave their supposedly threatened homeland. Other small tribes, especially the more mobile nomadic people like the Crows, Assiniboins, and Shoshonis also remained willing to fight well past the times when they were supposedly in great danger from the Sioux or Blackfeet. The Sioux were a threat to a number of tribal societies, but it would be hard to prove that they were actually on the brink of destroying or annihilating those small cultures.

The crucial impact on intertribal conflict not yet adequately covered in history or ethnology is the long-term influence of the Americans and other whites. From the beginning of the fur trade through the late 1800s, traders, missionaries, cattlemen, government officials, and others made conscious efforts to mold tribal war to their own uses and, especially, to control it and bring it to an end.

The various policies, even of the government, were not consistent, but in general, they pointed toward the need to end the conflict. United States officials saw raiding as a practice that interfered with the white man's economic pursuits, the settlement of the plains, and, finally, the civilizing process laid out for the Indian people. Ultimately, the future of tribal war and the question of its destructive potential became a moot point. The movement of Americans onto the plains, the elimination of the buffalo, and finally the government's policy of stopping intertribal raiding, all led to the end of the warriors' days of glory.

The British, Canadian, and American impact on tribal war was an important part of the total intercultural dealings between whites and Indians. The historical sources make this clear as one goes from the earliest writings through the 1880s. During the late 1800s, the concern about Indian warfare and how to stop it became an increasingly important part of most historical documents. This is a topic little researched up until now and is therefore a major subject of this study.

ENDNOTES

ABBREVIATION GUIDE FOR NATIONAL ARCHIVES

1. Archival Depositories

CU	Colorado University Libraries
DFRC	Denver Federal Records Center
KCFRC	Kansas City Federal Records Center
NA	National Archives Building

2. National Archives Microfilm Publications

Adjutant General's Office

M666	Letters Received Main Series, 1871-80
M689	Letters Received Main Series, 1881-89

Bureau of Indian Affairs

M5	Records of the Washington Superintendency of Indian Affairs
M21	Letters Sent by the Commissioner of Indian Affairs, 1824-81
M234	Letters Received by the Commissioner of Indian Affairs, 1829-81

3. Record Groups (RG) of the National Archives

RG 48	Records of the Office of Secretary of Interior
RG 75	Records of the Bureau of Indian Affairs
RG 94	Records of the Adjutant General's Office, 1780's-1917
RG 107	Records of the Office of Secretary of War
RG 393	Records of the United States Army Continental Commands, 1821-1920

4. Titles

A.G.	Adjutant General
A.A.G.	Assistant Adjutant General
LB	Letterbook

Note to Readers: Endnotes are greatly abbreviated. See Bibliography for complete citations.

Chapter 1 Endnotes

[1] Smith, *Verendryes*, 52-61, 88-94; Wood and Theissen, *Fur Trade*, 3-5; Verendrye, *Journals*, 26-7, 322-3, 332-6, 366.

[2] Verendrye, *Journals*, 412-6, 418-21, 428-9; Ewers, "Intertribal Warfare," 397-8.

[3] Verendrye, *Journals*, 412-6, 418-21.

[4] *Ibid.*, 1-2.

[5] *Ibid.*, 454-6.

[6] Isham, *Observations*, 113-4.

[7] Hendry, *Journal*, 333-5, 339, 346-7, 351.

[8] Cocking, *Journal*, 106, 110-2; Graham, "Observations on Hudson's Bay," Appendix B of Isham, *Observations*, 310-1.

[9] Secoy, *Military Patterns*, Chapters III-VI.

[10] Thompson, *Narrative*, xvi-xix, lxi-lxiv.

[11] *Ibid.*, 327-36; Verendrye, *Journals*, 412.

[12] Thompson, *Narrative*, 327-36, 339, 348.

[13] *Ibid.*, 327-8, 345, 348; Umfreville, *Hudson's Bay*, 177, 200; Hyde, *High Plains*, 117-44, 146-58.

[14] Hyde, *High Plains*, 164-5; Wood and Theissen, *Fur Trade*, 6.

[15] Hyde, *High Plains*, 164-5, 171-4; Thompson, *Narrative*, 337-44.

[16] Thompson, *Narrative*, 337-44.

[17] Secoy, *Military Patterns*, 51-3; Lewis, *Blackfoot Culture*, 52-6; Ewers, *Horse*, 173-5.

[18] McDonnell, "Red River," 281; M'Gillivray, *Journal*, 26-7, 39, 62-3, 70, 73; MacKenzie, *Voyages*, xlix.

[19] M'Gillivray, *Journal*, 14-6, 34, 44-5, 56, 62-3, 76, 78.

[20] McDonald, "Autobiographical Notes," 19, 81-2.

[21] Trudeau, "Description," 167-70, 172-3; Trudeau, "Journal," 9, 12, 15-6, 22-3, 28-9, 38-9. 45-8.

[22] Trudeau, "Journal," 22, 35-45, 45-7.

[23] MacKenzie, *Voyages*, lxx, lxxi; Thompson, *Narrative*, 345.

Chapter 2 Endnotes

[1] The word Sioux, used by their enemies, meant "enemy." The Sioux called themselves "Dakota", meaning "friend" or "ally". The Dakota tribes were originally a woodland and lake culture, living near the western end of Lake Superior. Beginning in the 1600s they began to migrate south and west into the prairie regions of present-day Minnesota because of the pressure of the Ojibwa, or Chippewa, tribe and the attraction of European trade. The term Dakota is used in this work to refer to all the Sioux, on or near the plains, but in actuality the word had three derivations corresponding to the three divisions of the Dakota nation. The four eastern tribes, collectively referred to as the Santees, called themselves Nakotas. They remained in present-day

Minnesota and the eastern portions of North and South Dakota, combining their woodland culture with the buffalo hunting of the prairie culture. The term Dakota officially was the name for the central division of Sioux. Consisting of the two large tribes — the Yankton and Yanktonai — they were prairie, buffalo hunting people who lived on the eastern side of the Missouri River. The Lakotas made up the western division, consisting of seven tribes. They migrated west of the Missouri River and became nomadic plains hunters. Popularly called the Teton Sioux, these western Sioux became the dominant force on the northern plains.

² Lewis and Clark, *Journals*, I, 102, 111-2, 26-32, 167; VII, 315.

³ Tabeau, *Narrative*, 127-9.

⁴ *Ibid.*, 129-30, 173; Lewis and Clark, *Journals*, VII, 248, 285-6.

⁵ Lewis and Clark, *Journals*, VII, 248, 285-6.

⁶ Thompson, *Narrative*, 212; Henry and Thompson, *New Light*, I, 314, 334, 336, 372-3; II 512-3, 516, 520.

⁷ Henry and Thompson, *New Light*, I, 354, 377-95; Cronon and White "Indians in the Land," 23-4.

⁸ Tabeau, *Narrative*, 204-5.

⁹ Lewis and Clark, *Journals*, III, 29-30.

¹⁰ Jackson ed., *Letters*, 282; Lewis and Clark, *Journals*, I, 241, 249, 252; VII, 306.

¹¹ MacKenzie, "Mississouri [sic] Indians," 327, 373-82; Larocque, "Missouri Journal," 301, 306; Lewis and Clark, *Journals*, I, 222-3, 229-33, 241, 267, 286.

¹² Clark and Edmonds, *Sacagawea*, 7-8.

¹³ *Ibid.*, 23-9; Lewis and Clark, *Journals*, II, 252, 350, 373-4.

¹⁴ Lewis and Clark, *Journals*, II, 383-4; III, 29-30; V, 19, 23, 24-5, 223-6.

¹⁵ *Ibid.*, VII, 381, 383.

¹⁶ Larocque, "Assiniboine to the Yellowstone," 22, 24, 44; see also Bruner, "Mandan," 201.

¹⁷ Larocque, "Assiniboine to the Yellowstone," 39-40, 65.

¹⁸ *Ibid.*, 65; MacKenzie, "Mississouri [sic] Indians," 345-6.

¹⁹ Henry and Thompson, *New Light*, II, 530-1, 726.

²⁰ Thompson, *Narrative*, LXXX, 375.

²¹ *Ibid.*

²² *Ibid.*, 379-84

²³ *Ibid.*, 423-8; Henry and Thompson, *New Light*, II, 643-4.

²⁴ Henry and Thompson, *New Light*, II, 712-3, 726.

²⁵ *Ibid.*, II, 643-4, 658; Thompson, *Narrative*, 423-8.

²⁶ Thompson, *Narrative*, 465-6, 546-55.

Chapter 3 Endnotes

¹ Bradbury, *Travels*, 49, 77-8, 80, 103-4, 108.

² Irving, *Astoria*, 186-197.

³ *Ibid.*, 195, 201; Bradbury, *Travels*, 176-7.

⁴ Bradbury, *Travels*, 136-7, 168-72.

[5] *Ibid.*; Brackenridge, *Journal,* 117-8.

[6] Brackenridge, *Journal,* 119, 123, 128-9.

[7] Irving, *Astoria,* 221.

[8] *Ibid.,* 224-5; Catlin, *Letters and Notes,* I, 53-4.

[9] Irving, *Astoria,* 252; Cox, *Columbia,* 135, 188, 263, 264; Bradley, "Manuscript, Book II," 156-61.

[10] Stuart, *Oregon Trail,* 4-18.

[11] *Ibid.,* 76, 98, 118-9, 82, 132-3.

[12] *Ibid.,* 4-18; Bradley, "Manuscript, Book II," 153-4.

[13] Bradley, "Various Selections," 307-10.

[14] *Ibid.,* 299-307, 312-3; Bradley, "Manuscripts, Book II and Book F," 156-61, 224-8.

[15] Bradley, "Manuscript, Book F," 236-44.

[16] Maximillian, *Travels,* 232-3.

[17] James, *Account,* XV, 157-60; XVI, 214-8.

[18] *Ibid.,* XVII, 154.

[19] *Ibid.,* XV, 79-93.

[20] Nichols, ed., *Missouri Expedition, 1818-1820,* 1109; Reid and Gannon, eds., "Atkinson-O'Fallon Expedition," 30-2.

[21] Simpson, *Journal,* 21-2, 55-6, 224; Ross, *Fur Hunters,* 122-3, 150-1, 155-9, 161, 169-71.

[22] Athearn, *Forts,* 6-11.

[23] William Clark to James Barbour, March 1, 1826, St. Louis Superintendency, RG75, M234, 747/341, DFRC; P. Wilson to Benjamin O'Fallon, October 23, 1824, Upper Missouri Agency, RG 75, M234, 883/20-2, DFRC; Kappler ed., *Indian Affairs,* 219-62.

[24] Athearn, *Forts,* 18.

Chapter 4 Endnotes

[1] Denig, *Five Indian Tribes,* 161-9.

[2] *Ibid.,* 93-4; De Smet, *Life,* III, 948, 1187-9; J. J. Abert to the Secretary of War, May 7, 1847, RG 107, M222, 34/4011, DFRC.

[3] Work, *Snake Country,* 11, 30, 41-9, 71, 76-7; *Journal,* 110-3, 122-3, 137-8; Leonard, *Adventures,* 42-6; Irving, *Bonneville,* 57-63, 50, 102, 217; Miller, *West,* 148; Ferris, *Life,* 183-4.

[4] De Smet, *Life,* II, 584-99; II, 953-4; Point, *Kingdom,* 102-3.

[5] De Smet, *Life,* III, 1122; II, 519-21.

[6] Mandelbaum, *Plains Cree,* 195, 295, 297.

[7] De Smet, *Life,* III, 1122; II, 519-21.

[8] Maximilian, *Travels,* 146-53; Chittenden, *Fur Trade,* I, 336, 388, 673-6.

[9] Denig, *Five Tribes,* 172-83; Bradley, "Affairs at Fort Benton," 210-6 and "Various Selections," 340-1; Algier, "Meldrum," 38-40.

[10] Catlin, *Indians,* I, 36, 42, 48, 53-4, 59-60, 44-6 , 33-4.

¹¹ Denig, *Five Tribes*, 11-3; Ewers, *Blackfeet*, 64-5.

¹² Bradley, "Manuscript — Book II," 153-4; Denig, *Five Tribes*, 142; Maximilian, *Travels*, XXII, 351-3.

¹³ Leland, ed., *Beckwourth*, 147, 256; Irving, *Bonneville*, 33, 35; Ferris, *Life*, 303-5; Bradley, "Various Selections," 288; Leonard, *Adventures*, 142-3, 140; Lowie, *Crow Indians*, 216-7; Ewers, *Horse*, 213-4.

¹⁴ Leonard, *Adventures*, 51; Ferris, *Life*, 305-6; Russell, *Journal*, 70-3, 145-6, 149; Miller, *West*, 144, 145, 39, 15; Hamilton, *Sixty Years*, 136-7.

¹⁵ Denig, *Five Tribes*, 58; Maximilian, *Travels*, XXIII, 394; Irving Jr., *Sketches*, 189-90.

¹⁶ Ferris, *Life*, 312-3, 29, 32; Irving, *Bonneville*, 34, 38; Anderson, *Journal*, 190-1; Hyde, *Red Cloud's Folk*, 51.

¹⁷ White, "Winning of the West," 335-7; Denig, *Five Tribes*, 21, 25; Preuss, *Exploring*, 30; De Smet, *Life*, II, 629-31.

¹⁸ Denig, *Five Tribes*, xv-xxv, 89-90, 145-6; White, "Winning of the West," 319-20.

¹⁹ Denig, *Five Tribes*, 152, 161-9, 195, 200, 148; Joshua Pilcher to William Clark, September 15, 1838, Upper Missouri Agency, RG 75, M234, 884/369, DFRC; Ewers, *Blackfeet*, 185-8; De Smet, *Life*, II, 524-5.

²⁰ Catlin, *Indians*, I, 48-9; Irving, *Bonneville*, 366-8; Denig, *Five Tribes*, 204; John C. Ewers also supports this theory, using as evidence Denig, Catlin, and statements of some of his Blood and Piegan informants in the 1940s. See Ewers, "Intertribal Warfare," 406.

Chapter 5 Endnotes

¹ Denig, *Five Tribes*, 57-9 ff.

² Catlin, *Indians*, I, 211, 166-74; Maximilian, *Travels*, XXIII, 261.

³ Joshua Pilcher to William Clark, September 18, 1838, Upper Missouri Agency, RG 75, M234, 884/357-8, DFRC; Chardon, *Journal*, 124-5.

⁴ Denig, *Five Tribes*, 73-8, 90-1, 94-5, 89; Kurz, *Journal*, 179; Bradley, "Various Selections," 288; Rodnick, *Assiniboine*, 1-4.

⁵ Maximilian, *Travels*, XXIII, 230-2; XXIV, 13-4, 54; Chardon, *Journal*, general coverage.

⁶ Catlin, *Indians*, I, 211; Denig, *Five Tribes*, 22-4; Report of Alfred D. Vaughan, September 20, 1853, Report of the Commissioner, 1853, 353; Warren, *Exploration*, 632-3.

⁷ Denig, *Five Tribes*, 24-7, 46-7; Warren, *Exploration*, 632-3, 662-4.

⁸ John Dougherty to William Clark, July 29, 1831; David D. Mitchell to W. P. Richardson, February 2, 1842, St. Louis Superintendency, Vol. 6, 2/238-41, Vol. 7, 2/151-2, KCFRC; Dougherty to Clark, November 20, 1832 and August 20, 1835, Upper Missouri Agency, RG 75, M234, 883/261-2, 490, DFRC; Dougherty to Clark, June 8, 1836, Council Bluffs Agency, RG 75, M234, 215/5, DFRC.

⁹ Parkman, *Oregon Trail*, 137-8.

¹⁰ Maximilian, *Travels*, XXII, 274.

¹¹ Thomas Harvey to William Medill, July 4, 1847, St. Louis Superintendency, RG 75, M234, 754/160, DFRC; John Miller to William Marcy, January, 1848, Council Bluffs Agency, RG 75, M234, 217/137, 143, DFRC; Daniel Miller to Mitchell, July 1, 1843, St. Louis Superintendency, Vol. 8, frames 113-4, KCFRC.

¹² Thomas Fitzpatrick to Harvey, June 27, 1848, Upper Platte Agency, RG 75, M234, 889/56, DFRC; Irving Jr., *Indian Sketches*, 184-8; Weltfish, *Lost Universe*, 106-18; Wissler, *Indians*, 155-6; See also De Smet, *Life*, IV, 976-88.

¹³ Kappler, ed., *Indian Affairs*, 417; Report of James Gatewood, October 16, 1853, Report of the Commissioner 1853, 348, 246-7; Daniel Miller to Mitchell, December 23, 1843, Council Bluffs Agency, RG 75, M234, 216/31-2, DFRC; John Dunbar to David Greene, November 14, 1843 and Samuel Allis to Greene, July 21, 1843, "Presbyterian Mission," 659-60 and 730-1; White, "Winning of the West," 337-8; Grinnell, *Pawnee Hero Stories*, 308-10; Harvey to Medill, October 7, 1847, St. Louis Superintendency, RG 75, M234, 754/335-6.

¹⁴ Andrew Drips to Harvey, December, 1844, Upper Missouri Agency, RG 75, M234, 884/466 and 369-70, DFRC.

¹⁵ Pilcher to Clark, September 15, 1838, Upper Missouri Agency, RG 75, M234, 884/369-70, see also 242, 575, DFRC; Harvey to Medill, November 22, 1847, St. Louis Superintendency, RG 75, M234, 754/3465-9 and 755/178-9, DFRC; Miller to Mitchell, June 10, 1843, St. Louis Superintendency, Vol. 8 frames 108-9, KCFRC.

Chapter 6 Endnotes

¹ Report of David D. Mitchell, October 13, 1849, Report of The Commissioner, November 30, 1849, 1070-1, 938-9.

² Report of the Commissioner, 1851, 289; De Smet, *Life*, II, 674-5, 679-80.

³ Kappler ed., *Indian Affairs*, 594-5.

⁴ H. W. Wharton to A. A. G., June 6, 1852, Council Bluffs Agency, RG 75, M234, 218/10-1, DFRC; De Smet, *Life*, II, 687-8.

⁵ B. L. E. Bonneville to D. C. Buell, June 6, 1849, Western Division and Department, 1821-56, RG 393, Box 2, NA.

⁶ Wharton to George Manypenny, January 21, 1854 and Wharton to A. A. G., June 6, 1853, Council Bluffs Agency, RG 75, M234, 218/208-14 and 10-1, DFRC; Thomas Twiss to Alfred Cumming, April 30, 1857, Upper Platte Agency, RG 75, M234, 890/7, DFRC.

⁷ Praus, *Winter Count*, 18; Report of A. H. Redfield, November 9, 1857, Report of the Commissioner, 1857, 423-4.

⁸ W. J. Wessels to A. A. G., Department of the West, July 7, 1858, Central Superintendency, RG 75, M234, 56/486-7, DFRC; Report of Redfield, September 9, 1856, Report of the Commissioner, 1856, 416; Reports of Redfield

and Twiss, September 1 and 23, 1858, Report of the Commissioner, 1858, 437-9, 446-7.

⁹ Report of Alfred J. Vaughan, September 20, 1853 and Report of the Commissioner, November 26, 1853, 353-5 and 246.

¹⁰ Goetzmann, *Army Exploration*, 278; Chittenden, *Fur Trade*, I, 388; Ewers, *Blackfeet*, 208-10, 73.

¹¹ Ewers, *Blackfeet*, 210, 104-5; Marquis, *Last Bullet*, 56-7; Lowie, *Crow Indians*, *186-92*.

¹² Ewers, *Blackfeet*, 211-19; Report of the Commissioner, 1855, 530; Partoll, ed., *Indian Council*, 4-10; Treaty of 1855, Blackfoot Agency, RG 75, M234, 30/8-12.

¹³ Report of Redfield, September 1, 1858. Report of the Commissioner, 1858, 443; John Owen to Superintendent Gray, December 21, 1860, Washington Superintendency, RG 75, M5, roll 22, NA.

¹⁴ "Fort Benton Journal, 1854-1856," and "Original Journal of James H. Chambers, Fort Sarpy, 1855-1856," 1-79 and 100-87; Ewers, *Blackfeet*, 213.

¹⁵ Report of Redfield, September 1, 1858 and Report of the Commissioner, November 6, 1858, 441 and 364.

¹⁶ White, "Winning the West," 334-8; Kappler, ed., *Indian Affairs*, 610-7.

¹⁷ Kappler, ed., *Indian Affairs*, 774-5; I. Shaw Gregory to A. M. Robinson, August 27, 1859; Gregory to A. B. Greenwood; J. B. Hoffman to H. B. Branch, July 18, 1861; Hoffman to William Dole, November 1, 1862; Hoffman to John Hutchinson, September 4, 1863; Ponca Agency, RG 75, M234, 670/44-53, 345, 576-7, 826-9, 947-8, DFRC.

¹⁸ R. Furnas to Superintendent Albin, October 25, 1864; Furnas to Dole, May 3, 1864; Furnas to Superintendent Taylor, October 25, 1865, Omaha Agency, RG 75, M234, 605/67-8, 141, 329-32, DFRC.

¹⁹ Central Superintendency, RG 75, M234, 55/991, DRFC; Kappler, ed., *Indian Affairs*, 417, 571-2, 765-6.

²⁰ Grinnell, *Pawnee Hero Stories*, 308-10, 312-6; J. L. Gillis to John Black, June 24, 1860, Pawnee Agency, RG 75, M234, 659/206, DFRC.

²¹ Stands in the Timber and Liberty, *Cheyenne*, 61-3.

²² Gillis to Greenwood, June 22 and 24, 1860, Gillis to Superintendent Robinson, July 12 and October 25, 1860, Alfred Sully to Gillis, September 10, 1860, Sully to A. A. G., September 27, 1860, Pawnee Agency, RG 75, M234, 659/119-20, 124-5, 168-70, 134-7, 208-10; Charles Mix to Gillis, July 9, 1860, Letters Sent, RG 75, M21, 64/89, DFRC.

²³ Henry Depuy to Branch, July 30, 1861, Depuy to Dole, December 29, 1861 and January 2, 1862, Letter of Henry Hudson, October 6, 1863, D. H. Wheeler to E. B. Taylor, May 4, 1866, B. F. Lushbaugh to Dole, February 17, 1865, Pawnee Agency, RG 75, M234, 659/262, 332-7, 660/124-5, 57, 416-8, 303-4, DFRC.

²⁴ Report of T. Hartley Crawford, November 25, 1844, Report of the Commissioner, 1844, 216; Report of C. F. Smith, December 30, 1856, Report of the Secretary of War, December 6, 1858, 434; Warren, *Explorations*, 667, 632-3.

[25] Morgan, *Journals, 1859-60,* 163-4; Vaughan to Cumming, July 3, 1854 and May 19, 1855, Bernard Schoonover to Robinson, July 12, 1860, Upper Missouri Agency, RG 75, M234, 885/50-1, 115-6, 365, DFRC; Boller, *Indians,* 59, 300-17; Athearn, *Forts,* 169-70, 174, 177-80.

[26] Linderman, *Plenty-Coups,* 47-9.

[27] Reports of Redfield and Thomas Twiss, September 1 and 23, 1858, Report of the Commissioner, 1858, 439-40 and 446-7; Twiss to Greenwood, January 4, 1860, Upper Platte Agency, RG 75, M234, 890/157, 218, also see 104, 220-3, DFRC.

[28] James Doty to Stevens, December 28, 1853, Washington Superintendency, RG 75, M234, 907/182-3, DFRC.

[29] Denig, *Five Tribes,* 81-2.

[30] Ewers, *Horse,* 174.

[31] Schultz, *Blackfeet,* 271-81; Ewers, *Blackfeet,* 243.

[32] Ewers, "Intertribal Warfare," 405; Henry A. Morrow to O. D. Greene, November 19, 1869, Dakota Superintendency, RG 75, M234, 251/522, 554, 557-8, CU; F. D. Pease to J. A. Viall, December, 1870, Montana Superintendency, RG 75, M234, 490/436-7, DFRC; William Quinton to M. C. Danbourne, May 19, 1871, Montana Superintendency, RG 75, M234, 491/1106, 1116, DFRC.

Chapter 7 Endnotes

[1] David S. Stanley to O. D. Greene, August 20, 1869, Montana Superintendency, RG 75, M234, 489/10-14, DFRC; Report of John Loree, 1862, Upper Platte Agency, RG 75, M234, 890/317, DFRC.

[2] Ewers, "Intertribal Warfare," 397-8.

[3] Hyde, *Bent* 164-99.

[4] Hyde, *Red Cloud's Folk,* 123-4, 220-1; Grinnell, *Fighting Cheyennes,* 220-1; Sandoz, *Crazy Horse,* 164-6; Hyde, *Bent,* 216-22, 226.

[5] McGinnis, "Strike and Retreat," 34-6 and "Wits and Daring," 25-6.

[6] Kappler, ed., *Indian Affairs,* 883, 885, 896, 898, 899-900, 901, 903, 905, 907, 1052-3, 1055.

[7] Report of the Northwestern Treaty Commission, Report of the Commissioner, 1866, 169.

[8] McGinnis, "Strike and Retreat," 37 and "Wits and Daring," 31-2; Grinnell, *Fighting Cheyennes,* 235-7.

[9] McGinnis, "Strike and Retreat," 38; Ewers, *Horse,* 206-7; Dodge, *Our Wild Indians,* 102,180-2.

[10] Utley, *Frontier Regulars,* 131-2.

[11] Kappler, ed., *Indian Affairs,* 905, 907, 998, 1002, 1008, 1012, 1020-1, 1052-3, 1055.

[12] Report of Charles Whaley, August 20, 1868, Report of the Commissioner, 1868, 694-5; Whaley to Nathaniel G. Taylor, February 20, 1869 Pawnee Agency, RG 75, M234, 660/721, DFRC; Grinnell, *Two Great Scouts,* 18-21, 72-4, 77-81.

13 Report of W. Clifford, September 1, 1869, Report of the Commissioner, 1869, 754; J. C. Kelton to Jacob D. Cox, September 17, 1869 and Clifford to Superintendent Burbank, September 10, 1870, Fort Berthold Agency, RG 75, M234, 292/143-4, DFRC.

14 Report of the Acting Commissioner, November 15, 1867, 3.

15 Report of Luther Mann, July 29, 1867, Report of the Commissioner, 1867, 182-3; J. A. Campbell to Ely Parker, November 7, 1870, Wyoming Superintendency, RG 75, M234, 953/81-5, 172-5, DFRC.

16 Henry A. Morrow to A. A. G., November 19, 1869, Fort Berthold Agency, RG 75, M234, 292/485-6, DFRC.

17 Report of Augustus Chapman, August 31, 1866, Report of the Commissioner, 1866, 315; Report of Alvin Galbreath, September 6, 1869, Report of the Commissioner, 1869, 739; Statement of Big Canoe to Chapman, October 28, 1866, Montana Superintendency, RG 75, M234, 488/331-2, DFRC.

18 Ewers, *Horse*, 173.

19 Dempsey, *Crowfoot*, 59-61; Ewers, *Blackfeet*, 249-53.

20 Superintendent Janney to Parker, October, 1871 and August 5, 1871 and Barclay White to Parker, December 26, 1872, Pawnee Agency, RG 75, M234, 661/24-5, 382-3, 603-4, DFRC; White to Francis A. Walker, January 23, 1873, Pawnee Agency, RG 75, M234, 662/317-20, DFRC.

21 White to Edward P. Smith, November 18, 1873, Pawnee Agency, RG 75, M234, 662/952-4, DFRC.

22 Reports of White, E. Painter, and William Burgess, September 27, 29, and 20, 1873, Report of the Commissioner, 1873, 554, 561-3; Hyde, *Pawnee*, 310-14.

23 Hyde, *Pawnee*, 315; E. A. Howard to Smith, August 20, 1873, Whetstone Agency, RG 75, M234, 926/167, DFRC.

24 Parker to Jacob D. Cox, February 26, 1870, Report Books, 1838-1885, RG 75, M348, 19/211, DFRC.

25 Hyde, *Pawnee*, 315-22; Grinnell, *Two Great Scouts*, Chapters 18, 19, 20.

26 John Hutchinson to A. B. Hoffman, April 5, 1863, Correspondence, Box 2, Dakota Superintendency, RG 75, NA.; Prucha, *Great Father*, I, 567.

27 John Clum to Charles Birkett, March 17, 1873, Letters Sent, RG 75, M21, 109/424, DFRC; Clerk of the Secretary of War to Secretary of the Interior, September 30, 1875, Ponca Agency, RG 75, M234, 673/777-9, DFRC; Birkett to Commissioner, June 9, 1873, Ponca Agency, RG 75, M234, 672/635-8, DFRC.

28 Report of the Commissioner, November 1, 1877, 417; Petition to the President of the United States from some citizens of Yankton, Dakota Territory, 1879, Ponca Agency, RG 75, M234, 676/332-7, DFRC.

Chapter 8 Endnotes

1 Stanley to O. D. Greene, August 20, 1869, Montana Superintendency, RG 75, M234, 489/10-4, DFRC.

² De Trobriand, *Military Life*, xx-xxv, 62, 82, 46-7.

³ *Ibid.*, 95, 150, 336, 370; Daniel Husolon to A. A. G., June 15, 1874, Fort Berthold Agency, RG 75, M234, 294/1085-8, DFRC.

⁴ De Trobriand, *Military Life*, 248, 57.

⁵ Greene to Clifford, October 4, 1869, Department of Dakota Letters Sent, RG 393, 517, NA.

⁶ S. B. Hayman to Greene, November 22, 1870, Fort Berthold Agency, RG 75, M234, 293/3-5, DFRC; Greene to Hayman, December 27, 1870, Dakota Superintendency, RG 75, M234, 252/20-1, CU.

⁷ Secretary of War to Secretary of Interior, July 18, 1872, Fort Berthold Agency, RG 75, M234, 293/848, DFRC; Alfred Terry to George Armstrong Custer, May 26, 1874, Department of Dakota Letters Sent, RG 393, Vol. 6, 37, NA; D. W. Sperry to Commissioner, June 3, 1874, Fort Berthold Agency, RG 75, M234, 294/796-7, DFRC.

⁸ Report of L. B. Sperry, September 1, 1875 and Report of the Commissioner, November 1, 1875, 744, 547; John Q. Smith to John Young, December 27, 1876 and Edward P. Smith to E. A. Howard, December 6, 1875, Commissioner Letters Sent, RG 75, M21, 132/311-2 and 128/132, DFRC.

⁹ James Irwin to Edward P. Smith, February 16, 1872, August 21, 1873, November 5, 1873, July 6, 1874, Wyoming Superintendency, RG 75, M234, 954/231-3, 808-9, 850-1, 1106-7, DFRC.

¹⁰ J. Mix to Irwin, July, 1876 and Irwin to John Q. Smith, July 8, 1876, Wyoming Superintendency, RG 75, M234, 955/580-1, DFRC; Marquis, ed., *Wooden Leg*, 199-200; Sandoz, *Crazy Horse*, 319, 322.

¹¹ William Dye to G. D. Ruggles, November 20, 1868, Upper Platte Agency, RG 75, M234, 893/649-51, DFRC; Sully to Commissioner, April 6, 1870, Montana Superintendency, RG 75, M234, 490/391, DFRC.

¹² Sandoz, *Crazy Horse*, 274.

¹³ Report of G. L. Tyler, undated, 1875, Montana Superintendency, RG 75, M234, 503/497-8,. DFRC.

¹⁴James Wright to Edward P. Smith, September 20, 1873, Montana Superintendency, RG 75, M234, 497/474-7, DFRC; B. F. Potts to Columbus Delano, July 8 and 9, 1875, Montana Superintendency, RG 75, M234, 503/486-9, DFRC; Potts to B. R. Cowen, June 24, 1874, Montana Superintendency, RG 75, M234, 500/159-61, DFRC.

¹⁵ N. B. Sweitzer to A. A. G., November, 1873, Montana Superintendency, RG 75, M234, 497/754-8, DFRC; Sweitzer to A. A. G., January 10, 1874, Montana Superintendency, RG 75, M234, 500/569-73, DFRC; Report of E. M. Camp, August, 1870, Report of the Commissioner, 1870, p. 663; Story and Hoffman Traders to Wright, February 13, 1874, Montana Superintendency, RG 75, M234, 500/642-3, DFRC.

¹⁶ Delano to Potts, May 22, 1874, Letters Sent, 1849-1903, RG 48, M606, 14/297/8, NA; Nelson Miles to A. A. G., December 17, 1876, Dakota Superintendency, RG 75, M234, 262/70-1, CU.

¹⁷ Linderman, *Pretty Shield*, 133, 168, 232-40.

18 Marquis, *Last Bullet*, 71; Marquis, ed., *Wooden Leg*, 218-22.

19 Redington, "Scouting," 30.

20 George Clendinin to J. A. Viall, December 12, 1870, Montana Superintendency, RG 75, M234, 491/1051, 1052, DFRC.

21 Viall to Parker, October 20, 1870 and A. J. Simmons to Parker, May 12, 1871, Montana Superintendency, RG 75, M234, 490/736-7 and 491/635-52, DFRC; Report of Simmons, August 31, 1871, Report of the Commissioner, 1871, 846-8; Report of the Commissioner, November 1, 1872, 436; Report of Alfred Sully, September 20, 1870, Report of the Commissioner, 1870, 653; Phil Sheridan to Edward D. Townsend, July 1, 1870, Montana Superintendency, RG 75, M234, 490/15-6, DFRC.

22 Koch, "Muscleshell [sic]," 300-1.

23 Koch, "Muscleshell [sic]," 299; Stanley to A. A. G., July 30, 1871, Dakota Superintendency, RG 75, M234, 252/45-6, CU; Report of Simmons, May 12, 1871, Montana Superintendency, RG 75, M234, 491/635-52, 657-9, DFRC.

24 W. H. Lewis to the Secretary of War, July 18, 1871, Report of the Commissioner, 1871, 849.

25 E. C. Watkins to Edward P. Smith, November 9, 1875, Dakota Superintendency, RG 75, M234, 255/823-3, CU.

26 Report of the Commissioner, October 30, 1876, 392-3.

27 Report of H. W. Bingham, September 1, 1875, Report of the Commissioner, 1875, 738-9.

Chapter 9 Endnotes

1 John Bourke to C. O. Camp Brown, April 16, 1877 and George Crook to General Williams, April 25, 1877, Department of the Platte, Telegrams Sent, 1877-8, RG 393, NA; Utley, *Frontier Regulars*, 209, 400; Report of J. I. Patten, September 1, 1877, Report of the Commissioner, 1877, 605-6; Patten to Ezra A. Hayt, April 15, 1879, Wyoming Superintendency, RG 75, M234, 957/421-5, DFRC; Charles Hatton to Hiram Price, May 3, 1881, Commissioner Letters Received, No. 7757, RG75, NA.

2 Edwin Alden to Hayt, January 29, 1879, William Courtenay to Hayt, May 12, June 7, July 8, 1879, Fort Berthold Agency, RG 75, M234, 297/505, 1030/2, 1125-7, 1208-9, DFRC; Courtenay to Hayt, July 25, 1879, Fort Berthold Agency, RG 75, M234, 298/11-2, DFRC.

3 Reports of William Courtnay, August 19, 1879 and J. A. Stephan, August 21, 1879, Report of the Commissioner, 1879, pp. 136, 154-5; Hayt to Alden, February 10, 1879, Commissioner Letters Sent, RG 75, M21, 150/47-8, DFRC.

4 James Brisben to A. A. G., April 17, 1879, Montana Superintendency, RG 75, M234, 515/648, DFRC; Report of W. E. Daugherty, September 9, 1880, Report of the Commissioner, 1880, 159; Daugherty to Jacob Kauffman and Daugherty to W. D. E. Andrea, August 9, 1881, Crow Creek Agency, Letters Sent, RG 75, No. 561878, 397 and 396, KCFRC.

5 A. Bell to John Cook, July 2, 1880 and Kauffman to Cook, November 6, 1880, Rosebud Agency, General Correspondence, 1880, RG 75, No. 235 and No. A255, KCFRC; T. M. Nichol to Leonard Love, February 18, 1881, Commissioner Letters Sent, RG 75, M21, 154/199, DFRC; Love to Commissioner, March 31, 1881, Commissioner Letters Received, RG 75, No. 7364, NA; Kauffman to Price, January 21, 1882, Commissioner Letters Received, RG 75, No. 1837 and No. 16205, NA; Love to Kauffman, March 1, 1880, Cheyenne River Agency Letters Sent, RG 75, No. 518485, KCFRC; Price to Cook, July 15, 1881, Rosebud Agency, General Correspondence, RG 75, No. 356, KCFRC.

6 D. W. Brotherton to Kauffman, September 11, 1880 and Kauffman to R. E. Trowbridge, September 22, 1880, Fort Berthold Agency, RG 75, M234, 299/672 and 673-4, DFRC; James Taylor to John Hay, October 30, 1880 and Williams Evarts to Carl Schurz, December 17, 1880, Dakota Superintendency, RG 75, M234, 273/564-7, 541-7, CU.

7 Ewers, Blackfeet, 212, 284; Utley, Frontier Regulars, 220-1; John Davidson to A. A. G. Department of Dakota, Letters Received, RG 393, No. 904, NA; E. M. Marble to John Young, April 4, 1881 and Marble to A. R. Keller, April 4, 1881, Commissioner Letters Sent, RG 75, M21, 159/258-60, DFRC.

8 Schulz, Blackfeet and Buffalo, 37, 41-3, 48, 59; Dempsey, Crowfoot, 115-30.

9 Schultz, Blackfeet and Buffalo, 7-13, 14-25, 158-63.

10 Ibid., 5; C. O. Fort Keogh to A. A. G., April 15, 1881, Department of Dakota Register of Letters Received, Vol. B, p. 672, RG 393, NA; Report of the Commissioner, 1880, pp. 364-71; N. S. Porter to Price, January 26, 1882, Letters Received, No. 2420, RG 75, NA; C. O. Poplar River Camp to A. A. G., November 14, 16, 19, 1880 and May 15, 1881, RG 94, M666, 582/90-7 and M689, 30/124, NA.

11 W. L. Lincoln to Hayt, June 26, 1878 and January 21, 1879, Montana Superintendency, RG 75, M234, 511/132-5 and 514/375-82; Report of Lincoln, August 1, 1879, Report of the Commissioner, 1879, 204-6; Daniel Huston, Jr. to A. A. G., January 17, 1878, Dakota Superintendency, RG 75, M234, 266/732-3, CU; Report of William Bird, August 17, 1878, Report of the Commissioner, 1878, 587; Hayt to Bird, November 20, 1878 and March 10, 1879, Commissioner Letters Sent, RG 75, M21, 144/413 and 150/110-1, DFRC; Report of N. S. Porter, August 12, 1880, Report of the Commissioner, 1880, pp. 235-6.

12 Utley, Frontier Regulars, 284-5, 288; Report of the Commissioner, November 1, 1877, 412-3; James MacLeod to Alexander MacKenzie, May 30, 1877, Dakota Superintendency, RG 75, M234, 261/583, CU.

13 Dempsey, Crowfoot, 88-92, 108-9, 115-30.

14 Guido Ilges to A. A. G., November 22, 1877 and George Buell To A. A. G., February 16, 1879 and Nelson Miles to A. A. G., July 31, 1879, Dakota Superintendency, RG 75, M234, 266/559-60 and 270/456 and 270/650-1, CU; Report of Lincoln, August 11, 1880, Report of the Commissioner, 1880, 236.

15 Constant Williams to A. A. G., February 6, 1878 and E. D. Townsend to Commanding Officer Division of the Missouri, February 18, 1878, Montana Superintendency, RG 75, M234, 512/58-71 and 39, DFRC; Report of Lincoln,

August 1, 1879, Report of the Commissioner, 1879, 204-6; Report of Miles, September, 1879, RG 94, M666, 545/94, NA; Report of Alfred Terry, October 4, 1880, Report of the Secretary of War, 1880, 62; Young to J. M. Walsh, April 28, 1879, Walsh to Young, September 30, 1879, and William T. Sherman to Philip H. Sheridan, July 24, 1879, Montana Superintendency, RG 75, M234, 515/1148-50 and 795, DFRC.

¹⁶ Report of Young, July 25, 1878, Report of the Commissioner, 1878, 578-9.

¹⁷ William Courtenay to Hayt, February 16, 1879, Dakota Superintendency, RG 75, M234, 267/499-500, CU; Lincoln to Hayt, December 9, 1878, Montana Superintendency, RG 75, M234, 511/271-2, DFRC.

¹⁸ Neihardt, *Black Elk*, 151-4.

¹⁹ Nabakov, ed., *Two Leggings*, xiii-xv, 62-3, 73, 167-76, 188-92, 212.

²⁰ Report of Terry, October 1, 1879, RG 94, M666, 545/310, NA; C. O. Fort Custer to A. A. G., October 31, 1881, Department of Dakota Letters Received, RG 393, No. 6941, NA; Miles to A. A. G., August 5, 1879, Dakota Superintendency, RG 75, M234, 270/635-6, CU.

²¹ Davidson to A. A. G., May 2, 1880 and A. A. G., to Davidson, May 24, 1889, RG 94, M666, 566/516-7, NA.

²² Alden to Hayt, November 18, 1878, Fort Berthold Agency, RG 75, M234, 297/8-9, DFRC; Utley, *Frontier Regulars*, 289-90, 287; Miles to A. G., July 22, 1879, Montana Superintendency, RG 75, M234, 515/811, DFRC.

Chapter 10 Endnotes

¹ Sandoz, *Buffalo Hunters*, 339-58; Gard, *Buffalo Hunt*, 270-4; Ridge and Billington, eds., *Frontier Story*, 582-3.

² Henry J. Armstrong to Lewis Merrill, August 24, 1882 and Armstrong to Alfred Terry, October 31, 1882, Department of Dakota Letters Received, RG 393, No. 5395 and No. 6672, NA; John Young to Hiram Price, August 15, 1882 and November 14, 1882, Commissioner Letters Received, RG 75, No. 15749 and No. 21403, NA; Schultz, *Life*, 115-9.

³ Price to Young, November 29, 1882, Civil Division Letters Sent, RG 75, Vol. 38, lst LB, pp. 10-2, NA; Armstrong to Merrill, August 24, 1882 and Endorsement by Merrill, August 30, 1882, Department of Dakota Letters Received, RG 393, No. 5395, NA; Merrill to A. A. G., August 31, 1882, RG 94, M689, 153/98, NA.

⁴ Secretary of War to Secretary of the Interior, April 26, 1883, Commissioner Letters Received, RG 75, No. 7901, NA — including enclosed telegrams; A. G. of the Army to Terry, June 6, 1883 and F. D. Holton to T. W. Schley, August 14, 1883, RG 94, M689, 215/381 and 228/111-3, NA; Thomas Hatch to A. A. G., April 28, 1883, Department of Dakota Letters Received, RG 393, No. 3056, NA.

⁵ Price to Young, May 8, 1883, Civil Division Letters Sent, RG 75, Vol. 39, 2nd LB, 246-7, NA; L. Sackville-West to Secretary of State, June 8, 1883, RG

94, M689, 93/454-9, NA; E. L. Stevens to Secretary of the Interior, June 15, 1883 and Price to Secretary of the Interior, September 1, 1883, Civil Division Letters Sent, RG 75, Vol. 40, lst LB, pp. 126-9 and Vol. 41, lst LB, pp. 331-3, NA — Sherman's recommendations included in the first letter.

6 Guido Ilges to A. G., April 18, 1883, Commissioner Letters Received, RG 75, No. 8383, NA; Ilges to A. A. G., May 7, 1883 and Ilges to Albert Shurtliff, May 7, 1883 and Shurtliff to Ilges, May 9, 1883, RG 94, M689, 205/209-10 and 93/481-99, NA.

7 James Wright to Lower Brulé Agent, May 1, 1883, Rosebud Agency Outgoing Correspondence, LB B-8, 326, FRC No. B-9, KCFRC; George W. Wilkinson to Commissioner, September 17 and 19, 1883, Commissioner Letters Received, RG 75 No. 17533 and No. 18528, NA: James McLaughlin to Jacob Kauffman, January 10, 1883, Standing Rock Agency Letters Received, RG 75, FRC No. 517091, KCFRC; Hatch to A. A. G., October 1, 1883, RG 94, M689, 233/394, NA; Report of Terry, October 6, 1884, Report of the Secretary of War, 1884, 109; Report of Price, October 10, 1883, Report of the Commissioner, 1883, 23-4.

8 H. J. Armstrong to Price, February 24, 1884, Commissioner Letters Received, RG 75, No. 4127, NA; Report of Terry, October 6, 1884, Report of the Secretary of War, 1884, 110; Edward Moale to A. A. G., October 19 and 20, 1885 and F. C. Armstrong to Secretary of the Interior, November 18, 1885, RG 94, M689, 390/77-83, 117, NA; John D. C. Atkins to Secretary of the Interior, November 23, 1885, Land Division Letters Sent, RG 75, LB 142, 105-6, NA; Terry to A. G., October 5, 1885, RG 94, M689, 390/90-8, NA.

9 C. O. Fort Assiniboine to A. A. G., June 6, 1885, Department of Dakota Letters Received, RG 393, No. 4147, NA; Stands in the Timber and Liberty, *Cheyenne Memories*, 249-55; Thomas Ruger to A. G., June 5, 1884, Division of the Missouri Letters Received, RG 393 No. 3389, NA; Reports of John Harris, August 29, 1884 and Abram J. Gifford, August 5, 1884, Report of the Commissioner, 1884, 110, 80; Report of A. L. Cook, July 1, 1885, Report of the Commissioner, 1885, 292.

10 Schultz, *Blackfeet and Buffalo*, 210-24; Ewers, *Blackfeet*, 302-3.

11 Report of Henry M. Teller, November 1, 1884, Report of the Secretary of the Interior, 111; Henry Williamson to V. T. McGillycuddy, May 8, 1885 and H. G. Armstrong to McGillycuddy, October 8, 1885, Pine Ridge Agency Letters Received, RG 75, FRC No. 516023, KCFRC; Alfred Smith to A. A. G., April 13, 1885, RG 94, M689, 341/155, 191-2, NA; Schultz, *Life*, 115-9; Grinnell, *Lodge Tales*, 242-4.

12 Report of R. A. Allen, no date, Report of the Commissioner, 1885, 344; James Terrell to Senator J. B. Beck, February 8, 1885 and related correspondence, RG 94, M689, 341/41-2, 48-51, 56-8, 97, 132-43, 154-5, 209-12; J. R. Dilworth to Secretary of the Interior, December 8, 1886, Commissioner Letters Received, RG 75, No. 33488, NA.

13 J. K. Toole to Secretary of the Interior, February 5, 1886, Commissioner Letters Received, RG 75, No. 4185, NA; Stuart, *Forty Years*, II, 218; Report of Ruger, September 6, 1886, Report of the Secretary of War, 1886, 128.

14 Report of N. D. Baldwin, August 20, 1887, Report of the Commissioner, 1887, 218.

15 Report of Henry E. Williamson, September 15, 1886, Report of the Commissioner, 1886, 395; F. C. Armstrong to Secretary of the Interior, October 17, 1887, Commissioner of Letters Received, RG 75, No. 2741, NA; F. C. Armstrong to Secretary of the Interior, June 3, 1886 and Secretary of War to Secretary of the Interior, July 3, 1886 and Ruger to A. A. G., September 29, 1886, RG 94, M689, 455/287, 291-7, 483/206-7, NA; A. B. Upshaw to H. Heth, September, 1886, Land Division Letters Sent, RG 75, LB 153, p. 304, NA; Heth to Commissioner, September 1, 1886 and September 28, 1886, Commissioner Letters Received, RG 75, No. 24401 and 26507, NA; C. O. Fort Custer to A. A. G., January 14, 1887, RG 94, M689, 512/97, NA.

16 Ruger to A. A. G., October 6, 1886 and October 18, 1886 and November 16, 1886, RG 94, M689, 483/279-81 and 486/192-216, NA; Upshaw to Secretary of the Interior, April 14, 1887, Land Division Letters Sent, RG 75, LB 158, p. 421, NA; Report of Privy Council for Canada, March 18, 1887 and Ruger to A. A. G., April 22, 1887, RG 94, M689, 483/314-27 and 376-7, NA; Edwin Fields to Commissioner, April 27, 1887 and W. E. Smith to Commissioner, April, 1887, Commissioner Letters Received, RG 75, Nos. 11812, 1183 and 1224, NA; Report of Fields, August 16, 1887, Report of the Commissioner, 1887, p. 224; Lieutenant J. F. Huston to Post Adjutant, Fort Assiniboine, June 12, 1887, RG 94, M689, 483/405-13, NA; C. O. Fort Assiniboine to A. A. G., October 22, 1887, Department of Dakota Letters Received, RG 393, No. 6136, Register Vol. C, 1939, NA.

17 Dempsey, *Crowfoot*, 165-72, 189-92; Report of the Ruger, September 1, 1889, Report of the Secretary of War, 1889, 161-2.

18 Report of Ruger, September 6, 1886, Report of the Secretary of War, 1886, 126-32; Ruger to A. A. G., October 26, 1886, RG 94, M689, 488/287-9, NA; Report of Ruger, August 6, 1887, Report of the Secretary of War, 1887, 137.

19 Ruger to A. A. G., November 6, 1886 and F. C. Armstrong to Secretary of the Interior, November 14, 1885, RG 94, M689, 486/192-216 and 390/117, NA; Report of M. D. Baldwin, August 20, 1887, Report of the Commissioner, 1887, 213; General Order Number 38, June 21, 1886, General Orders, RG 94, NA; Report of Williamson, August 31, 1887, Report of the Commissioner, 1887, 215-6; Report of Ruger, August 6, 1887, Report of the Secretary of War, 1887, 146.

20 Atkins to Secretary of the Interior, February 19, 1886, Land Division Letters Sent, RG 75, LB 145, 60-2, NA; Report of the Secretary of the Interior, November 24, 1888, LXVII-LXVIII.

21 Calloway, "Sword Bearer," 39-42; Secretary of the Interior to Secretary of War, October 18, 1887, Commissioner Letters Received, RG 75, Nos. 27841 and 27842, NA; Report of Sheridan, November 1, 1887, Report of the Secretary of War, 1887, 73; Report of Ruger, September 15, 1888, Report of the Secretary of War, 1888, 146-53; Ruger to A. A. G., November 30, 1887, Lieutenant Wainwright to Colonel Campbell, February 16, 1888, James Howard to Commissioner, April 27, 1888, R. C. Drum to George Crook, May 10, 1888, Ruger

to A. A. G., July 15, 1889, President Grover Cleveland to Secretary of the Interior, November 7, 1887, Commissioner Letters Received concerning Crow outbreak, NA.

[22] Report of Ruger, September 15, 1888, Report of the Secretary of War, 1888, 146.

[23] Edwin Fields to Commissioner, May 9 and 31 and September 21, 1888, Commissioner Letters Received, RG 75, Nos. 12769 and 14571, NA; Upshaw to Fields, June 9, 1888, Land Division Letters Sent, LB 174, 361, NA.

[24] C. O. Fort Custer to A. A. G., June 17, 1888, RG 94, M689, 632/471-4, NA; C. O. Poplar River Camp to A. A. G., August 27, September 4, October 1, 1888, and C. O. Fort Custer to A. A. G., August 30, September 6, 1888, Department of Dakota Letters Received, RG 393, Nos. 4682, 4913, 5418 and 4711, No. 4908, NA.

[25] C. O. Fort Assiniboine to A. A. G., June 4, 1889 and L. Wheaton to A. A. G., June 4 and 23, Department of Dakota Letters Received, RG 393, Nos. 3194 and 3158, No. 3579, NA; Report of Ruger, September 1, 1889, Report of the Secretary of War, 1892, 116.

[26] Ewers, *Blackfeet*, 302; Report of Wesley Merritt, September 1, 1892, Report of the Secretary of War, 1892, 116.

[27] Stands in the Timber and Liberty, *Cheyenne Memories*, 281, 183-5; Marquis, ed., *Wooden Leg*, 355-9; Burbank and Royce, *Among the Indians*, 128, 152, 154; Report of Ruger, September 15, 1888, Report of the Secretary of War, 1888, 146.

[28] Ewers, *Blackfeet*, 303; Linderman, *Plenty-Coups*, 557; Nabokov, ed., *Two Leggings*, 193, 197; Stands in the Timber and Liberty, *Cheyenne Memories*, 249-55; Marquis, ed., *Wooden Leg*, 383-4.

[29] Ironwood Singers, "Traditional Songs of the Sioux," (cassette tape recording) Live at Rosebud (Taos: Indian House, 1980).

BIBLIOGRAPHY

A. PRIMARY SOURCES

1. Government Documents

Annual Reports of the Commissioner of Indian Affairs to the Secretary of the Interior, 1849-92.

Annual Reports of the Commissioner of Indian Affairs to the Secretary of War, 1825-7 and 1830-48. Washington: Government Printing Office, 1825-7 and 1830-48.

Annual Reports of the Secretary of the Interior to the President, 1877, 1881, 1882, 1884, 1888. Washington: Government Printing Office, 1877, 1881, 1882, 1884, 1888.

Annual Reports of the Secretary of War to the President, 1867-92. Washington: Government Printing Office, 1867-92.

Kappler, Charles J. ed. *Indian Affairs, Laws and Treaties.* 2 vols. 58 Cong., 2 sess., *Sen. Doc. 319.* Washington: Government Printing Office, 1904.

Records of the Adjutant General's Office, 1780s-1917, Record Group 94. Letters Received Main Series, 1822-60. National Archives Microfilm Publication M567. National Archives Building.

—. Letters Received Main Series, 1861-70. National Microfilm Publication M619. National Archives Building.

—. Letters Received Main Series, 1871-80. National Microfilm Publication M666. National Archives Building.

—. Letters Received Main Series, 1881-9. National Microfilm Publication M689. National Archives Building.

Records of the Bureau of Indian Affairs, Record Group 75. Agency Records, 1867-93: Cheyenne Rvier, Crow Creek, Pine Ridge, Rosebud, Spotted Tail, Standing Rock, and Whetstone. Kansas City Federal Records Center.

—. Letters Received, 1881-92. National Archives Building.

—. Letters Received, 1824-81. National Archives Microfilm Publication M234. Denver Federal Records Center.

—. Letters Sent, 1881-92. National Archives Building.

—. Letters Sent, 1824-1881. National Archives Microfilm Publication M21. Denver Federal Records Center.

—. Records of the Dakota Superintendency of Indian Affairs, 1859-78. National Archives Building.

—. Records of the Montana Superintendency of Indian Affairs, 1867-73. National Archives Microfilm Publication M833. National Archives Building.

—. Records of the Washington Superintendency of Indian Affairs, 1853-74. National Archives Microfilm Publication M5. National Archives Building.

Records of the Office of the Secretary of the Interior, Record Group 48. Letters Received by the Indian Division, 1849-1903. National Archives Microfilm Publication M825. National Archives.

—. Letters Sent by the Indian Division, 1849-1903. National Archives Microfilm Publication M606. National Archives Building.

—. Territorial Papers of Montana, 1867-89. National Archives Publication M192. University of Colorado.

Records of the Office of the Secretary of War, Record Group 107. Letters Received Unregistered Series, 1789-1861. National Archives Microfilm Publication M222. Denver Federal Records Center.

—. Department of Dakota, Letters Received, 1868-87. National Archives Building.

—. Department of Dakota, Letters Sent, 1874-5 and 1887-8. National Archives Building.

—. Department of the Northwest, Letters Sent, 1862-5. National Archives Building.

—. Department of the Platte, Telegrams Sent, 1887-8. National Archives Building.

—. Military Division of the Missouri, Letters Received, 1866-91. National Archives Building.

—. Military Division of the Missouri, Letters Sent, 1866-91. National Archives Building.

—. Western Division and Department, 1821-56, Letters Received by General Henry Atkinson, 1822-33. National Archives Building.

Records of the United States Superintendency of Indian Affairs, St. Louis, 1831-44. Microfilm rolls 1 and 2 of the "William Clark Papers." Kansas State Historical Society, Topeka.

U.S. Congress. *Report of the Joint Special Committee on the Condition of the Indian Tribes, 1867.* Washington: Government Printing Office, 1867.

U.S. Department of Interior. *Letter of the Secretary of the Secretary of the Interior,* April 10. 1869. *Sen. E. Doc.* 5, 41 Cong., 2 sess.

U.S. Department of State. Territorial Papers of Montana, 1864-72. National Archives Microfilm Publication M356. University of Colorado.

U.S. House of Representatives. *Letter from the Secretary of War Respecting the Movements of the Expedition Which Lately Ascended the Missouri River. House Doc.* 117, 19 Cong., 1 sess.

U.S. President. *Message from the President of the United States. House Ex. Doc.* 2, 43 Cong., Sp. sess.

—. *Message from the President of the United States. House Ex. Doc.* 154, 44 Cong., 1 sess.

2. Published Journals, Narratives, and Letters

Anderson, William Marshall. *The Rocky Mountain Journals of William Marshall*

Anderson: The West in 1834. Ed. by Dale L. Morgan and Eleanor T. Harris. San Marino: The Huntington Library, 1967.

Barrows, John R. "A Wisconsin Youth in Montana in the 1870s." *Way out West: Recollections and Tales.* Ed. by H.G. Merriam. Norman: University of Oklahoma Press, 1969.

Belden, George P. *Belden, The White Chief; or Twelve Years Among the Wild Indians of the Plains.* Ed. by General James S. Brisbin. New York: C.V. Vent, 1872.

Bent, George. "Forty Years with the Cheyennes." Ed. by George E. Hyde. *The Frontier,* 1905-1906.

Boller, Henry A. *Among the Indians: Eight Years in the Far West, 1858-1866.* Ed. by Milo Milton Quaife. Chicago: R.K. Donnelly and Sons Company, 1959.

Booth, Margaret ed. *Overland from Indiana to Oregon, The Dinwiddie Journal. Sources of Northwest History No. 2.* Missoula: State University of Montana, 1928.

Bourke, John G. *On the Border with Crook.* London: Sampson Low, Marston, Searle and Rivington, 1892.

Brackenridge, Henry Marie. *Journal of a Voyage up the River Missouri Performed in Eighteen Hundred and Eleven.* Vol. VI of *Early Western Travels, 1748-1846.* Ed. by Reuben Gold Thwaites. 32 vols. Cleveland: Arthur H. Clark Company, 1904-1907.

Bradbury, John. *Travels in the Interior of America in the Years 1809-1811.* Vol. VI of *Early Western Travels.* Ed. by Thwaites.

Bradley, James H. "Account of the Attempts to Build a Town at the Mouth of the Musselshell River," *Collections of the Historical Society of Montana* (hereafter abbreviated *CHSM*), II. Helena: State Publishing Company, 1896, 304-13.

—. "Affairs at Fort Benton from 1831 to 1839; from Lieutenant Bradley's Journal." *CHSM*, III. Helena: State Publishing Company, 1900, 201-88.

—. "Bradley Manuscript, Book F." *CHSM*, VIII. Helena: Montana Historical and Miscellaneous Library, 1917, 197-250.

—. "Bradley Manuscript, Book II." *CHSM*, VIII. Helena: Montana Historical and Miscellaneous Library, 1917, 127-96.

—. "History of the Sioux." *CHSM*, IX. Helena: Montana Historical and Miscellaneous Library, 1923, 29-140.

—. "Journal of James H. Bradley; The Sioux Campaign of 1876 under the Command of General John Gibbon." *CHSM*, II. Helena: State Publishing Company, 1896, 140-228.

—. "Various Selections from His Manuscript." *CHSM*, IX. Helena: Montana Historical and Miscellaneous Library, 1923, 226-351.

Burbank, E.A. and Ernest Royce. *Burbank Among the Indians.* Ed. by Frank J. Taylor. Caldwell: The Caxton Printers, Ltd., 1946.

Carrington, Colonel Henry B. *AB-SA-RA-KA, Land of Massacre, Being the Experience of an Officer's Wife on the Plains with an Outline of Indian Operations and Conferences from 1865 to 1878.* Philadelphia: J.B. Lippincott and Company, 1879.

Catlin, George. *Episodes from Life Among the Indians and Last Rambles.* Ed. by Marvin C. Ross. Norman: University of Oklahoma Press, 1959.

—. *North American Indians: Being Letters and Notes on Their Manners, Customs, and Conditions, Written During Eight Years' Travel Amongst the Wildest Tribes of Indians in North America, 1832-9.* 2 vols. Philadelphia: Leary, Stuart and Company, 1913.

—. *O-KEE-PA: A Religious Ceremony and Other Customs of the Mandans.* Ed. by John C. Ewers. New Haven: Yale University Press, 1967.

Chambers, James H. "Original Journal of James H. Chambers, Fort Sarpy, 1855-6." *CHSM,* X. Helena: Naegale Printing Company, 1940, 100-87.

Chardon, Francois A. *Chardon's Journal at Fort Clark, 1834-1839: Descriptive Life on the Upper Missouri; of a Fur Trader's Experiences Among the Mandans, Gros Ventres and Their Neighbors; of the Ravages of the SmallPox Epidemic of 1837.* Ed. by Annie Heloise Abel. Pierre: Department of History, State of South Dakota, 1932.

Clough, Wilson O. ed. *Fort Russell and Fort Laramie Peace Commission in 1867. Sources of Northwest History No. 14.* Missoula: State University of Montana, 1931.

Cocking, Matthew. "An Adventurer from Hudson Bay: Journal of Matthew Cocking, from York Factory to the Blackfeet Country, 1772-73." Ed. by Lawrence J. Burpee. *Proceedings and Transactions of the Royal Society of Canada.* Series 3, Vol. II (1908), 89-121.

Cox, Ross. *The Columbia River: Or Scenes and Adventures during a Residence of Six Years on the Western Side of the Rocky Mountains Among Various Tribes of Indians Hitherto Unknown.* Ed. by Edgar I. Stewart and Jane R. Stewart. Norman: University of Oklahoma Press, 1957.

Denig, Edwin Thompson. *Five Tribes of the Upper Missouri.* Ed. by John C. Ewers. Norman: Univrsity of Oklahoma Press, 1961.

De Smet, Pierre Jean, S.J. *Life, Letters and Travels.* Ed. by Hiram Martin Chittenden and Alfred Talbot Richardson. 4 vols. New York: Francis P. Harper. 1905.

de Trobriand, Philippe Regis. *Military Life in Dakota: The Journal of Philippe Regis de Trobriand.* Ed. and Trans. by Lucile M. Kane. St. Paul: The Clarence Alvord Memorial Commission, 1951.

Dodge, Colonel Richard Irving. *Our Wild Indians: Thirty-Three Years' Personal Experience Among the Red Men of the Great West. A Popular Account of Their Social Life, Religion, Habits, Traits, Customs, Exploits, etc., With Thrilling Adventures and Experience on the Great Plains and in the Mountains of our Wide Frontier.* New York: Archer House, Inc., 1959, 1882.

Drannon, Captain William F. *Thirty-one Years on the Plains and in the Mountains or, The Last Voice from the Plains.* Chicago: Rhodes and McClure Publishing Company, 1906.

Dunraven, The Earl of. *The Great Divide: Travels in the Upper Yellowstone in the Summer of 1874.* 2nd Ed. Rev. London: Chatto and Windus, Piccadilly, 1876.

Edgar, Henry. "Journal of Henry Edgar, 1863." *CHSM,* III. Helena: State Publishing Company, 1900.

Ferris, Warren Angus. *Life in the Rocky Mountains: A Diary of Wanderings on the Sources of the Rivers Missouri, Columbia, and Colorado from February, 1830, to November, 1835.* Ed. by Paul C. Phillips. Denver: The Old West Publishing Company, 1940.

Finerty, John F. *War-Path and Bivouac, or The Conquest of the Sioux.* Norman: University of Oklahoma Press, 1961.

"Fort Benton Journal, 18541856," *CHSM*, X. Helena: Naegale Printing Company, 1940, 1-99.

Garfield, James A. *James A. Garfield's Diary of a Trip to Montana in 1872.* Ed. by Oliver W. Holmes. *Sources of Northwest History No. 21.* Missoula: State University of Montana, 1934-5.

Gass, Patrick. *A Journal of the Voyages and Travels of a Corps of Discovery.* Minneapolis: Ross and Haines, Inc. 1958.

Grant, Peter. "Sauteaux Indians, about 1804." In Vol. II of *Les Bourgeois de la Compagnie du Nord-Ouest; Recite de Voyages, Lettres et Rapports Inedits Relatifs au NordOuest Canadien.* Ed. by L.R. Masson. 2 vols. New York: Antiquarian Press, 1960, 1889-90, 303-66.

Hamilton, William T. "A Trading Expedition Among the Indians in 1858 from Fort Walla Walla to the Blackfoot Country and Return." *CHSM*, III. Helena: State Publishing Company, 1900, 33-124.

—. *My Sixty Years on the Plains: Trapping, Trading, and Indian Fighting.* Ed. by E.T. Sieber. Norman: University of Oklahoma Press, 1960, 1905.

—. "Trapping Expedition, 1848-9." *CHSM*, III. Helena: Montana Historical and Miscellaneous Library, 1910, 231-52.

Harkness, James. "Diary of James Harkness of the Firm of La Barge, Harkness and Company: St. Louis to Fort Benton by the Missouri and to the Deer Lodge Valley and Return in 1862." *CHSM*, II. Helena: State Publishing Company, 1896, 343-61.

Harris, Edward. *Up the Missouri with Audubon: The Journal of Edward Harris.* Ed. by John Francis McDermott. Norman: University of Oklahoma Press, 1951.

Healy, John T. *An Adventure in the Idaho Mines.* Ed. by Clyde McLemore. *Sources of Northwest History No. 26.* Missoula: State University of Montana, 1937-8.

Hendry, Anthony. "Journal of a Journey Performed by Anthony Hendry, to Explore the Country Inland, and to Endeavor to Increase the Hudson's Bay Company's Trade, A.D. 1754-1755." Ed. by Lawrence J. Burpee. *Proceedings and Transactions of the Royal Society of Canada.* Series 3, Vol. I, Section II (May, 1907), 307-354.

Henry, Alexander and David Thompson. *New Light on the Early History of the Greater Northwest: The Manuscript Journals of Alexander Henry and of David Thompson.* Ed. by Elliott Coes. 3 vols. New York: Francis P. Harper, 1897.

Henry, Alexander. *Travels and Adventures in Canada and the Indian Territories Between the Years 1760 and 1776.* New York: I Rily, 1809.

Hosmer, Allen J. *A Trip to the States in 1865.* Ed. by Edith M. Duncan. *Sources of Northwest History No. 17.* Missoula: State University of Montana, 1932.

Hulbert, Archer Butler ed. *The Oregon Trail Centennial: The Documentary Back-*

ground of the Days of the First Wagon Train on the Road to Oregon. Sources of Northwest History No. 9. Missoula: State University of Montana, 1930.

Irving, John Treat. Jr. *Indian Sketches Taken During an Expedition to the Pawnee Tribes, 1833.* Ed. by John Francis McDermott. Norman: University of Oklahoma press, 1955.

Isham, James. *James Isham's Observations on Hudson's Bay, 1743.* Ed. by E.E. Rich. Vol. XII of *The Publications of the Hudson's Bay Record Society.* Toronto: The Champlain Society, 1949.

Jackson, Donald ed. *Letters of the Lewis and Clark Expedition, 1783-1854.* Urbana: University of Illinois Press, 1962.

James, Edwin. *An Account of an Expedition from Pittsburgh to the Rocky Mountains Performed in the Years 1819, 1820.* Vols. XIV, XV, XVI, XVII of *Early Western Travels.* Ed. by Thwaites.

Kane, Paul. *Wandering of an Artist Among the Indians of North America from Canada to Vancouver's Island and Oregon Through the Hudson's Bay Company's Territory and Back Again.* in *Paul Kane's Frontier.* Ed. by J. Russel Harper. Austin: University of Texas Press. 1971.

Koch, Peter. "A Trading Expedition Among the Crow Indians, 1873 1874." Ed. by Carl B. Cone. *The Mississippi Valley Historical Review,* XXXI, No. 3 (December, 1944), 407-31.

—. "Life in Muscleshell [sic] in 1869 and 1879." *CHSM,* II. Helena: State Publishing Company, 1896, 292-303.

Kurz, Rudolph Friedrich. *Journal of Rudolph Friedrich Kurz: An Account of His Experiences among Fur Traders and American Indians on the Mississippi and Upper Missouri Rivers During the Years 1846 to 1852.* Ed. by J.N.B. Hewitt. Bureau of American Ethnology *Bulletin 115.* Washington: Government Printing Office, 1936.

Larocque, Francois-Antoine. *Journal of Larocque from the Assiniboine to the Yellowstone, 1805.* Ed. by Lawrence J. Burpee. *Publications of the Canadian Archives,* No. 3. Ottawa: Government Printing Bureau, 1910, 1-82.

—. "The Missouri Journal, 1804-1805." in Vol. I of *Les Bourgeois de la Compagnie du Nord-Ouest.* Ed. by Masson, 297-313.

Larpenteur, Charles. *Forty Years a Fur Trader on the Upper Missouri, 1833-72.* Ed. by Elliott Coues. 2 vols. New York: Francis P. Harper, 1898.

La Verendrye, Pierre Gaultier de Varennes de. *Journals of Pierre Gaultier de Varennes de la Verendrye and His Sons; With Correspondence Between the Governor of Canada and the French Court, Touching on the Search for the Western Sea.* Ed. by Lawrence J. Burpee. Vol. XVI of the *Publications of the Hudson's Bay Record Society.* Toronto: The Champlain Society, 1927.

Leonard, Zenas. *Adventures of Zenas Leonard, Fur Trader.* Ed. by John C. Ewers. Norman: University of Oklahoma Press, 1959.

"Letters Concerning the Presbyterian Mission in the Pawnee Country near Bellvue, Neb., 1831-1849." *Collections of the Kansas State Historical Society, 1915-1918.* XIV (1918).

Lewis, Meriwether and William Clark. *Original Journals of the Lewis and Clark*

Expedition, 1804-1806. Ed. by Reuben Gold Thwaites. 8 vols. New York: Dodd, Mead, and Company, 1904.

MacKenzie, Alexander. *Voyages from Montreal, on the River St. Laurence [sic] through the Continent of North America, to the Frozen and Pacific Oceans; In the Years 1789 and 1793.* London: Cadell and W. Davies, 1801.

MacKenzie, Charles. "The Mississouri [sic] Indians; A Narrative of Four Trading Expeditions to the Mississouri, 1804 - 1805 - 1806." in Vol. I of *Les Bourgeois de la Compagnie du Nord-Ouest.* Ed. by Masson, 315-93.

Maximilian, Alexander Philip (Prince of Wied Neuwied). *Travels in the Interior of North America.* Vols. XXII, XXIII, XXIV of *Early Western Travels.* Ed. by Thwaites.

McDonnell, John. "Some Account of the Red River (About 1797) with Extracts from His Journal, 1793-1795." in Vol. I of *Les Bourgeois de la Campagnie du Nord-Ouest.* Ed. by Masson, 265-95.

Mengarini, Gregory. *Mengarini's Narrative of Rockies: Memoirs of Old Oregon, 1841-1850, and St. Mary's Mission.* Ed. by Albert J. Partoll. *Sources of Northwest History No., 25.* Missoula: State University of Montana, 1938.

M'Gillivray, Duncan. *The Journal of Duncan M'Gillivray of the North West Company at Fort George on the Saskatchewan, 1794-5.* Ed. by Arthur S. Morton. Toronto: The MacMillan Company of Canada, 1929.

Miller, Alfred Jacob. *The West of Alfred Jacob Miller, 1837.* rev. ed. Ed. by Marvin C. Ross. Norman: University of Oklahoma Press, 1968, 1951.

Mirrieleas, Lucia B. ed. *Pioneer Ranching in Central Montana: From the Letters of Otto Maedian, Written in 1882-1883.* Sources of Northwest History No. 10. Misoula: State University of Montana, 1959.

Morgan, Lewis Henry. *The Indian Journals, 1859-62.* Ed. by Leslie A. White. Ann Arbor: University of Michigan Press, 1959.

Newell, Robert. *Robert Newell's Memoranda: Travles [sic] in the Teritory [sic] of Missouri [sic]; Travle to the Kayuse War; together with A Report on the Indians South of the Columbia River.* Ed. by Dorothy O. Johansen. Portland: Champoeg Press, Inc., 1959.

Nichols, Roger L. ed. *The Missouri Expedition, 1818-1820; The Journal of Surgeon John Gale with Related Documents.* Norman: University of Oklahoma Press, 1969.

Parkman, Francis. *The Oregon Trail: Sketches of Prairie and Rocky-Mountain Life.* Intro. by H.S. Comager. New York: The Modern Library, 1949, 1847.

Point, Nicholas, S.J. *Wilderness Kingdom: Indian Life in the Rocky Mountains, 1840-1847. The Journals and Paintings of Nicholas Point, S.J.* Trans. and Intro. by Joseph P. Donnally, S.J. New York: Holt, Rinehart and Winston, 1967.

Preuss, Charles. *Exploring with Fremont: The Private Diaries of Charles Preuss, Cartographer for John C. Fremont on His First, Second, and Fourth Expeditions to the Far West.* Ed. and Trans. by Edwin G. and Elisabeth K. Gudde. Norman: University of Oklahoma Press, 1958.

Quivey, Addison M. "Yellowstone Expedition of 1874." *CHSM,* I. Helena: Independent Publishing Company, 1876, 236-50.

Redington, J.W. "Scouting in Montana in the 1870s." in *Way Out West: Recollections and Tales*. Ed. by H.G. Merriam. Norman: University of Oklahoma Press, 1969.

Ross, Alexander. *The Fur Hunters of the Far West*. Ed. by Kenneth A. Spaulding. Norman: University of Oklahoma Press, 1956, 1855.

Rothernick, Captain A.E. ed. *Early Days at Fort Missoula. Sources of Northwest History No. 23*. Missoula: State University of Montana, 1936.

Russell, Osborne. *Journal of a Trapper*. Ed. by Aubrey L. Haines. Lincoln: University of Nebraska Press, 1955.

Simpson, George. "Remarks Connected with the Fur Trade in the Course of a Voyage from York Factory to Fort George and Back to York Factory, 1824-25." in *Fur Trade and Empire: George Simpson's Journal with Related Documents*. Ed. by Frederick Merk. Cambridge: Belknap Press of Harvard University Press, 1968, 1931.

Stuart, Granville. *Forty Years on the Frontier as Seen in the Journals and Reminiscences of Granville Stuart, Gold-Miner, Trader, Merchant, Rancher, and Politician*. Ed. by Paul C. Phillips, 2 vols. Cleveland: The Arthur H. Clark Company, 1925.

Stuart, James. "The Yellowstone Expedition of 1863." *CHSM*, I. Helena: Independent Publishing Company, 1876, 132-205.

Tabeau, Pierre Antoine. *Tabeau's Narrative of Loisel's Expedition to the Upper Missouri*. Norman: University of Oklahoma Press, 1939.

"The Expedition of Major Clifton Wharton in 1844." *Collections of the Kansas State Historical Society, 1923-1925*. XVI (1929).

Thompson, David. *David Thompson's Narrative of His Explorations in Western America, 1784-1812*. Ed. by J.B. Tyrell. Vol. XII of *The Publications of the Hudson's Bay Record Society*. Toronto: The Champlain Society, 1916.

Townsend, John K. *Narrative of a Journey Across the Rocky Mountains to the Columbia River*. Part II in Vol. XXI of *Early Western Travels*. Ed. by Thwaites.

Trudeau, Jean Baptiste. "Journal of Jean Baptiste Trudeau Among the Arikara Indians in 1795." Ed. and Trans. by Mrs. H.T. Beauregard. *Missouri Historical Society Collections*. IV (1912-1923), 9-48.

—. "Trudeau's Description of the Upper Missouri." Ed. by Annie Heloise Abel. *Mississippi Valley Historical Review*. VIII, Vol. 1 and 2 (June-September, 1921), 148-79.

Umfreville, Edward. *The Present State of Hudson's Bay. Containing a Full Description of that Settlement, and the Adjacent Country; and Likewise of the Fur Trade With Hints for its Improvement*. London: Printed for Charles Stalker, No. 4 Stationers-Court, Ludgate Street, 1790.

Warren, Gouverneur Kemble. *Explorations in Nebraska. Preliminary Report of Lieutenant G.K. Warren*, in *Sen. Ex. Doc. 1*, 35 Cong., 2 sess., December 6, 1858.

Wentzel, W.F. "Letters to the Hon. Roderic McKenzie, 18071824." in Vol. I of *Les Bourgeois de la Compagnie du Nord-Ouest*. Ed. by Masson, 67-153.

Wislizenus, Frederick Adolphus. *A Journey to the Rocky Mountains in the Year*

1839. Glorieta, New Mexico: The Rio Grande Press, Inc., 1969.

Work, John. *The Journal of John Work: A Chief-Trader of the Hudson's Bay Co. During His Expedition from Vancouver to the Flatheads and Blackfeet of Pacific Northwest*. Ed. by William S. Lewis and Paul C. Phillips. Cleveland: The Arthur H. Clark Company, 1923.

—. *The Snake Country Expedition of 1830-1831; John Work's Field Journal*. Ed. by Francis D. Haines, Jr. Norman: University of Oklahoma Press, 1971.

3. Memoirs

Hyde, George E. *Life of George Bent, Written from His Letters*. Norman: University of Oklahoma Press, 1968.

Leland, Charles G. ed. *The Life and Adventures of James P. Beckwourth, Mountaineer, Scout, Pioneer, and Chief of the Crow Nation of Indians; Written from His Own Dictation by T.D. Bonner*. New York: MacMillan and Company, 1892.

Linderman, Frank B. *Plenty-Coups, Chief of the Crows*. Lincoln: University of Nebraska Press, 1962, 1930.

—. *Pretty-Shield, Medicine Woman of the Crows*. Lincoln: University of Nebraska Press, 1972, 1932.

Marquis, Thomas B. ed. *Memoirs of a White Crow Indian*. New York: The Century Company, 1928.

—. *Wooden Leg: A Warrior Who Fought Custer*. Lincoln: University of Nebraska Press, 1957.

McDonald of Garth, John. "Autobiographical Notes, 1791-1816." in Vol. II of *Les Bourgeois de la Compagnie du Nord-Ouest*. Ed. by Masson, 159.

Nabokov, Peter ed. *Two Leggings: The Making of a Crow Warrior*. New York: Thomas Y. Crowell Company, 1967.

Neihardt, John G. *Black Elk Speaks, Being the Life Story of a Holy Man of the Oglala Sioux*. Lincoln: University of Nebraska Press, 1962, 1932.

Schultz, James Willard. *My Life as an Indian*. Greenwich: Fawcett Publications, Inc., 1935.

—. *Blackfeet and Buffalo: Memories of Life Among the Indians*. Ed. by Keith C. Seele. Norman: University of Oklahoma Press, 1962.

4. Unpublished Materials

Bent Letters. George Bent to George E. Hyde, June 10, 1904 to December 31, 1906. Colorado Historical Society.

Buntin, Arthur Roy. *Battleground: A Narrative and Evaluation of Intertribal Warfare on the Buffalo Plains of Eastern Montana and in Adjacent Areas Prior to 1880*. M.A. Thesis, Montana State University, 1952.

Bushotter, George. *Lakota Texts by George Bushotter*. Trans. by James Owen Dorsey. Washington, D.C., 1887. National Anthropological Archives.

Calloway, Donald Goodwin. *Raiding and Feuding Among Western North Amer-*

ican Indians. PhD Dissertation, University of Michigan, 1978.

Chamberlain, Alexander F. *The Culture-Relations and Status of the Kutenai and the Blackfeet*. Washington, D.C., 1937. National Anthropological Archives.

Riggs, Stephen R. and Thomas L. Riggs. *Notes on Dakota Culture*. Washington, D.C., 1880s. National Anthropological Archives.

Rodnick, David. *The Fort Belknap Assiniboine of Montana*. PhD Dissertation, University of Pennsylvania, 1938.

Sword, George. *Lakota Texts*. Ed. and Trans. by Ella Deloria, in *Dr. James R. Walker Collection*, Microfilm No. W152d. Colorado Historical Society.

5. Cassette Recordings

Ironwood Singers. "Traditional Songs of the Sioux." Recorded live at Rosebud. Taos, New Mexico: Indian House, 1980.

B. SECONDARY SOURCES

1. Books

Ambrose, Stephen E. *Crazy Horse and Custer: The Parallel Lives of Two American Warriors*. Garden City: Doubleday and Co., 1975.

Anderson, Gary Clayton. *Kinsmen of Another Kind: Dakota-White Relations in the Upper Mississippi Valley, 1650-1862*. Lincoln: University of Nebraska Press, 1984.

Berkhofer, Robert F., Jr. *Salvation and the Savage: An Analysis of Protestant Missions and American Indian Response, 1787-1862*. New York: Atheneum, 1972.

Clark, Ella E. and Margot Edmonds. *Sacagawea of the Lewis and Clark Expedition*. Berkeley: University of California Press, 1979.

Dempsey, Hugh A. *Crowfoot, Chief of the Blackfeet*. Norman: University of Oklahoma Press, 1972.

Densmore, Frances. *Mandan and Hidatsa Music*. Bureau of American Ethnology *Bulletin 80*. Washington: Government Printing Office, 1923.

—. *Teton Sioux Music*. Bureau of American Ethnology *Bulletin 61*. Washington: Government Printing Office, 1918.

Dunlay, Thomas. *Wolves for the Blue Soldiers: Indian Scouts and Auxiliaries with the U.S. Army, 1860-90*. Lincoln: University of Nebraska Press, 1982.

Ewers, John C. *Indian Life on the Upper Missouri*. Norman: University of Oklahoma Press, 1968.

—. *The Blackfeet: Raiders on the Northwestern Plains*. Norman: University of Oklahoma Press, 1958.

—. *The Horse in Blackfoot Indian Culture, With Comparative Material from Other Western Tribes*. Bureau of American Ethnology *Bulletin 159*. Washington: Government Printing Office, 1955.

Flynn, A.F. *The American Indian as a Product of Environment with Special Reference to the Pueblos.* Boston: Little, Brown and Company, 1908.

Gard, Wayne. *The Great Buffalo Hunt.* Lincoln: University of Nebraska Press, 1968.

Goble, Paul and Dorothy. *Lone Bull's Horse Raid.* New York: Bradbury Press., 1973.

Goetzmann, William H. *Army Exploration in the American West, 1803-1862.* New Haven: Yale University Press, 1959.

Grinnell, George Bird. *Blackfoot Lodge Tales: The Story of a Prairie People.* New York: Charles Scribner's Sons, 1892.

—. *Pawnee, Blackfoot, and Cheyenne.* Ed. by Dee Brown. New York: Charles Scribner's Sons, 1961.

—. *Pawnee Hero Stories and Folk Tales with Notes on the Origin, Customs, and Character of the Pawnee People.* Intro. by Maurice Frink. Lincoln: University of Nebraska Press, 1961, 1889.

—. *The Fighting Cheyennes.* Norman: University of Oklahoma Press, 1956, 1915.

—. *Two Great Scouts and Their Pawnee Battalion.* Lincoln: University of Nebraska Press, 1973.

Hassrick, Royal B. *The Sioux: Life and Customs of a Warrior Society.* Norman: University of Oklahoma Press, 1964.

Hodge, Frederick Webb. ed. *Handbook of American Indians North of Mexico.* 2 vols. Bureau of American Ethnology *Bulletin 30.* Washington: Government Printing Office, 1912.

Hutton, Paul Andrew. *Phil Sheridan and His Army.* Lincoln: University of Nebraska Press, 1985.

Hyde, George E. *Indians of the High Plains, From the Prehistoric Period to the Coming of the Europeans.* Norman: University of Oklahoma Press, 1959.

—. *Red Cloud's Folk: A History of the Oglala Sioux Indians.* Norman: University of Oklahoma Press, 1937.

—. *Spotted Tail's Folk: A History of the Brule Sioux Indians.* Norman: University of Oklahoma Press, 1961.

Irving, Washington, *Astoria, Or Anecdotes of an Enterprise Beyond the Rocky Mountains.* Ed. by Edgeley W. Todd. Norman: University of Oklahoma Press, 1964.

—. *The Adventures of Captain Bonneville, U.S.A.* Ed. by Edgeley W. Todd. Norman: University of Oklahoma Press, 1961.

Johnson, Olga Weymemeyer. *Flathead and Kootenay: The Rivers, the Tribes, and the Region's Traders.* Glendale: Arthur Clark Company, 1969.

Kennedy, Michael Stephen ed. *The Assiniboines: From the Accounts of the Old Ones Told to First Boy (James Larpenteur Long).* Norman: University of Oklahoma Press, 1961.

Lewis, Oscar. *The Effects of White Contact Upon Blackfoot Culture with Special Reference to the Fur Trade.* New York: J.J. Augustin, 1942.

Lowie, Robert H. *Indians of the Plains.* Garden City: Natural History Press, 1963.

—. *The Crow Indians.* New York: Holt, Rinehart and Winston, 1956, 1935.

Mallery, Garrick. *Picture Writing of the American Indians.* 2 vols. New York: Dover Publications, Inc., 1893.

Marquis, Thomas. *Keep the Last Bullet for Yourself: The True Story of Custer's Last Stand.* New York: Two Continents Publishing Group, Ltd., 1976.

Meyer, Roy. *A History of the Santee Sioux: United States Indian Policy on Trial.* Lincoln: University of Nebraska Press, 1967.

Miskin, Bernard. *Rank and Warfare Among the Plains Indians. III. Monographs of the American Ethnological Society.* New York: J.J. Augustin Publishers, 1940.

Nasatir, Abraham Phineas. *Before Lewis and Clark: Documents Illustrating the History of the Missouri, 1785-1805.* 2 vols. St. Louis Historical Documents Foundation, 1952.

Oliver, Symmes C. *Ecology and Cultural Continuity as Contributing Factors in the Social Organization of the Plains Indians.* Vol. 48. No. 1. *University of California Publications in American Archeaology and Ethnology.* (1963).

Paullin, Charles O. *Atlas of the Historical Geography of the United States.* Ed. by John K. Wright. Carnegie Institution of Washingrton and the American Geographical Society of New York, 1932.

Praus, Alexis. *The Sioux, 1798-1922: A Dakota Winter Count.* Cranbrook Institute of Science, *Bulletin Number 44* 1952.

Prucha, Francis Paul. *The Great Father: The United States Government and the American Indians.* 2 vols. Lincoln: University of Nebraska Press, 1984.

Ridge, Martin and Ray Allen Billington eds. *American Frontier Story: A Documentary History of Westward Expansion.* New York: Holt, Rinehart and Winston, 1969.

Robinson, Doane. *A History of the Dakota or Sioux Indians.* Minneapolis: Ross and Haines, Inc., 1904.

Roe, Frank Gilbert. *The Indian and the Horse.* Norman: University of Oklahoma Press, 1955.

Sandoz, Mari. *Crazy Horse, The Strange Man of the Oglalas.* Lincoln: University of Nebraska Press, 1961.

—. *The Battle of the Little Bighorn.* New York: Modern Literary Editions Publishing Company, 1966.

—. *The Buffalo Hunters.* New York: Hastings House, 1954.

Secoy, Frank Raymond. *Changing Military Patterns on the Great Plains (17th Century-Early 19th Century).* New York: J.J. Augustin, 1953.

Stands in the Timber, John and Margot Liberty. *Cheyenne Memories.* New Haven: Yale University Press, 1961.

Storm, Hyemeyohsts. *Seven Arrows.* New York: Harper and Row, Publishers, 1972.

Teit, James A. *The Salishan Tribes of the Western Plateaus.* Ed. by Franz Boas. Bureau of American Ethnology *Forty-fifth Annual Report.* (1927-1928). Washington: Government Printing Office, 1930.

Trenholm, Virginia Cole and Maurine Corley. *The Shoshonis: Sentinels of the Rockies.* Norman: University of Oklahoma Press, 1964.

Turney-High, Harry Holbert. *Primitive War: Its Practice and Concepts.* 2nd ed. Columbia: University of South Carolina Press, 1934.

Utley, Robert M. *Frontier Regulars: The United States Army and the Indian, 1866-1891.* Bloomington: Indiana University Press, 1973.

Vestal, Stanley. *New Sources of Indian History, 1850-1891.* Norman: University of Oklahoma Press, 1934.

—. *Sitting Bull, Champion of the Sioux.* Norman: University of Oklahoma Press, 1932.

Wagner, Glendolin Damon and William A. Allen. *Blankets and Moccasins: Plenty Coups and His People, the Crows.* Caldwell: The Caxton Printers, Ltd., 1936.

Wedel, Waldo R. *Prehistoric Man on the Great Plains.* Norman: University of Oklahoma Press, 1961.

Weltfish, Gene. *The Lost Universe.* New York: Basic Books, 1965.

Wood, W. Raymond and Thomas D. Thiesson eds. *Early Fur Trade on the Northern Plains: Canadian Traders Among the Mandan and Hidatsa Indians, 1738-1818.* Norman: University of Oklahoma Press, 1985.

2. Articles

Algier, Keith. "Robert Meldrum and the Crow Peltry Trade." *Montana, The Magazine of Western History,* 36 (Summer, 1986), 36-47.

Anderson, Gary Clayhton. "Early Dakota Migration and Intertribal Warfare." *Western Historical Quarterly,* XI, (Jan., 1980), 17-36.

Bruner, Edward M. "Mandan." *Perspectives in American Indian Culture Change.* Ed. by Edward H. Spicer. Chicago: University of Chicago Press, 1961.

Calloway, Colin G. "Sword Bearer and the 'Crow Outbreak,' 1887," *Montana, The Magazine of Western History,* XXXVI (Autumn, 1986), 38-51.

—. "The Inter-tribal Balance of Power on the Great Plains, 1760-1800." *Journal of American Studies,* XVI (April, 1982), 25-47.

Cronon, William and Richard White. "Indian in the Land." *American Heritage,* XXXVII (August-September, 19860, 18-25.

Ewers, John C. "Deadlier Than the Male." *American Heritage.* XVI (June, 1965), 10-13.

—. "Intertribal Warfare as a Precursor of Indian-White Warfare on the Northern Plains." *The Western Historical Quarterly,* VI (October, 1975), 397-410.

—. "The Blackfoot War Lodge: Its Construction and Use." *American Anthropologist,* XLVII, No. 2 (1944).

—. "The Indian Trade of the Upper Missouri before Lewis and Clark: An Interpretation." *Missouri Historical Society Bulletin,* X, No. 4 (July, 1954), 429-46.

Grinnell, George Bird. "Coup and Scalp Among the Plains Indians." *American Anthropologist,* vol. 12 (1910), 296-310.

Howard, James H. "Yanktonai Ethnohistory and the John K. Bear Winter Count." *Plains Anthropologist* (August, 1976).

Mandelbaum, David G. "The Plains Cree." *Anthropological Papers of the American Museum of Natural History,* XXXVII, Pt. 2, New York City, 1940.

McGinnis, Anthony. "A Contest of Wits and Daring: Plains Indians at War with the U.S. Army." *North Dakota History: Journal of the Northern Plains,* 48 (Spring, 1981), 24-32.

—. "Economic Warfare on the Northern Plains, 1804-1877." *Annals of Wyoming,* 44 (Spring, 1972), 57-71.

—. "Intertribal Conflict on the Northern Plains and Its Suppression, 1738-1889." *Journal of the West,* XVIII (April, 1979), 49-61.

—. "Intertribal Raiding on the Northern Plains after the Surrender of Sitting Bull." *Red River Valley Historical Review,* II (Fall, 1975), 349-362.

—. "Strike and Retreat: Intertribal Warfare and the Powder River War, 1865-1868." *Montana: The Magazine of Western History,* XXX (Autumn, 1980), 30-41.

Murray, Genevieve. *Marias Pass: Its Part in the History and development of the Northwest. Sources of Northwest History No. 12.* Missoula: State University of Montana, 1938.

Newcomb, W.W. "A Reexamination of the Causes of Plains Indian Warfare." *American Anthropologist.* Vol. 52 (1950), 317-29.

Partoll, Albert J. ed. *The Blackfoot Indian Peace Council. Sources of Northwest History No. 3.* Missoula: State University of Montana, 1937.

Sheehan, Bernard W. "Indian-White Relations in Early America: A Review Essay." *The William and Mary Quarterly,* XXVI (April, 1969), 267-86.

Smith, Marian. "The War Complex of the Plains Indians." *Proceedings of the American Philosophical Society,* LXXVIII (1936), 425-64.

Stands in the Timber, John. "Last Ghastly Moments at the Little Big Horn." *American Heritage,* XVII (April, 1966) 15-21.

White, Richard. "The Winning of the West: The Expansion of the Western Sioux in the Eighteenth and Nineteenth Centuries." *Journal of American History* LXV (Sept., 1978), 319-343.

Wissler, Clark. "Material Culture of the Blackfoot Indians." *Anthropological Papers of the American Museum of Natural History,* V, Pt. 1. New York City, 1910, 1-175.

Woody, F.H. "A Sketch of the Early History of Western Montana." *CHSM,* II. Helena: State Publishing Company, 1896, 88-106.

INDEX

ABOUT THE AUTHOR

Anthony McGinnis holds a B.A. from Colorado College and M.A. and Ph.D. degrees from the University of Colorado. He has published a number of well-received articles on Indian history. This is his first book.